# ARDKINGLAS

**Christina Noble** was born and brought up in Ardkinglas, Cairndow. After gaining a degree in English Literature, she moved to the Indian Himalayas, where she lived from 1970 to 1990. She ran a Himalayan trekking company and wrote about her life in India in two books, *Over the High Passes* (1987) and *At Home in the Himalayas* (1991). After leaving India she returned to Cairndow, where she now lives. She is Director of Here We Are, a project which aims to sustain the local community and enable it to prosper in the modern world.

# ~ ARDKINGLAS ~

## THE BIOGRAPHY OF A HIGHLAND ESTATE

Christina Noble

BIRLINN

First published in 2018 by Birlinn Ltd
West Newington House
10 Newington Road
Edinburgh
EH9 1QS
*www.birlinn.co.uk*

ISBN: 978 1 78027 486 7

British Library Cataloguing in Publication Data
A catalogue record for this book is available from the
British Library

Typeset in ITC Galliard at Birlinn

Printed and bound in Great Britain by
Bell & Bain Ltd, Glasgow

*'Generations pass while some trees stand and old families*
*last not three oaks'*
Sir Thomas Browne, 1605-1682

For Alice Beattie and her daughter Dot Chalmers, without whom
this book wouldn't have been written

In thanks for what I learnt about a way of life from
my mother Elizabeth, my Aunt Anastasia and my brother Johnny

# Contents

# Plates

Looking up Loch Fyne from Laglingarten.

Lorimer Cottage, The Stables and Ardkinglas House in the 1930s.

Ardno Farm in the 1950s.

Gilbert Livingstone and an old ewe.

Jean MacDiarmid and Janet Callander with a plucked hen at Ardkinglas in 1956.

Tasia and her deerhounds on the front drive at Ardkinglas.

Tasia and Johnny Noble at Sarah's wedding in 1957.

View across Loch Fyne from above Kilmorich Church, 1963.

The coalboat unloading on Ardkinglas foreshore in 1969.

Donnie MacDonald, John Beattie and Colin Callander watching as the coalboat is unloaded.

Jimmy Waddell and Donald MacPherson with 'improver' tups in front of Achadunan in 1975.

Cairndow Estate shepherds at Butterbridge in 1975.

The Phantom 1 Rolls Royce at the Square.

George Knight with a crop of his onions in the bicycle shed.

Morag Keith and Greta Cameron.

Christina at Mossariach, above the head of Glen Fyne, 2016.

# Acknowledgements

In memory of the many who are mentioned in the book who participated in the Estate in the past, and in thanks to all those who feature in the book and to the many who have encouraged me and contributed to it over the years:

Alastair MacCallum, Alexander Miles, Andy Lane, Angus Robertson, Annie McKee, Annie Tindley, Bob Craig, Christine MacCallum, David Sumsion, Donald Peck, Ernie MacPherson, Greta Cameron, Hugh Raven, Ian Jack, Janet Callander, Jean Maskell, John Keay, John MacDonald, Lizzie Maguire, Lindy Sharpe, Lucy Peck, Malcolm McKay, Margaret Mackay, Morag Keith, Neal Ascherson, Nigel Callander, Peter Beaton, Roddy MacDiarmid, Sam Millar, Sarah Skerrat, Sarah Sumsion, Tara North, Timothy Noble, Vanessa Thomas.

In thanks to Ardkinglas Estate archive and to Here We Are archive and all those who have contributed to it; see *www.hereweare-uk.com*, *www.ourhouses-theirstories.com*, *www.glenfyne.org.uk*, *www.shepherding-cairndow.org.uk*.

And finally, thank you to my consistently encouraging editor, Tom Johnstone at Birlinn.

# Foreword

This book begins when Sir Andrew Noble, my great-grandfather, bought the 45,000 acre Ardkinglas Estate, at the head of Loch Fyne in Argyll, in 1905. He bought it as a sporting estate and commissioned the architect Sir Robert Lorimer to build a mansion house there. Two years later Sir Andrew was ceremoniously pulled along the drive in his car by estate staff and tenants to be welcomed at his newly completed house. This book ends in 2002 with the death of my brother, Johnny Noble, owner of Ardkinglas Estate at the time and founder of Loch Fyne Oysters, and I have added a short afterword on Ardkinglas as it is today.

I was born in the Kinglas bedroom in Ardkinglas House in 1942. I live now a couple of miles along the shore road from the Big House at Maggie Luke's, these days more often known as Policy Gate. There were Lukes here from 1861, and the elderly sisters Maggie and Julie lived here until the 1950s. Janet Callander remembers how, in the 1930s, when she and her brother Archie walked to school from their Granny's house, they would stop here for a 'jam piece', and Maggie would give them a threepenny piece out of the little dish she kept on the dresser. The dresser is still here.

For some years I had thought that a biography of Ardkinglas Estate could be an interesting book. Then I came across a letter I had forgotten from Johnny, written in 1999, three years before he died. It asked me to do just that. He mentioned *100 years in the Highlands*, by Osgood Mackenzie, as an earlier example that I might try to follow. Finding Johnny's letter gave strength to my elbow and I determined to carry on and to try not to be down-hearted at the thought of how much better he would have done it himself.

When I began to write what I had envisaged as a biography about the place and about the people who lived here, I thought it would be relatively easy to patch together a chronological 'scrapbook' which would tell the story. As I worked on it, it became much more difficult than I had anticipated. I became increasingly aware, not just that Johnny would have written the book much better himself, but that it lacks the conversation I would have had with him about it – 'What's the point of an estate? For whom?' And increasingly this question has troubled what I have been writing: no clear answers have emerged. So much has changed over the last hundred years, including the mindsets of landowners and those who worked for them.

A historian would not be troubled by such questions; she would simply write the history as a curious and (with luck) sympathetic outsider. But I have known this place for sixty of the hundred years that the book describes, and that familiarity has both helped and hindered me. As I wrote I became aware of the difficulty of my identity. What was my relationship with Ardkinglas? Did my privileged early life on the estate mean that I couldn't see it clearly from a detached perspective? And did my 'social position' – such as it was – inevitably affect how others in the district saw me? Again, no clear answer.

And another difficulty began to emerge to do with my identity, in a different way. All my life the place hasn't just been a home to me: it, and some people here, are a part of who I am. So sometimes as I was writing, the book churned vivid feelings that disturbed my sleep.

When Sir Andrew bought it in 1905, Ardkinglas Estate was the whole of the parish of Kilmorich. The village and the terrain marked by the parish boundary is better known as Cairndow, which covers all of the land around the head of Loch Fyne from Dunderave to St Catherine's, and all of Glen Fyne and

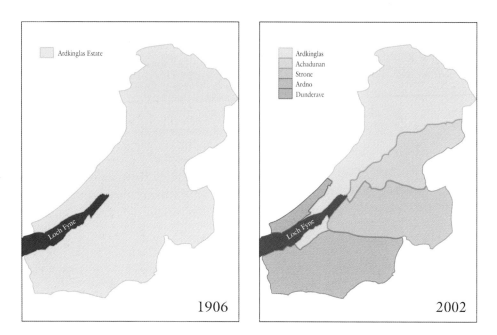

*The area of Ardkinglas Estate in 1906 and how ownership had changed at the beginning of the twenty-first century.*

Glen Kinglas. Loch Fyne is the longest sea loch in Scotland, once renowned for its herring, but now more often known for oysters. In 1966 the original Ardkinglas Estate was divided into Ardkinglas Estate and Cairndow Estate, and subsequently there have been further subdivisions. For the purposes of this book I have taken Ardkinglas Estate to mean roughly the area of land my great-grandfather bought.

I hope that this biography of Ardkinglas Estate will give an idea of what it was like for those of us who lived there during the twentieth century. At the outset I should try to describe what a Highland estate was in the past, and to some extent still is.

The old-established Scottish families had owned large tracts of land with fine houses for centuries. But it was Queen Victoria and particularly Prince Albert who in the mid-nineteenth century, with the purchase of Balmoral, began a new trend of ownership for Victorians and Edwardians. With many variations and diminutions, this continued well into the twentieth century and even into the twenty-first. The estate and its mansion house might be referred to, in today's terms, as a 'second home', as the owners' principal home was elsewhere, most often London. The well-to-do owners and family and friends would come there only for lengthy holidays in the summer months, into the autumn and perhaps for Christmas. Many of them would, however, feel a strong attachment to their estate and to its people.

On the estates the mansion house, or the Big House, as it was usually referred to, was the fulcrum point of the community. These days, because of the expense of heating a huge house and of maintaining it without an estate team, it is more often felt to be a white elephant unless it has been turned into holiday flats or a hotel.

Much the largest area of the extensive acres would be hill ground, providing rough grazing for cattle, sheep and/or deer – their numbers in various proportions according to terrain, owner's priorities and the prices or subsidies current at the time. Near the Big House there would be a byre for dairy cattle, stables, a cart shed, garage, lofts and sheds, along with dwelling-houses for the estate employees. Some of the household staff, cooks, kitchen-maids and housemaids, lived in servants' quarters in the mansion house, some nearby. Many of the important household staff travelled with the family from London for the season (often romance flourished among the maids and the estate joiners, gardeners or keepers). There were extensive gardens including a kitchen garden and flower gardens, and often a park at the front or the back of the mansion house with ornamental trees. Further afield there were well-tended policies extending a mile or two from the Big House. At the drive gates there was a small lodge where the gatekeeper, often an elderly man or woman, lived.

The village buildings – post office, shop, hotel, village hall, would be owned and controlled by the estate, often on long leases. Certainly during the earlier years of the twentieth century many of the outlying farms were tenanted, along with cottages and bothies for their farmworkers and shepherds. The proportion of arable land to rough hillside was small and would be located near the farmhouse and its steading.

During the early years – and on some estates up to the present day – shooting and fishing, and particularly stalking red deer, were essential to the concept of a Highland estate; activities pursued for the owners' pleasure and as a source of income. Often there was a shooting lodge in a remote glen, used by the family and friends for a few weeks at a time, or let to visitors with the fishing. On the whole relationships between employers and staff were easy. The hours the staff would have been expected to work and to be at the beck and call of their employers, and the scrubbing and cleaning required, would seem well out of order today. But that is with hindsight. Friendship between staff and a member of the owner's family (or his friends) often grew out of adventurous days spent together on the hill or by the river.

A composite portrait of this way of life, *Strathalder, a Highland Estate*, by Robert Grant, was first published in 1978 (re-published by Birlinn in 2007). There is no such estate as Strathalder, but the book is based on a number of real examples. Grant was the son of a gamekeeper on an estate and suggested that without the communities formed by such Highland estates the more remote areas of Scotland would become depopulated. He observed that the framework established by the estates, each one with its laird, had stood the test of time and was still in place, in 1978.

Grant goes on to make an interesting point:

> In the course of my childhood I came into contact with many people from all walks of life; surprisingly for such a remote place, far more than I could have expected to meet in a town . . . farm worker, kitchen maid, chauffeur, the laird himself and his guests, people with wealth beyond the bounds of my imagination.

This book is about a place, the people who make it and have made it and the context in which they have lived and worked. There is an inconsistent level of information about different periods, and inconsistency in the type of information available. In the earliest section, 1905 to 1938, there is information on the proprietors but little detail about employees. In later sections the source material is more varied, though not more consistent: there are letters and household diaries covering some periods and quotes from estate journals that were only compiled over a year or two. More recent decades are coloured by memories, mine and many others', and greatly enhanced by photographs and by oral records that have been collected thanks to Here We Are, the community organisation I have worked with over the last fifteen years.

This is not a nostalgic memoir of the Noble family, nor of life in 'The Big House'. I have wanted to convey an idea of what life was like on a Highland estate for all of the community. I have also tried to give an idea of the finances that underpinned it (or more often didn't).

The book is about belonging to a place; whether this comes about by ownership or because it is home. In 1945 John and Michael Noble saw the place as their responsibility. In *Ardkinglas and the Future*, a booklet sent to all employees and tenants at New Year, 1945, they wrote:

> It is within your knowledge that the income of the estate has fallen far short of the outgoings, and that income from 'other capital' has had to balance the accounts. [I don't think employees at that time or ever were aware of this.] We aren't complaining, happiness and success aren't be measured exactly in money. Neither we nor our predecessors have regrets . . . Our affection for all of you and for the place has firm roots and we are determined to remain at Ardkinglas, if we are able to do so. We believe all rights and privileges carry corresponding duties, our responsibility is to maintain and increase the welfare of all who live here.

The place as home is described in 2017 by Roddy MacDiarmid (shepherd and international sheepdog-trialist):

> I was born in Glen Fyne, I worked here shepherding when I left school at fifteen in 1959, I worked right on here and I knew every hill like the back of my hand . . .
>
> Both Mr Michael and your father were good at trying to find a wee house for someone to give them a start and that helped to make the community such a tight-knit place.

My home was always Cairndow. I don't know if I could have settled anywhere else as well as I have settled in Cairndow, it's such a nice area and I knew everyone, and I knew all the hills here.

In my work on this book I have been flattered and encouraged by academics – Margaret Mackay of the School of Scottish Studies, Sarah Skerratt of Scotland's Rural College (SRUC), Annie Tindley of Newcastle University and Annie McKee of the James Hutton Institute. What I have written is far from academic, however: I don't claim it to be an objective view, it is written through the prism of my eyes. Writing it has been an interesting challenge.

# ARDKINGLAS

# The Beginning: 1905 to 1938

## The Glory Days

When Prince Albert and Queen Victoria bought Balmoral Estate and in 1856 rebuilt the house in what came to be known as the Scots Baronial style, they set a trend. It became a style of architecture and the Highland estate a style of recreation for wealthy industrialists to follow – George Bullough at Kinloch Castle on Rum, Octavius Smith at Ardtornish, and Andrew Carnegie at Skibo. And in 1905 Sir Andrew Noble, my great-grandfather, bought the 45,000 acres of Ardkinglas for £62,000.

Sir Walter Scott's novels, Landseer's and other artists' romantic Highland scenes had whetted the public appetite for such places, and improved roads and the penetration of the railway had facilitated easy access. The grand old Highland families, like the Stuarts of Bute, the MacLeods of Dunvegan in Skye and the Dukes of Argyll had retained their (increasingly) large houses on their huge Highland estates throughout the nineteenth century. But from time to time they had had to sell portions of their land, creating an opportunity for a purchaser with new money to buy a Highland estate. In the Duke of Argyll's case, falling rents and his spendthrift nephews, Henry and George Callander, had brought the Ardkinglas Estate near to bankruptcy.

Andrew Noble was born in 1832 in Union Street, Greenock. He went briefly to Edinburgh Academy and then, when fifteen, to the Royal Military Academy at Woolwich. At the age of seventeen he was commissioned in the Royal Artillery and was sent to Canada, where he met and married a Margery Campbell.

At twenty-nine he was back in Britain and joined Armstrong's armaments and engineering firm at Elswick near Newcastle. Clearly he was a talented physicist of great value to the firm; for instance he invented an Electro Mechanical Chronoscope which measured speeds inside a gun-barrel. Then he and Sir Frederick Abel improved muzzle velocities, which increased the energy produced by the weapons. These developments meant that both guns and their mountings had to be redesigned at Armstrong's. This gave the firm a competitive advantage, enabling the company to expand into shipbuilding,

1

locomotives, tanks and aircraft, so by 1914 it had become one of the world's largest armament firms.

Sir Andrew was not just a brilliant physicist, he was also a businessman. He took over from Sir William Armstrong as Chairman of Armstrong's during the 1890s and masterminded much of the growth of the company. Sir Andrew claimed that all the Japanese guns which sank the Russian fleet at the battle of Tsushima in 1905 had been manufactured at Elswick. He was knighted in 1893 and made a baronet in 1902.

The Noble family's main residence was Jesmond Dene house near the Armstrong works at Elswick. The fashionable Scottish architect Norman Shaw, who had introduced technical innovations like electrical lifts and electric spits at Cragside for Sir William Armstrong, was commissioned by Andrew to build extensive conversions and installations at Jesmond Dene. Andrew had come a long way from Union Street, Greenock. There are formal photographs of the extended family arranged over the steps at Jesmond, dressed in their Edwardian best, posing with guests and dogs. Sir Andrew and Lady

*Sir Andrew and Lady Noble with Admiral Togo and other Japanese guests at Jesmond in 1900.*

2

*The old house at Ardkinglas, 1905.*

Noble entertained dignitaries and useful international ship and armaments clients like Prince Fushimi, brother of the Emperor of Japan. Of the Japanese Admiral Togo, Lady Noble wrote: 'We were delighted with him, with his simplicity and dignity. We had a large reception for him and later on in the evening I asked if he would like to slip off and go to bed, after a tiring evening and shaking hands with a hundred people. He said "No, I thank you, I should like to play billiard with your son."'

As did many of the well-to-do in the later Victorian era, over the years Sir Andrew took large houses and sporting estates for sport and recreation with friends and family, sometimes for a season, sometimes for years at a time. But these were rented, he did not own them. What made him, at seventy-three, decide to buy an estate in Argyll, we don't know. An urge to come back near to his childhood home? Encouragement from his Campbell wife, or from Lilly, his elder, unmarried daughter, who was said to be an enthusiast for the Highlands as depicted in Sir Walter Scott's novels? Maybe he had been looking for a Highland property in Campbell territory.

He might have heard that Ardkinglas was on the market from Cameron Corbett, later Lord Rowallan, the philanthropist and politician. At the time when Sir Andrew bought a part of the Ardkinglas Estate from the Duke of

Argyll, Cameron Corbett bought the other part, the Ardgoil section, which lay round Loch Goil, and gave it to the city of Glasgow for the benefit of its citizens.

Duke Niall of Argyll, trustee for the two spendthrift nephews, was ashamed to have to write to the tenantry in 1905 explaining why the Estate was being sold:

> For those of you who have at all studied the question with close attention, it will not be difficult to perceive that in these days the ordinary burdens upon land are so grievous, that when independent sources of support are either slender or totally lacking, it becomes increasingly difficult to hand on an Estate unimpaired to succeeding generations. More especially is this the case when the Estate is so heavily burdened by an accumulation of debts inherited by its present Possessor from the unwisdom of their forefathers. *A point is ever reached in such cases when the interests on money borrowed can no longer be paid and the lands themselves have to be sold.* [My italics.]

The problems caused by borrowing would haunt generations of Ardkinglas owners.

In 1905 Sir Andrew had become a very wealthy man. At the time, Armstrong's was one of the largest companies in Britain, even in the world. It represented 5% of the total capitalisation of the London Stock Exchange and Sir Andrew was one of the largest shareholders of the company. He bought the 45,000 acre estate for £62,000 and commissioned Robert Lorimer to build a mansion house, which would cost another £55,000. (In today's money that £117,000 would be in the region of £11.5 million.) Moreover Sir Andrew is said to have been able to pay for the construction of Ardkinglas, which cost him almost as much as the purchase of the entire estate, out of one year's income from Armstrong's – his salary plus his dividends.

It may have been Corbett who introduced Sir Andrew to the fashionable architect Sir Robert Lorimer; he had been appointed as the architect for the restoration of Rowallan Castle, (never completed). Daughter Lilly Noble was an enthusiast for Lorimer. The land purchase was finalised in November, and by 7 January 1906 Sir Andrew and Sir Robert Lorimer met at Ardkinglas and the commission was fixed. Lorimer wrote, 'The ground is to be broke on 1st May and the dear old gent wants to eat his dinner in the house on 1st August 1907.'

The proposed mansion house was to face onto Loch Fyne, its grounds stretching down to the shore. Here, situated north east from the Royal Burgh of Inveraray, Loch Fyne is narrow and, seen from the far side, the house would be set into the sweep of high hills – Beinn an Lochan and Ben Ime – framing the view up Glen Kinglas. The house stands in a handsome and carefully considered position: both when looking at it and looking out from it.

Two piers had to be built in order to be able to ship in fine timber for the panelling, the ironwork, the Orkney slates and the sandstone. Teams of skilled plasterers, panellers and electrical fitters were brought in, two hundred of them, encamped in the field by the church. At this time there was no telephone; communication was post or telegram.

When Lorimer tackled Ardkinglas he was at the height of his powers; as mentioned he had been working on the new building at Rowallan Castle. He was renowned for the sensitivity with which he restored historic houses and Sir Andrew's commission – an entirely newly built mansion house – would

*Sir Andrew and Lady Noble at the laying of Ardkinglas*
*foundation stone, 1906.*

5

*Ardkinglas under construction.*

be Lorimer's only completed large house. He became known as the Scottish Lutyens; he took much from the Arts and Crafts movement, and is known for his care in the choice of building materials and the craftsmanship of his teams of tradesmen. At Ardkinglas, probably at Sir Andrew's request, he showed a zest for the modern and the innovative. Ardkinglas was the first house in Scotland to have electricity built into it; the silver plate 'electroladas' – chandeliers with hanging bulbs – are renowned; the central-heating radiators are hidden by iron grilles, each with a different design; the principal bedroom has a shower with nozzled pipes that squirted water in a 200-degree spray from floor to head height, and there is an experimentally low lavatory pedestal. At the back of the lavatory pan is the word 'Remirol' – Lorimer spelt backwards; Sir Robert had married a Miss Shanks.

Considering the problems of communication and transportation, and the complexity of the building, its construction, its detail and the materials and craftsmen involved, it is hard to believe that it was completed in the required eighteen months. Sir Andrew travelled north by train to Arrochar and was driven (in his car, no old-fashioned horses for him) over the Rest and Be Thankful. The family processed from what was called the Old House, a converted stables where the Callanders had lived, to the entrance to the new house. Celia, wife of Sir Andrew's second-eldest son Saxton, commented acerbically that it was like a scene from Wagner's Valhalla. Sir Andrew was ceremoniously pulled along the drive in his car by estate employees and tenants.

6

The pipers played and the children followed in a procession round the house. 'At night a great bonfire was lit, while the full moon sparkled. A more lovely evening could not be imagined,' Lady Noble wrote in her autobiography *A Long Life.*

It had been an incredible achievement, a miracle of organisation of tradesmen and materials and a meld of traditional craftsmanship with modern innovations. A few weeks later Lorimer and his wife visited the Nobles. Mrs Lorimer went to Church with Lilly. Robert wandered around – 'and I tell you I had a lump in my throat as if I was saying goodbye to a child. I made a tour –

*The 'Remirol' lavatory pan.*

the power house, the dam, the waterworks, then downhill to the home farm, the garage, the kennels, the pier, the gardens. All done and finished up. Never in my life have I *enjoyed* a job like that, it all went with such a swing.' (Peter Savage, *Lorimer and the Edinburgh Craft Designers.*)

However, it wasn't a triumphant swing for everyone. Alexander Stewart, a plumber of Ardrishaig, was one of the few local suppliers. Between his quoting for the job and beginning the installation the price of lead shot up. He was expected to keep to his original quote, his firm went bust and in shame he drowned himself in the Crinan Canal.

No one could have foreseen that the first decade of the twentieth century would mark the end of grandiose houses in the Highlands. Indeed Formakin, a Lorimer commission from John Holms, a Glasgow stockbroker, which had been started in 1909, was never finished. Holms ran out of cash as a result of a bad speculation, and then the 1914–18 war brought an end to such schemes; and to some extent to a way of life.

Bon (Lady Gainford), one of Sir Andrew's older granddaughters, wrote this nice vignette describing Sir Andrew's tea-time:

On sunny afternoons Grandpapa strolled down to the Caspian [the ornamental lake that predated Lorimer's Ardkinglas] and sat in the shade of a large rhododendron bush near the water. He carried an enamel bowl of Indian corn to feed the ornamental duck. Presently the butler and footman would bring afternoon tea. A white cloth was spread on the teak garden table, silver tea pot and kettle, green dragon china. There was bread and butter and buttered toast and two sorts of jam, besides Grandpapa's special glass pot with a silver lid and spoon that held the sugared caraway seeds which he always used instead of jam. There was Patum Peperium (the Gentleman's Relish) and spring onions and radishes and two or three sorts of cake. Grown-ups sat on garden chairs and children on the grass. Several dogs had their bowls set out and were given milky tea.

(Lady Gainford, *Ardkinglas Thoughts and Memories*, unpublished.)

At the death of Lady Noble (aged 101, in 1929), the same granddaughter wrote: 'I think this was the end of an era for the whole family . . . a cousin wrote of Grandmama's death "it was like the closing of a lovely book", and looking back it seems as if it pointed an end of stability and security in our lives.' The family's idea of itself as stable and secure may have been prolonged by Lady Noble's long life, and maybe it took time for the family members to grasp the reality of changed circumstances.

Sir Andrew died when my father (John) was six. The old boy was in the habit of giving each of his grandchildren a sovereign on his birthday, so my father must have had some memory of him. But I don't ever remember him talking of him. My image of my great-grandfather is as in the Jacques-Émile Blanche portrait of Sir Andrew and Lady Noble that hangs in the dining room at Ardkinglas. They are sitting on a sofa, she upright, haughty and handsome, he whiskered and a little slumped, his head resting on a red cushion. My children used to say that he looked as if he was on the phone. My brother Johnny's explanation was that by then the old boy had lost his marbles and had to be propped up. As a child I was told that the front stairs at Ardkinglas were shallow and easy because Sir Andrew was so old he couldn't manage steep steps. So he went up these gentle ones or was put in the electric luggage lift (which we were not meant to play in, but did). When Noble relations visited I don't remember them talking about Great Grandpapa, but their overheard conversations did convey a sense of a lost era, so I suppose I was aware that the man in the portrait headed a revered dynasty.

*Foresters clearing a fallen tree in the Pinetum in 1900. Nicol Luke is on the left.*

I do have a real link with the remote world of 1905 and the Valhalla procession to the entrance of the newly completed mansion house, through a man called Nicol Luke. Nicol was born on the estate in 1876, and lived here all his life; I knew him well.

There is a photograph of foresters, including Nicol, at work clearing a huge silver fir in the Pinetum, taken early in the twentieth century. But for me Nicol is more than just a name and a faded black and white photo of a sturdy old-fashioned man in braces. In my mind's eye I can see him clearly standing by the footbridge across the Kinglas to the Ladies Walk. Apparently, aged three, I had set off to the Post Office, a mile's walk. I was well on my way to it when Nicol saw a familiar little figure passing his house, and retrieved me. My vivid memory of Nicol at the bridge and the feel of his firm warm hand at that spot must be because it was there that he and I met my mother who was searching for me. I have no memory of being at all worried.

While gathering material for this book I was interested to find a mention of Nicol even in pre-Noble days. In Duke Niall's diary of 1905, about walking through the estate prior to the sale, he wrote:

*Cairndow Post Office in 1910.*

Told Luke to clear out some of the trees in the Pinetum, in which I
found many rare species doing splendidly, several of which are not
at Inveraray at all. Some fine Picea Nobilis were quite smothered by
beastly Austrian pines. I marked out all the trees to be taken out to let
in air and light.
(Quoted by David Gray, 'Ardkinglas Woodland Garden: A Historical
          Perspective', in *Scottish Forestry*, Vol. 54, No. 2, 2000.)

In 1907, at the time of the arrival ceremony at Ardkinglas, Nicol was
twenty-one, and as an estate employee, a forester, surely he would have been
one of those pulling Sir Andrew's car to the entrance of the new house.

Nicol fought in the Great War. Then in the 1920s he was head forester on
5 shillings a week, with an allowance of cottage and garden, and in charge of
four under-foresters. (Foresters and gardeners were paid on a different scale:
at that time the head gardener was paid 10 shillings a week and had four men
under him.) Nicol was to become the elder statesman of Cairndow village,
elder of the Kirk and Registrar of births, marriages and deaths.

# The Estate

As already mentioned, the Estate that Sir Andrew bought comprised some 45,000 acres, largely rough hill ground around the head of Loch Fyne, from Dunderave Castle on the north-west side to Tighcladich on the south-east. It included the ownership of the village of Cairndow, all of Glen Fyne and its surrounding towering hills, and most of Glen Kinglas and its surrounding hills. There was little arable, or 'in-by' land round the loch and on the floor of the glens, but this was of no matter as farming was of little consequence to the new owner. The three significant farms – Clachan, Achaduan and Ardno – the small farms at Laglingarten and most of the dwelling houses were rented out to private tenants or to the tenant farmers for their employees. In 1906 the total rental income from all properties, farms, dwelling houses and pasturage, was £1,174 as against the purchase price of £62,000; an insignificant amount that would have taken some sixty years, without inflation, to break even. The houses within the vicinity of the Big House, Garden Cottage, Pier Cottage, Mid Lodge, North and East Lodge and the dwellings at the Square which existed at the time, would have been occupied by gardeners, chauffeurs, dairymen, laundresses and joiners.

By correlating the list of Rental Properties of Ardkinglas Estate in 1906, and the information on employees from even before Sir Andrew arrived (those like Nicol Luke and Archie MacVicar), with the Census for the Parish of Kilmorich of April 1911, an idea of who was who on the Estate and what they did begins to emerge.

The total population of the parish was about two hundred and forty; fifteen were over seventy (some people lived to old age then too); many children lived with parents and grandparents. Out of the working-age population there were about twenty men who would have been directly employed by the Estate – five gamekeepers, some gardeners and a few masons and joiners. The joiners included Winton, who was to play a pivotal role in the Estate and who began the records in the square red notebook from which so much of my information for the period has been gathered. But it's clear that many other men are labourers who from time to time might work for Ardkinglas Estate, or for the tenant farmers, or on any construction work. There are seventeen men, including shepherds, who are farm workers: the workers also include the tenant famers themselves, and often their sons. As will be seen from shepherd Archie MacIntyre's poem on page 14, by March 1914 the Estate was clearing sheep from the land in favour of deer.

11

*Duncan Luke at Clachan Beg in 1911.*

The houses that feature in the photographs of the period look adequate, whitewashed and neat; they would have been short of windows, running water, and WCs – in most cases these facilities would not be installed until after the 1950s. All houses would have had their own garden, and some people kept a cow. The garden and the cow's pasturage would be added to the rent, or deducted from the wage – depending whether the householder was an employee or a tenant. Most of the houses were located round the loch, and faced onto it; many people kept a boat and had rudimentary jetties. In the 1911 Census there are only three inhabited houses in Glen Fyne, and two, at Butterbridge, in Glen Kinglas. On Ordnance Survey maps of the end of the nineteenth century and as recorded in the 1901 Census there were many more hamlets in the outlying areas – like the head of Glen Fyne – and at Acharioch, around Strone and above Laglingarten. Remnants of a recent time with a much larger population in the area, by the turn of the century some of the buildings may have been lived in during the summer, others may have become byres and sheds.

When Sir Andrew bought the Estate, Henry Callander, one of the spend-thrift brothers, had shifted from the old mansion house to Strone House. But by the time of the 1911 census he had moved again, down the loch to St Catherines. Strone House must have been of a decent size as it had a rate-

12

able value second only to the Hotel. In the late 1920s the old Strone House would be demolished and rebuilt larger and grander; though not as grand as originally envisaged. The story I was told that was that my grandmother had run though too much money, and so Strone had to be completed, and the roof put on, one storey short.

In 1911 Henry Callander had moved out and a Mr William Mason, the factor, had replaced him at Strone. A factor's role was to make sure tenants paid their rent in full and timely and that employees worked diligently. To an extent what should be done, with an eye both to the welfare of the place and to budgets and expenditure, was his decision. Also he would be expected to represent the owner's views, whether the owner was at home or absent. I think it was frequently an unenviable role. He was often caught between what he knew was needed and what the owner would agree to pay; added to that he might be in a tricky social position; often a factor was nobody's friend.

The Nobles, like other well-to-do families, didn't live on their Highland estate for more than a few months in the year. (For example, on 2 April 2011, Census day, there was only a skeleton staff in the house of two housemaids, a cook, a dairymaid and a hallboy.) Though, in today's terms it would be considered a second home, for many of the family members this home was important. Its allure was to do with the freedom of the wild spaces, the romance of the Highlands, the sense of ownership and responsibility, the welcoming servants, the well-kept gardens and policies and a house designed for fun and hospitality. For these Edwardian grandees their estates were pleasure domes, for recreation and for entertaining friends and family. Sir Andrew had a motor yacht, the *Armeda*. A photograph shows Lady Noble and her daughter on deck, with the Captain, Andrew MacKellar. 'The Captain', as he was always referred to, with his distinctive long beard, appears in many photographs of Noble family ceremonies.

But it was sporting activities that were the predominant pastimes for the Edwardian gentry, and for later gentry too. Maybe with an eye on a sale, the Duke's Argyll Estates had kept an annual record of the game-bag at Ardkinglas until 1904, the last season before the sale. The list is extensive – some 360 brace of grouse, 90 head of black game (black grouse), 40 head of woodcock, 11 stags, 3,500 rabbits, 86 salmon and 330 seatrout (by rod). In 1903 and 1904 the numbers of stags killed had risen to 14 and 16. Apart from the stags these figures were never matched afterwards; so perhaps it was something of a sales-pitch.

In October 1905 Duke Niall walked from Dalmally over into the head of Glen Fyne as the sheep were being taken off the hills there, presumably to make way for deer. He was given oatcakes and milk by a Mrs MacPhee, wife of the shepherd there. She told him that she hadn't been down the glen since she arrived to live there four years before. Probably by 1905, hers was the only inhabited house at the head of the glen. For Mrs MacPhee, surviving there all through the long, wet winter months, it must have been lonely and boring. But for an autumn walk the stretch from the head of the glen along to Inverchorachan, with steep-sided Trosgiche towering above, is as beautiful as any, and with the rutting stags roaring, no wonder the Duke was affected.

Inverchorachan was, and still is, though now derelict, a single house a couple of miles down from the head of the glen. There the Duke would have greeted Archie MacIntyre, the shepherd there at the time, and discussed the weather, the flock and local knowledge. Both the shepherd and the Duke were Gaelic speakers.

A mile and a half further on down, was the MacCallums' house. Archie MacCallum had taken on the position of stalker on the Estate in 1902. In the early years of the century they had imported special large stags (I wonder how) to improve the red deer stock, and it was one of Archie's tasks to feed them during the winter. His son Colin would become a stalker too.

A few years later in Sir Andrew's day, and presumably in the interests of deer-stalking and the large stag project, Archie MacIntyre and his flock had been moved from Inverchorachan down to Clachan; and then not long after, when even Clachan hill was to be given over to deer, the sheep on Archie's hirsel (hill sheep grazing) had to be sold. So in March 1914 Archie was on his solitary, and jobless, way home from MacDonald Fraser's Mart in Stirling. His flock had been sold; hoggs, wethers, tups and in-lamb ewes and all had gone under the hammer of Paton the auctioneer. Archie had bought drams for the men at the mart (and maybe one or two for himself) and then, fond shepherd as he was, he wept for the unborn lambs he would never see. Making his forlorn way home, nearing the Rest and Be Thankful via Glen Croe, he composed a poem in Gaelic. There are sixteen stanzas to the poem (translated by Ronald Black of the Department of Celtic, University of Edinburgh). Two stanzas towards the end are as follows:

> The land . . .
> When I was a child.

Being sown and being tilled
By civilised folk;
It's now just a desert
With deer beyond number,
Giving sport to rapscallions
And some very strange people.

The deer of the cold hills
Are now on the move
With a rabble of toffs
Going out to meet them;
Some ungainly major
Scattering lead at them
And going sour and surly
If he doesn't wound them.

The issue of sheep versus deer was to continue on into the future. In March 1923 the farm tenant at Cuil complained vociferously about the increase in deer numbers. As he saw it, when he took on the tenancy in 1917, the average deer stock on the hill was 50 or 60, now it was 500 to 600. So, for lack of grazing, his sheep wander off and over to the Duke of Argyll's land. They have to be brought back, but each time they wander again. The tenancy agreement was to keep 800 sheep; at his expense he has improved the ground, but owing to the deer coming in and benefiting, the land will not carry more than 400 sheep.

Farming was of little consequence to Sir Andrew, nor was it to generations of Ardkinglas Estate owners. My uncle Michael was the only one who would be an enthusiastic farmer, as was my Aunt Anastasia (Tasia), but she was never an owner.

Nicol Luke and Archie MacCallum have already been mentioned, and as I explored the notebooks and estate journals among my parents' and aunt's papers and the Ardkinglas archives I came across the names of others I knew who had featured in my great-grandfather's day. There were other names familiar only from hearsay; I had never known them personally. But bit by bit these all began to complete the jigsaw of who was doing what on Ardkinglas Estate and who helped underpin its continued operation.

*Archie and May MacVicar's wedding in 1920.*

Among those whom I did know personally was Archie MacVicar. Before 1900 his father had had the contract to build a dam on the Fyne River for a Mr Strutt (the Strutt family rented the salmon fishing from the Estate for many years before Sir Andrew bought it). As a boy, Archie and his father camped by the Fyne while the dam was under construction. The pool there is still known as Strutt's pool and the dam still stands. Aged fifteen, Archie had worked with his father on the building of Ardkinglas. Like Nicol, Archie fought in the Great War. Back at Ardkinglas, by 1928 he was head mason, as he was to be late into the 1960s. I remember Archie for his moustaches, by then uncommon, and as for sharply waxed ones, his are the only ones I have ever seen.

Bob Cameron was another stalwart of the Estate and of the Nobles; particularly throughout the Second World War. By the time I knew him he sat in a shed at the Square with a rug over his knees, half-hiding his wooden leg, chopping kindling on a wooden block. He too had belonged to the sporting department, being a keeper or a stalker (I'm uncertain which). Paddy Noble, my uncle, said Bob 'had a soft and gentle voice, charming blue eyes, and was one of nature's gentlemen', and went on to praise his manners: 'Nobody ever missed an easy shot if they were out with Bob, as he could find you an easy excuse for the most futile of misses, and save your shame.'

During the 1920s he and Mrs Cameron and their six children lived up at Inverchorachan, by then the furthermost house in the glen (the house where Mrs MacPhee had been at the head of the glen had been abandoned). In 1928 the Lorimer 'Kennels' were refurbished (and renamed Lorimer Cottage) as a residence for a demoted farm-manager. It was converted into an eight-room cottage; a combination bath and a new Carron and Co stove was fitted; and electric light was installed and plugs for the five rooms without fireplaces for electric heating. What had been the storehouse was converted into a laundry with a boiler and two washtubs with hot and cold water. The whole house was decorated inside and out, about 60 shrubs were planted, the ground fenced off and a hen-run erected. Two unemployed miners were engaged to help with these improvements.

However the demoted manager soon left and Bob Cameron and family moved in. This newly refurbished house existed with exactly the same interiors well into the next century. And well into the next century it was lived in by keepers – the Mansons were moved in when the Camerons moved further up the Square.

Bob played a central role in the Estate community as secretary to the Recreation Club. At the December 1929 meeting it was decided to hold a shinty match on Rhu Mhor on New Year's Day, to be followed by dancing in the garage yard and then a dance in the Hall. Bob proposed that three bottles of whisky should be purchased and three bottles of Australian wine as refreshments on the day.

# The Twenties

Sir Andrew died at Ardkinglas in October 1915 at the age of 83. He left an estate with a gross value of £734,418. Estate duty on this was £136,877. The residue of the estate was left to his four sons – George, Saxton, John and Philip, 'equally' (except that George, considered by his father to be the wayward one, was only to have the interest on his share of the capital).

Sir Andrew provided in his will that each of the sons, in order of seniority, was to be allowed the chance to have Ardkinglas, on paying £85,000 to the residue of the estate. Assuming this sum was equivalent to three-quarters of the value of Ardkinglas Estate, as the purchaser would not be paying for his own quarter, the full value of Ardkinglas at the time would have been £113,000. Neither Saxton nor Philip wanted it. My grandfather, John Henry Brunel Noble, the third son, became the owner in 1917; presumably having paid up the £85,000 – equal to £6,251,000 in today's money.

At the time John was fifty. Like his brothers he had been to Eton and Balliol, Oxford. He had a nervous breakdown while at Oxford and was helped by John Meade Falkner, the novelist, who earlier had been a tutor to him and his brothers. John had joined Armstrong's when he left Oxford, in 1887, and was to continue there, on its financial side, including during the enforced merger with Vickers in 1927. He was also a Director of Martins Bank and of the London and North Eastern Railway Company (LNER).

A note from John to Lorimer in 1920 (they had become friends) shows that already the wealth that Sir Andrew enjoyed could no longer be assumed.

'Since you left I have been considering the problem you put to me as to the cost of building here [I don't know what the building referred to is] I have been forced to the conclusion that I can't afford to attempt any of the schemes considered.'

The brief boom time enjoyed in the first few years after the 14–18 war was soon over. There is a typed letter headed 'Finances', dated June 1921, unaddressed and unsigned, but probably to Sir John, listing some £10,000 of debts which had been paid, but also listing 'Supertax' which up to that point had been avoided: 'but you must be prepared to pay it at very short notice . . . The total amount due will be £10,029. And in addition £50 for income tax on untaxed interest.'

It was at around this time that the building of Strone House (not designed by Lorimer) was under way, then lack of funds curtailed it; as already mentioned, the house had to be constructed without the planned third storey.

In 1929 they had brought Achadunan Farm back into the Estate and, in a sign that now it was sheep which were taking precedence over deer, they owed an additional £11,500 for the purchase of the Achadunan sheep stock.

*Coalboat unloading in front of Ardkinglas in the 1920s.*

Their farming of Achadunan lasted only a short time, however, because from 1931 to 1935 it was let to Willie Weir, son of the Weirs at Ardno, and then in 1939 the house and the low-ground was let to John Lang as a dairy farm, with a herd of Ayrshire cattle.

The glory days of the Edwardian era may have been over, but for hedonists there was plenty of entertainment to be had during the 'roaring twenties'. Stanley Baldwin made John a baronet in 1923 (it's not clear why). That year he and his wife Amie replaced the rented home in Park Lane, London, splashing out and buying a large house in Portland Place. She was an enthusiastic socialite, he less so. There were Caledonian Balls, there were coaches decked with lilies and lace for the Eton and Harrow cricket match, and there were presentations at Buckingham Palace for debutante

*Duncan McKellar in the 1920s, at Dunderave Cottage.*

daughters. According to *The Times* Court Circular, a Juno Ball in aid of the YWCA was held in the Portland Place house in December 1926.

> Piper Duncan McKellar, from Ardkinglas, played for the foursome, eightsome, and sixteensomes. Miss Rosemary Noble and Mr Andrew Noble and their friends organised a game of 'living bridge' for which dresses representing playing cards were designed, the men (with the exception of the kings and knaves) wearing kilts. One hand was played early in the evening and the other during the supper interval.

I can dance a sixteensome, but dressed as a nine of diamonds and then to play a hand of bridge with fifty-one dancers at a Juno Ball, with Duncan MacKellar playing the pipes? To me this is as fanciful as Brigadoon.

In September of the same year, 1926 (the year of the General Strike, led by impoverished miners), the *Oban Times* gives an account of the splendid

Coming-of-Age Rejoicings at Ardkinglas for Andrew Noble (Paddy), Sir John's eldest son. Presentations were made to him by Mr Colin Brodie of Laglingarten, the oldest tenant, and by Captain Andrew MacKellar (with the long beard) the oldest employee. Mr Ballingal, the Factor, introduced them and expressed his confidence that the friendly spirit that existed between the house of Ardkinglas and the people would long exist. Duncan MacKellar (the Captain's son) played the pipes in splendid style at the banquet and for the reels. The guests who assembled in the dining room and other rooms of the mansion house included many family members and some society neighbours.

Many toasts were proposed and 'honoured'. The toast to 'The King' was given by Sir John Noble, while Graham Noble proposed the toast to old Lady Noble, now living with her daughter, Lilly, at Dunderave Castle (which had been restored by Lorimer in 1912). She replied that she was pleased that she had been spared to see the day and take part in the coming-of-age celebrations for her grandson among their people of Ardkinglas.

After the banquet, when darkness had set in, the guests went down to the foreshore for a display of fireworks carried out under the supervision of Donald MacGillivray, the electrician.

> The flames of a huge bonfire shot high into the air lighting the recesses of Glen Fyne and Glen Kinglas and other glens while its light shed far over the surface of Loch Fyne. Then in the drawing room dancing took place to the piano music of Miss Mina Stewart of Inveraray. Liberal refreshments were served during the night.
>
> *Oban Times*, 26 September 1926

Harry MacIntyre, the house joiner and Bard, presented a poem to young Andrew. It included the lines:

> All at the mansion the people are gathered
> To meet the young laird and due homage to pay,
> There will be joy at the House of the Nobles –
> Andrew of age is being honoured today.
>
> . . . With foot on the table, in true Highland honour,

[Except on a china tea cup I have never seen anyone making a toast with a foot on the table.]

20

*Harry MacIntyre, Katie McDougall, Mamie Cameron and Chrissie McIntyre at North Lodge.*

We pledge the young laird in his house by the sea.

Long may he live in the hearts of the people;
Long may he dwell in the home of his sire;
Long may the Noble name reign in Ardkinglas –
Honoured and cherished is all our desire.

Up then my hearties, three cheers for young Andrew!

I came across an odd little document scribbled on the back of a Christmas card. The writing is probably my grandmother Amie Noble's, it has the ring of her style. It is entitled 'The Assess'. It's not clear what its purpose was, perhaps a game for children? There is a little 'tag' about each employee, including Harry –

H MacIntyre Bard of Ardkinglas will make fun of you in rhyme. He will be ill-tempered at all times if you disturb his peace. But respect him as a real craftsman and he will show you how to spend happy hours making and carving beautiful furniture.

21

Harry had joined the estate in 1906 when he was forty-three. His carpentry and wood carving were admired, also his fiddle-playing and his songs and poems. He had composed a poem for the inauguration of the curling pond. Initially he lived at the North Lodge, by the Big Gates at the edge of the village. When it was demolished, and he was semi-retired, he built himself a cottage at Strone, finishing it in 1931. In April 1934, aged 71, he left the Estate to live at Inveraray.

There is an Estate Journal from 1921 to 1928, kept up until August 1928 by Mr Ballingal, the factor. That August he shot himself in the old office behind the bicycle shed at Ardkinglas. Tina Luke (soon to be Tina MacCallum), a parlourmaid, saw him going round the corner from the gun-room with a gun. No one knows why he did it. For the remaining months of 1928 the Journal was taken over by Winton. He had been a joiner on Ardkinglas Estate since 1878. He became head joiner, and must have been held in high regard, as after Ballingal's death he seems to have been promoted to be a *de facto* factor. Of Winton 'The Assess' says:

> Mr Winton will teach you how to succeed in life. He can build houses and it is men like him who built up our empire in its early days. His motto certainly is – I am able to do this job. I can do it. I ought to do it. And I will do it.

Winton's style in the Journal is more in command, it conveys more of a sense of what is going on than poor Ballingal did. This journal stops, without explanation, at the end of 1928, though there are plenty of empty pages in the book and though Winton didn't retire until 1936.

To me the most telling aspect of the Journal is that there is little mention of intervention by or interest in the Estate from Sir John. We know that during those years he had other preoccupations. Until the forced merger in 1927 he was still a director of the failing Armstrongs. In the Journal there is no indication of Estate strategy nor proposals; reading between the lines it seems the policy was – carry on as usual. The income to the Estate (such as it was) was still largely rental from the farms and cottages, and the lease of fishing and stalking; though the woods and timber were, and continued to be, Ardkinglas's most consistent source of income. The outgoings were largely the wages for the indoor and outdoor household staff, the estate gamekeepers, joiners and masons, and the materials for the yearly maintenance of all the dwellings and the Big House.

The December 1928 Journal entry is one of Winton's last:

McVicar [Archie] and his men have finished the work at Pier House where Donald MacGillivray lives, Mrs MacCallum's chimney at Glen Fyne and the stables at Clachan have also been done. Now they will make the annual round of each cottage to examine roofs and do essential repairs in rotation.

They will go over Ardkinglas House roof and see the slates are alright and they will clean the lead rhones, some of which are sagging rather badly and must soon be overhauled and straightened. There are 21 windows where rhones crossing sag and remain full of water to the brim. The nursery window and the one at the front of the house leak. Last winter's frost caused the soldered joints to burst and split open, the lead has been torn away for want of support as the average length between straps at different windows is 4ft 5in to 4ft 8in. [This, which might be considered a fault on Lorimer's part, is a continuing problem!]

In those days there were teams who kept up the maintenance, annually, on all the Estate buildings – a great contrast to what is possible today.

Because the sporting side of the estate was so valued, both for the Noble family's own pleasure and for the income from leasing it, facilities for gamekeepers and their dogs were given priority. At Lorimer Cottage new kennels and a run were constructed for the spaniels. The Journal contains details about keepers and gun-dogs:

Each keeper should have the chance of keeping and handling a dog, it is good rivalry and each man will aspire to have the best dog.

The price of a spaniel at the time was £28, a lot of money when a ton of coal was £1. 3s.

In 1928 three new kennels were constructed at Glen Fyne, with piped water; though the MacCallums' dwelling house didn't have piped water until the 1950s.

In November 1928, Winton wrote that the Estate accounts would now close at old Martinmas (11 November) and that from then onwards Miss

*Lady Noble in 1929, aged 100.*

Powell Jones would take over the account book for the 'outside staff' (perhaps until August this had been a Ballingal task). This meant she was to pay the five gardeners, the garden carters, two men at the garage, and the electrician, as these were 'outdoor household staff' rather than belonging to the Estate. The large number of garden staff were required to maintain the lawns and grounds and to provide flowers and vegetables while the family was in residence.

The Miss Powell Jones, who was mentioned in the guest list at Andrew's coming of age, was known as 'Daisy'. She had been private secretary to Sir John from 1914. She kept household accounts both in London and at Ardkinglas, often paid the wages and dealt with a variety of correspondence, always in her characteristic green ink. From time to time her daily household diaries give us insights into the goings on at Ardkinglas – though the insights are all too few and there is always too much about the weather:

> St Swithun's day, a nasty vile wet morning which became heavy showers in the afternoon. Too depressing, so 40 days more of this and the weeds have never been worse.

(St Swithun's day is 15 July and it is said that if it rains on that day it will rain for the next 40 days.)

Daisy was very much part of the family through until the 1970s.

It seems that during the 1930s Winton and Daisy were masterminding the Estate, or what there was of it to mastermind. Winton retired in 1936 at 78, after 58 years of service. He left an immaculate inventory of joiners' tools with his initials branded into them. A few of these sailed the seas to New Zealand with Jimmy Stewart (the next head joiner who was to emigrate in 1953); others of them are still here, and now used by Nigel Callander. Briefly

Winton went to live in Pitcairn, Perthshire, but died soon after his move and is buried in the graveyard at Ardkinglas.

# Decline

In 1927, the Governor of the Bank of England instigated a merger between Armstrongs and Vickers, as both businesses were nearly insolvent. Armstrongs had been brought to its knees by 'diversifying' into a pulp and paper mill in Newfoundland in 1922. It had also diversified into railway engines, cars, commercial aircraft, merchant ships and papermaking machinery. This was financed on borrowed money. Its debt increased from £5,000,000 in 1922 to £14,000,000 in 1926. It must have been demoralising, at the least, for Sir John and his older brother Saxton, who were directors on the financial side at Armstrongs.

The 1920s may have been the 'roaring twenties' for some, but for the UK economy it was depression and decline. The later 1920s and the early 1930s were dominated by the high levels of unemployment. For most people the 1930s were dark days. The Wall Street crash of 1929 lead to the Great Depression, and by 1932 some 20 per cent of the British workforce was unemployed.

Information on the 1930s at Ardkinglas is scant. Rosemary Noble and her brothers, Andrew and John, were all married between 1931 and 1934. The photographs and the professional films made of the weddings show that they were fashionable London occasions. None of them were held at Ardkinglas: perhaps it was customary for all 'society' weddings to be held in London. Sometime in the mid-1930s the family had to rent out the Portland Place house to produce needed income. In its place a more modest flat in Weymouth Mews was leased; from there Amie Noble continued her London social life. As the decade wore on Sir John spent more time at Ardkinglas, as his health, and perhaps his spirits, deteriorated.

These were tough times for the Highland estates. Many were sold or were having to sell off farms. In *Yesterday Was Summer: The Marion Campbell Story*, David Adams McGilp and Marian Pallister explain how Marion, devoted as she was to the Kilberry Esate she had inherited, viewed it as something of a poisoned chalice. The fact was that 'The accumulated debts and mortgages and the reality of constraints gripped estates such as Kilberry after the Great War . . . Many estates were being broken up and farms being sold off.'

No part of the Ardkinglas Estate was sold, though John too may have been thinking of it as a poisoned chalice, certainly as a difficult duty. Hugh Raven, a member of the family which has owned Ardtornish Estate in Morven since 1930, wrote this about his grandfather's purchase and ownership:

> Owen Hugh Smith was already sixty-one when he first saw Ardtornish. He came from a banking family, his principal business was chairman of Hay's Wharf, the international trading company on the south bank of the Pool of London. He visited Ardtornish in May 1930 and noted it was 45,000 acres, good stalking, 36 stags, good fishing, salmon and sea trout, the whole place very attractive but for the hideous house, though well found and comfortable. He bought it for £30,000, calculating £15k for the place, £5k for the furniture, £10k for the sheep. Then he sold on a portion to the Forestry Commission for £7k.
>
> In the 1930s he financed the running cost of the place out of income, the cost was Smith's largest single expense but was still less than a quarter of his annual expenditure . . . Ardtornish remained for its proprietor principally a sporting estate; but both to him and certainly to those who lived and worked there, it was also a great deal more than that.

This raises several points in relation to Ardkinglas. The first is that the value of Highland estates had fallen significantly since the early years of the century. Owen Hugh Smith bought his 45,000 acres (with spacious mansion house and many dwelling houses) for £30,000. Sir Andrew had paid £55,000 for his 45,000 acres without a proper mansion house. Even allowing for the fact that Ardtornish is more remote than Ardkinglas and further from a railway station, this is a significant difference in cost. The next point is that, despite the common complaints of draconian taxes in the 1920s and 1930s, there were men with a lot of money. Smith was able to finance the estate's running cost out of income, which was still less than a quarter of his annual expenditure. At Ardkinglas at the same time Sir John, though certainly well off by most ordinary people's standards, was not in the league of being able to finance his estate's running costs out of income, with seventy-five per cent more to spare. The demise of Armstrong's had put a major dent in his portfolio.

Hugh Raven's final point, that for his grandfather and friends and family it remained principally a sporting estate, 'but both to him and certainly to those who lived and worked there, it was also a great deal more than that' is important to this book. I am sure that it applied to Sir John and his family too. Inevitably with hindsight we view the past through a different lens. Much of that world seems like Brigadoon to me, and the leather-bound albums with photographs of 'After the Northern Meeting', with groups of lackadaisical young men and women on well-mowed lawns, Oban Ball dance cards with a pink pencil, noting a partner for the Duke of Perth and Hamilton House, and 'A Good day on the Fyne', with a row of salmon laid out on a bank, don't make me hanker

*Sir John and Amie Noble, 1935.*

for those days. However, because at the time that way of life was important to the Nobles, it does not follow that the place and its people there were unimportant to them.

On Ardkinglas Estate in the early 30s times weren't as bad as for people in Glasgow or Newcastle, but here too times were tough. In July 1932 all estate employees had their wages reduced (though farm wages weren't cut, presumably because of the need of food production). Winton's wages were reduced from £4 per week to £3 10s in 1932, and then in July 1933 reduced further to £3, in all a 25% reduction. This percentage roughly applied to all the Estate employees from 1932 onwards. Wages began to rise again, slowly, but didn't reach their previous level until 1937.

As far as I am aware, after Winton retired, no Factor or Manager was appointed. This may have been due to lack of funds but it may also have been that the situation was considered so unpromising there was no point; or it could have been a combination of both reasons.

There were Government interventions with an impact at Ardkinglas – BBBF, 'British Boys for British Farms', meant that boys from areas of severe unemployment were given accommodation and jobs on the land. Amie Noble became an enthusiast for the idea. There was also the Baldwin Unemployment Scheme. Under this scheme several employees came to Ardkinglas on a wage of £2 per week. What would turn out to be the most significant contribution to Ardkinglas Estate through any of these schemes was the arrival of John Taylor, or Jack Taylor as he was always known.

Jack, born in 1902, was from Motherwell. He had served some years with the RAF, and came to Ardkinglas in 1928 under the Baldwin Scheme, as an estate clerk. He had the use of a room at the garage which was electrically lit (from the Big House plant). The room was valued at £1 per annum and the electricity also valued at £1 per annum. His wages were £2 a week. He had 'meals indoors'; presumably that meant with the Big House staff. He married in 1930, a Margaret Humphrey, who had been a maid with the Nobles in London (the butler, ladies' maids and some others travelled backwards and forwards to London and Ardkinglas with the family). The married couple then moved to a new cottage by the garage which also was lit electrically. It came to be known as Dacia Cottage; previously it had been used as the Club Rooms, which had had a library room stocked with newspapers – the *Glasgow Herald*, *The Bulletin*, and *Strand Magazine* – and it had an allocation of 10 tons of coal per annum. Jack's wage was raised to £3 per week, but as with other employees was then reduced in July 1932 and again in 1933.

Though there will be much more about Jack Taylor, as he was to become a mainstay of Ardkinglas until his death in December 1980, here I want to acknowledge his invaluable contribution to this section of this book. There is a square red cloth-backed notebook entitled, in handwritten upper-case lettering that could grace a Bible or Royal records – *PARTICULARS OF ESTATE & FARM EMPLOYEES*. It is this notebook – in which there is a page per employee, I think initially entered by Winton and then in Jack's inimitable writing – that provides most of the information about employees from 1905 until 1936. It gives details about the employees already mentioned and introduces others who will be playing important roles.

*Jimmy Stewart (the baby) with his parents at Abyssinia in Glen Kinglas in 1905.*

Among these, for instance, Jimmy Stewart, born 1905, came to the estate aged fourteen. He was the son of Catherine and John Stewart, originally a shepherd at Abyssinia in Glen

*Ian McLachlan, William MacPherson, Ina Cameron, Kate
MacDougal, Donald MacPherson, Douglas Luke and Angus McInnes
in 1931.*

Kinglas. In 1928, when Winton became Estate Manager, Jimmy was promoted to head joiner and lived in the other part of Mid Lodge (where Winton had been), on a wage of £2 per week and an allocation of 5 tons of coal a year. In March 1936 he married a Miss Bashford, Lady Noble's lady's maid, always known as Bashie.

The notebook has a page each for two young men from familiar Cairndow families. William MacPherson, born 1919, was an apprenticed joiner with Jimmy in 1936 on 10 shillings per week. He was the son of Dougald MacPherson, at the time shepherd at Ardno Farm and brother of Donald MacPherson, later to become head shepherd for Michael Noble. There was Nicol Douglas Luke, known as Douglas (son of Nicol). He started work in May 1934 as a forester, but two years later was transferred to the masons. He was important to the community as he played the accordion for dances.

And there is Angus MacGillivray born in 1899, brother of Donald, Sir Andrew's electrician, who came to the estate in 1919 (it was Donald who masterminded the firework spectacular for Paddy's 21st birthday celebrations). In 1928 Angus was an under-gardener and groundsman. He was to become head gardener, a loner whom we feared when we tried to reach a long arm into the greenhouse to pick the tomatoes. He was married to May;

29

in the 1920s she was referred to as a second laundry maid, but by the 1950s she did all the laundry. I would go to her to request she press my ball gown, when reluctantly I was to attend one of those dance-card with pink pencil Oban Balls. Angus and May lived at Laundry Cottage, at the Square, opposite the Stables, until they retired well into the 1960s.

Archie MacCallum, the feeder of large stags, has already been mentioned. His eldest son Colin has a page in the red notebook; he became head stalker when his father retired. Colin married Tina Luke from Laglingarten, a parlourmaid at Ardkinglas. Old Archie lived some of the time with the younger shepherding son Duncan down at Mark Park, and some of the time with Colin and Tina. I remember him there, whiskery and with a white beard, sitting comfortably on the far side of the range. The MacCallum family were to live in what was always called 'Tina's house' until the 1970s, when she moved down to Clachan. Archie's grandson Alastair, granddaughter Janet, great-grandson Colin, and great-great-grandsons Alastair and Craig, are still here in Cairndow.

Well before the romantic concept of the Highlands and Highlanders was established by Sir Walter Scott or Edwin Landseer, around the time of Macpherson's *Ossian*, Robert Burns, though son of an Ayrshire farmer, played up the romance of the Highlands for his Southern admirers.

> Farewell to the Highlands, farewell to the North,
> The birth-place of Valour, the country of Worth;
> Wherever I wander, wherever I rove,
> The hills of the Highlands for ever I love.
>
> *Chorus*
> My heart's in the Highlands, my heart is not here,
> My heart's in the Highlands, a-chasing the deer;
> Chasing the wild-deer, and following the roe,
> My heart's in the Highlands, wherever I go.

For the Noble family there was (and is) something about Glen Fyne that epitomises the romance of a Highland glen: a tug at the heart-strings, a tightening to the rib-cage. Veronica Gainford, (née Noble), the only child of George Noble, wrote:

Oh glen of blessed memory . . . always the glen cast its spell over me . . . The line of hills are more beautiful than any I know, and there is an atmosphere with a quality unequalled anywhere else. How lucky we were to spend so much of our young lives in that perfect spot.

*John Noble, Archie MacCallum, a friend and a famous 30 lb salmon.*

She returned in her seventies and eighties to holiday at unelectrified Inverchorachan by herself, in September when the stags were beginning to roar.

Days on the hill with the companionship of stalkers like Archie and Colin, crawling through burn and heather to get a grand stag's antlers in the rifle's bead, were an experience to be treasured from stalking season to stalking season by men, and some women. The friendship with the stalker and a vision of his simple 'rustic' life was, perhaps to some still is, intrinsic to a sportsman's perception of the Highlands. The rural idyll was described by Oliver Goldsmith in *The Deserted Village* (1770):

A man he was to all the country dear . . .

Remote from towns he ran his godly race,
Nor e'er had chang'd nor nor wished to change his place;
Unpractised he to fawn, or seek for power,
By doctrines fashion'd to the varying hour.

Lord Cottesloe expressed a very similar sentiment about Colin MacCallum. Cottesloe was a crack rifle-shot and an old friend of the Noble family – he wrote 'The Ballade of Glen Fyne' to Sir John Noble in 1934. 'Ah, hills

31

*Young lairds at the Oban Games in 1933.*

of happy memory! The mail must bear me south tonight.' His sentimental poem expresses envy of the (supposedly), simple man and his simple life in the Highland hills.

> Son of the hills, of toil unsparing,
> Colin, the wise, the keen of eye –
> Still shall he hear the great harts blaring
> Defiance, and each brae reply;
> For him the storm that tears the sky,
> The silent snow, the winter's bite,
> Till jewelled spring return – and I?
> The mail must bear me south tonight.
>
> *Envoi*
> The sunset pales, its glories fly;
> So brief is all our best delight.
> Glen of my heart, goodbye, goodbye;
> The mail must bear me south to-night.

For many members of the Noble family, and their friends and tenants past and present, the MacCallum family became intrinsic to Glen Fyne. Tina's welcome, and Tina's pancakes, Tina's milk were meshed into Glen Fyne memories.

# The Later 1930s: Nothing Improving

Harry MacIntyre, once the esteemed joiner and the bard, had retired to Inveraray in 1934. He died in hospital in Glasgow in January 1936, aged seventy-three. Later that year, in October, there is a letter from Harry's widow, Chrissie, from Inveraray, asking Lady Noble for assistance to help pay the outstanding account for Harry's funeral. Chrissie explained that on that morning she had had a letter from the undertaker asking for a settlement of the account, but as she was on Parish Relief she didn't have much money coming into the house. Daisy, secretary to Sir John and Lady Noble, wrote to George Cardwell, the undertaker, to ask how much was owed. He replied that it was £9 10s. Daisy offered £6 in settlement. George Cardwell must have suggested that if that was all, perhaps Mrs MacIntyre might pay the balance later. Daisy knew that a widow on Parish Relief could not contribute, and she retorted: 'Unless you are prepared to accept this offer I should say the chances of your account being paid are remote.'

Poor George Cardwell wrote: 'I am in a very funny position for I do my job and have to hope for the best. The funeral is all over and the material used for same paid for by me and now I have to accept £3 less than I am due. I cut this job to the lowest figure and it means I am to be the sufferer.'

Ardkinglas was not moved, did not recall old Harry's loyal words at Andrew's 21st celebrations:

> Long may the Noble name reign in Ardkinglas
> Honoured and cherished is all our desire.

The Ardkinglas reply was: 'It is really up to you whether you decide whether to take the £6 or not . . . I should like to point out that from a business proposition you are getting £75% of the account which otherwise you would have had to consider the whole as bad debt, which everyone knows occurs in every line of business.'

George, surprised and disappointed, accepted the £6. Making a living as an undertaker in Govan in the late 1930s can't have been easy. Harry's underpaid funeral was probably not his only bad debt that year, but he might have hoped for better from the Nobles. Times were tough for everyone in the mid-1930s but measured on different scales: it was tough at Ardkinglas mansion house, but much tougher on Langlands Road, Govan.

Sir John grew increasingly ill. By 1937, nationally things had improved enough to reinstate Estate wages at least to where they had been in 1930, and a little better, but the future was far from promising. The levels of taxation caused those with money great anxiety. In the clubs of St James's was heard the ditty – 'There's a rumour going around that income tax is soon to be ten shillings in the pound.' And there was gathering gloom about what was happening in Germany.

Sir John was very ill during the autumn of 1937, with cirrhosis of the liver. He died at Ardkinglas in January 1938 aged seventy-three. I know that all his children, with the possible exception of Paddy who felt unloved, were very fond of him. I have little idea what he was like and unfortunately his diaries that were until relatively recently in book ends on a table in the billiard-room can't be found. Such letters as there are tell me little. From what I learnt from my parents, he loved and felt responsible for Ardkinglas and its people, but felt pessimistic about its future.

At the time of Sir John's death, Ardkinglas Estate was still the original 45,000 acres that Sir Andrew had bought. According to the probate registry, the gross value of all of Sir John's estate was pre-tax £703,289 (equivalent to £41,210,000 today). Of this, £185,000 (£10,840,000 in today's money) was the heritable estate, i.e. Ardkinglas, including the house, while £398,000 was his personal wealth. A receipt from the Inland Revenue shows that tax of £120,268 had been paid as estate duty and also the interest on the estate duty, thus amounting to almost 25% of the whole.

# Interim and Self-sufficiency: 1938 to 1945

## January 1938 to 1 September 1939

On the death of Sir John, his eldest son Andrew (always known as Paddy), in-herited the baronetcy. He had joined the Foreign Office in 1928, and married Sisi, a Norwegian. By 1938 they had two children, Iain and Laila. Whatever the future of Ardkinglas was going to be, Paddy let it be known that he didn't want to be involved; he wanted to continue his Foreign Office career and would sell out his share to his brothers John and Michael.

The probability is that for some time after Sir John's death, decisions about Ardkinglas's future were yet to be made. From what I gathered from my parents, the uncertain prospects for Ardkinglas's continued viability had saddened Sir John. There is a letter dated 17 January 1938 from Michael to Elizabeth (John's wife, my mother), thanking her for a letter of sympathy on his father's death. It is a charming letter; describing his love and his apprecia-tion of his father, he goes on to say: 'If there are any ways in which I can help John, of course I will, for I feel it depends so much on us whether we can carry on things that Daddy would have wanted us to do, and the least tribute we can pay to his memory seems to be this.'

At this point so soon after the death, was it assumed that John, being the next eldest son, would inherit? What certainly seems to have happened here at this moment, as in other cases of landed estates, was that the death of the owner, a beloved relation, whets a determination in the family to fight on. There is a strong sense of the duty to carry the inherited yoke, whether that be realistic or not.

John, said to be Sir John's favourite, was then 29. After Eton and Oxford, during the early 1930s he had spent time studying in Germany. In the later 1930s he had founded an underwriting business called John Noble and Co. He and his brother-in-law Harry Lucas had also set up the New Trading Company, with the Jewish refugees Heinz Grunfeld and Siegmund Warburg; it was to become S. G. Warburg and Co, the investment bank. In 1934 John had married Elizabeth (née Lucas). In 1938 their children were Sarah, aged three, and Johnny, aged two.

Michael, said to be his Mother's favourite, was also educated at Eton and Oxford. At the time of his father's death he was 25 and single. He was yet to decide on his profession, and for that reason was probably the one who had been most at Ardkinglas during his father's illness.

Both John and Michael at this time were mostly London-based; throughout the 1920s and 1930s they had London residences, though they spent holidays and family occasions at Ardkinglas.

As already mentioned, during the later 1930s it isn't clear who had been running the Estate and farms – nor how much there was to be run. There isn't any evidence of an Estate factor or manager; maybe it was felt there was too little money to spare for employing one, and too little point. Daisy Powell-Jones and Jack Taylor – whose involvement with the Estate spans four sections of this book – were keeping the accounts and the wage books.

On the farms, Miss Wallace, her brother and an invalid sister were living at Clachan, but not farming. The Weirs held the tenancy at Ardno and had done so since 1918, and would be there until 1962. John Weir had three sons, John, Willie and Robbie. Willie Weir was the tenant at Achadunan from

*John Noble in the Billiard Room at Ardkinglas in 1938.*

*John Lang at Achadunan.*

1928. Willie would give it up in 1939 when John Lang, with his family and his herd of Ayrshire cows, took it on. Bobby Johnstone (known as Gandhi because of his skinniness and swarthy colour) had been a shepherd off and on during the 1920s. He had married Bonella (Bonny) Payne, daughter of Payne the electrician. They lived in Garage Cottage at The Square. During the war years Bobby was to become a de facto farm manager and a source of support to the women in charge.

Sometime during the months after Sir John's death, it was decided that for the time being Ardkinglas House would be let out to sporting tenants for short and longer lets.

At Christmas 1938, John and his family and Michael and Tasia were all at Ardkinglas. Perhaps it was at this time that the decision was made to let Ardkinglas House itself. It was also decided that John and Michael would jointly buy out Paddy's share of the £185,000 estate, gradually, as their funds permitted. In January 1939 Christies came to carry out a valuation of Sir John's silver collection; in due course the sale of some of it would help John and Michael pay Paddy for his share of Ardkinglas.

Thus far in its history Ardkinglas had not been a place where any of its owners worked or lived permanently. In 1938 it is improbable that either of the brothers would have thought of doing so. No one would have envisaged that from the following year, for the best part of six years, the house and the estate would be largely run by women – Elizabeth Noble, Tasia Noble and Daisy Powell-Jones. Ostensibly they were 'holding the fort' until the war would be over, but in fact they were laying the foundations of a family home and future estate with a tight-knit community that would last generations.

Elizabeth née Lucas, known locally as Mrs John, was born in 1909 into a sophisticated Jewish family. She had lived at Oakash, in the Berkshire Downs, and in Mayfair in London. Before her marriage to John she had studied at Westminster Art School, and was a painter.

Anastasia (Tasia), born in 1911, known locally as Miss Anastasia, was Sir John and Amie's younger and unmarried daughter. (Rosemary, the oldest of Sir John's children, married in 1931, was living elsewhere.) She was an equestrian, and drove a coach and four then owned by Bertram Mills, the circus people. She kept a horse in London, which, with the groom, would travel to Arrochar on the train and she would ride over the Rest and Be Thankful to Ardkinglas. In 1930 she got her first deerhound; breeding deerhounds would become her lifelong occupation.

Constance (Daisy) Powell-Jones, known locally as Miss Daisy, was born in 1885 and died in 1973. She had arrived with the Nobles in 1914 (through her sister who was a nurse to Michael), as a private secretary to Sir John. By 1915 the household wage books were being kept in her distinctive writing, and during the 1930s she had handled the household accounts in Newcastle, London and at Ardkinglas; thereafter, with Jack Taylor, she kept the Estate ones too.

*Tasia driving a coach and four in Hyde Park, 1930s.*

*Daisy Powell-Jones at Arrochar Station.*

❦

For the moment, whether at Ardkinglas or in London, to an extent life was still led as it had been for years, though those who paid heed viewed war as inevitable. Elizabeth prepared for the two refugee children she was sponsoring from Germany. On 7 March 1939, Elizabeth's diary records, 'Mussolini has invaded Albania' and on 18 March 1939 she writes 'Hitler threatening Rumania, news very gloomy'. Because of this, or perhaps despite it, on 30 May, Amie Noble, Sir John's widow, an eccentric and always a travel enthusiast, set off for Hong Kong via Marseilles for a year travelling round the world (she didn't return until 1946).

From April 1939 onwards, Elizabeth divided her time between Ardkinglas, with the children Sarah and Johnny and their Nanny, called Mouse, and in London with John. Elizabeth's diary mentions that Nicol Luke, now sixty-three and still head forester, came to cut Sarah and Johnny's hair 'quite well'. Tasia and Michael were at Ardkinglas much of the time. There were many days when everyone participated in gardening, planting and weeding and cutting and sawing wood and making bonfires, which had always been everyday activities for everyone when at Ardkinglas. Now they were also sorting out cupboards, linen and carpets and china, preparing for the arrival of

39

the tenants. By the end of July all the sorting of cupboards, china, glass, linen etc was completed.

From June 1939 there is an invoice for an order of goods from Marcus Cockayne Ltd, Regent Street London. As it includes 12 packets of parrot food, it must have been ordered by the Fairhursts, the tenants-to-be, who had a parrot; its beak marks can still be seen at Ardkinglas on the pantry shelving. The order list also includes a stone of sultanas, 12 tins of Gospo cleaning paste, 3 gallons of malt vinegar, a hundredweight of scrubbing soap at £1.6s and a hundredweight of preserving sugar at £1.7s.1d. It seems they envisaged a lengthy tenancy.

In 1934 Elizabeth and John had spent their honeymoon in Glen Fyne Lodge; the MacCallum family lived close by. John must have known Colin from childhood; like his father Archie, he was a gamekeeper and stalker, and they had spent happy days on the river and hill together. Elizabeth soon became friends with Tina. She told Mrs John how, when she was first married, and lonely up the glen, her mother would stand out in front of her home at Laglingarten and swing a lantern. From some seven miles down the glen and the loch, Tina had been comforted by the sight of the swinging glimmer. On 29 July, along with children, dogs, Tasia's hawks and horses, all the family moved up to Glen Fyne Lodge and the Bungalow, and with excitement and pleasure prepared to settle in for the summer.

And the Fairhursts arrived to take over Ardkinglas House. Elizabeth commented: 'they had masses of stuff and very messy staff, crowds of dogs, two doves and a monkey, the parrot and, by the next day, a yacht.'

My sister Sarah remembers the excitement of seeing a monkey downstairs by the store cupboard. Janet MacCallum remembers that when the Fairhursts came up the glen to fish, her mother was asked to set the table outdoors with a tablecloth for their tea. And she remembers their yacht *Cuil*, a steam yacht with a funnel. Janet thought it enormous.

During August 1939 the international crisis worsened; Ribbentrop went to Moscow to sign a pact with Russia agreeing that the two countries would not fight each other, nor help any another country against either of them. Elizabeth spent some of the time in London with John. He went to the city every day, to John Noble & Co. and the New Trading Co. She might go to a picture gallery while he was there, then they would have dinner at the Berkeley Grill or have people to dinner at their house in Palace Gardens Terrace.

❧

*Tina MacCallum, a friend, Mrs MacDiarmid and children and Sarah and Johnny, at Glen Fyne Lodge in 1939.*

When not in London, Elizabeth was at Glen Fyne Lodge with the children and Mouse, along with Paddy's wife, Sisi, their children Iain and Laila and their nanny. The MacCallums – Old Archie, Colin, Tina and the children Janet, Archie and little Colin – were at their house nearby. By mid-August holidays were over for Janet and Archie, and for them once again it was the four-mile walk down to the school. The Roddy MacDiarmid family (he was a shepherd) were at Mark Park, a mile down river, on the right bank. The older MacDiarmid children would join Janet and Archie for the walk down to school. The Langs, who had moved in that year, were at Achadunan, yet further down the Glen. So the Nobles were among a little community in Glen Fyne.

Saturday 19 August was the Sheep Dog Trials. Tasia, Michael, John (who was there for the event) and Elizabeth went down to Ardkinglas to take out the china for the lunch. Lunch for eighty or ninety of the county society at set tables in the dining room had been a regular event during the 1930s. This year it had to be in the village hall, as the Fairhursts were ensconced in Ardkinglas. John went back to London on the Sunday evening. On Monday the china was put back into a cupboard at Ardkinglas, the one in the oak-panelling behind the door in the dining room (where it would remain untouched for forty years). Then Tasia, Michael and Elizabeth went over to Clachan to help with the haymaking, the work cooled and thirst-quenched by drinking oatmeal in water. Finally, in the evening on their way back up the Glen, on foot or bicycle, or maybe on horseback, they bathed in the Whirlpool on the Fyne.

*Tasia and Michael at sheepdog trials in 1938.*

*Elizabeth Noble, Tasia Noble and Daisy Powell-Jones haymaking at*
*Ardkinglas.*

A day or two later Elizabeth went down to London to join John. On 29
August 1939, five days before the outbreak of war, she wrote in her diary:
'John and I had a cosy dinner and evening. Parliament met today. Chamberlain made a long speech. He isn't able to divulge Hitler's note but he has
replied to it.'

The next day Elizabeth went to offer her services at the Town Hall Air
Raid Precaution offices. Then home to Palace Garden Terrace to 'garden a
little and paint a picture of the house from the garden'. This was the last picture she painted until the 1960s. This is also her last ever personal diary entry.
She had kept a daily diary since childhood.

At 11 am on 31 August the directive had come to 'evacuate forthwith'.
120,000 children were to leave Glasgow within three days. I found two letters she wrote to John, both written on 31 August. The first is a note left in
their house, at Palace Gardens Terrace, for John in case he didn't get back
from the office before she left for Kings Cross to catch the sleeper train, telling him that she had hidden the keys to his gold cup box and her jewel case

behind the bookcase. The second letter was written when she was on the train; it is a cry of anguish and passion at having left him in London. She felt she had made the wrong decision: 'My beloved, I don't think I've ever, ever been more miserable. How could I ever have left you today I can't imagine.' And she questioned herself: should she get off the train at York and try to get back to London? In the end she stayed on the train and got the sleeping car attendant to send John a telegram.

During the war years (for my parents they were from this 31 August until May 1946, when John came back to Ardkinglas) they were not together for anything more than short holidays. Neither of them were in direct danger. A bomb might have fallen somewhere in London where John happened to be, or on a train that one of them happened to be in. But those years were to change Elizabeth's life for ever, also Daisy and Tasia's; and maybe John's too, to a lesser extent. Afterwards, even when I was grown up, people didn't talk about what those years were really like, not what they thought or felt or knew. Incidents mentioned were trivial, like finding an onion washed up on the shore (it was so rare and exciting they didn't know what to do with it) and the thrill of seeing the King's train waiting at Arrochar station. It may have been partly that, after the first year, John was working with the Government Code and Cypher School decoding at Bletchley Park, and the lifting of the secrecy restrictions wasn't until after his death. But I think their, perhaps unconscious, reluctance to talk about those years came about because they didn't want to remind themselves. Looking back on that time it's as though we see the ripples on the surface of the water, with little idea of the currents below.

Unfortunately the last existing letter from Elizabeth to John is March 1940. If we still had later ones they would be invaluable, as she did write about what she felt and thought and saw. After John's death in 1972 she burnt a lot of letters.

# From September 1939 Ardkinglas Becomes a Home to Many

After arriving off that sleeper train at Arrochar on the morning of 1 September Elizabeth went straight to join the others at Glen Fyne Lodge. Then that morning, she and Tasia, Michael, Sisi and the children and nannies moved down from the Lodge back to Ardkinglas, so that evacuee families could go to the Lodge. The Nobles were going to have to share Ardkinglas with

*Paddy, Sisi, Rosemary, Ernest, John, Elizabeth, Michael Noble and the children Iain and Laila.*

the Fairhurst tenants until they could move out the following week. It was thought that evacuees with their mothers would need to use the Lodge and the Bungalow. None of the evacuees were to go to Ardkinglas; it was planned that the big houses were to be kept in reserve in case there was a sudden rush of evacuees later, or else they were to be needed as hospitals or convalescent homes.

That night, or rather in the early hours of 2 September, Elizabeth wrote to John: 'I've had to play bridge tonight, Mike, Mrs Fairhurst and Sisi and I. It was hateful. The hammer in my head went on and on "War! War! War!" I don't know if they enjoyed it. They seemed to. I tried to seem to, Johnnie, I know you would have wanted me to.'

She complained of a numbness, of not being able to think. And of how difficult it was living with all these people around.

On 3 September, the day war was formally declared, what must have been long-planned preparations swung into action and eighty evacuees arrived from Glasgow, off the steamer at Lochgoilhead. Five charabancs were there to meet them. But there was a change of plan as to where they were to go. The previous day the Glaswegian evacuees had rioted when they had been placed in remote lonely places. So it was now decided neither the Lodge nor the Bungalow were suitable: the Glen was considered too remote for school-children and mothers with babies. Instead mothers and families were to go to

Strone, and a number of children were allocated to Ardkinglas House itself and to houses round the village.

Sixty-seven years later, in 2006 Helen Hepburn (married name Dunion) wrote to us from Canada about her childhood in Cairndow.

I had my 9th Birthday on Sept 1st 1939 & 2 days later war was declared. I was fortunate to be sent to Mr and Mrs Ure, my granny & grandad's at East Lodge Cairndow [she would be there for 3½ years].

I was considered a 'private evacuee' & was allowed to go to Kilmorich School, Miss Munro was the teacher there. A one-room school was very new to me, but I soon got to know my classmates & the other children. They soon became my friends.

The Square was the gathering place for us to play & have some fun but I always had to be back in time to lock up the chicken house & get in to the house before the 9.00 o'clock news came on. Sometimes there was only enough juice in the battery to hear the news.

The Square (dated 1764) is about 400 yards from the 'Big House'. The Square itself is a courtyard with various buildings surrounding it or within its vicinity. It must once have been the yard for stables and carriage horses. During the war years there were at least six dwelling houses here. From there it would have been a fifteen-minute scamper for Helen up the drive to get back home to East Lodge. She named her playmates:

Isabel, Margaret & Avril [Johnstone, daughters of Bobby and Bonella] lived in the groom house at the Square. Eileen & Peggy Taylor at Pier Cottage were also close friends and I played with them a lot. Andrew & Vickie were younger. There was Ishie Shaw & Walter [daughter and son of Dougie] who lived near Mr & Mrs [Angus] MacGillivray in the laundry house. I spent many hours with Mr MacGillivray [Angus the gardener] when he was bedridden. He showed me how to do embroidery stitches & gave me all the short ends to take home.

Evacuee children were taken in by many families. It wasn't all plain sailing, either for the visitors or for the hosts. Mrs Bobby (Bonella) Johnstone in Garage Cottage at the Square took three evacuee children. Mrs Bob Cameron at Lorimer Cottage at the Square had a boy and a girl and didn't want the boy, so he came to Ardkinglas. Mrs Taylor at Pier Cottage had a boy and wanted a girl, and so on. The rate for boarding a child was 8s 6d per week. Michael thought this inadequate and suggested that the estate people who were providing boarding should receive a special coal allocation and an additional 1s 6d. There was quite a bit of confusion about the payments. Two evacuees at Mrs Bobby John-

*Angus and May MacGillivray and a friend at Laundry Cottage in the 1930s.*

stone's went back to Glasgow as the parents couldn't afford to pay for their lodgings, though both the boys and their parents wanted them to stay.

The evacuees without relations in Cairndow went to school in the Village Hall. Mrs Hall was the teacher. Their letters home give a wonderfully vivid picture of the journey to and arrival at Ardkinglas and Cairndow village in 1939. John Farrell, aged about twelve (his home was in Avenpark Street, Glasgow), wrote a letter home in pencil, in excellent handwriting giving his view of the adventure:

> This house belongs to a certain Mrs Noble who was kind enough to take in a party of children who were evacuated from Glasgow.
>
> The children started out from Maryhill station on the Sunday morning to land at Craigendoran where they got on the boat which took them through some of the most beautiful scenery in Scotland. They were then landed at Lochgoilhead where a tea was provided for them by the inhabitants of that village.
>
> After their tea they were put on busses which would take them to their new homes. There are eleven of us in the Ardkinglas House and all of us are very happy to be here, which I am sure is much better than staying at home in Glasgow.

He illustrates his letter with an impressive pencil drawing of Ardkinglas House (which is not an easy building to draw).

Eric Phillips from Maryhill, in Glasgow, who was of a similar age to John Farrell, described the place they found themselves in.

Cairndow is a little village in Argyllshire. It is just a collection of houses and it has a little church and post office. There is a school house along the road nearby the outskirts of the village and as you go along the road towards it you pass the village hall, which at present is our school. Along the road towards the War Memorial there are bramble bushes growing at the side of the road. Where we are living is at Ardkinglas house, it is situated in the middle of a vast estate and there is a large garden in which there are pear trees and vegetables in plenty. At the front of the big house there is a large field and there in the field there is a little pony. Well, we are very contented where we are and I do not think we will get lonely.

John and Eric's letters are particularly vivid records, but there are many letters from young Glaswegians during those early days, all admirably literate. It seems unlikely that there was much intervention by the teacher, as none of the letters are like each other.

During those first days of September so much happened for so many people it must have been a turmoil of emotions, of fears and of work that had to be done. On that 3 September, John, in London, was going to have dinner with his Uncle Saxton, in Kent House in Knightsbridge. He was going on foot, as he didn't want to drive in the blackout. Before he set out he wrote to Michael at Ardkinglas. He described how fantastic and unreal it was in London, with the blackout and balloons and soldiers moving about.

If only it was the nightmare that it seems . . .
   I want to write to send my sympathy as I am sure you feel as unhappy as I do at the dreadful and catastrophic news, and to say quickly
how anxious I am that you should stay at Ardkinglas . . .

He goes on to say he isn't sure how Michael will feel on the question of fighting:

It is in any case a difficult question, and it will get worse, as one
will see all one's friends and acquaintances going to fight the Nazi
regime which is an intolerable monstrosity and really feeling one
would like to be with them and yet to feel that it is wrong to do so.
For myself I have no intention of doing non-violent propaganda – If
I can be useful in some humanitarian capacity like ambulance driving

or stretcher parties I shall do so . . . My point in putting down my feelings to you is that if you feel somewhat the same, you should know you have my support for what it's worth. More particularly you should feel you are doing really useful work by being at Ardkinglas, keeping things running smoothly there with evacuees and organising the production of food. This must be of great importance. Whatever criticism you get and I expect it will be plenty, you can feel certain you are not doing something trivial. At Ardkinglas use your powers of moderation in all quarters – these will be needed in times of strained nerves.

This was a momentous week for Elizabeth and it was to be pivotal for Ardkinglas Estate: from then on Elizabeth made it not just her home but her life's work. Afterwards her pre-war world wouldn't exist. Her mother had died in 1937; by the time the war was over their family properties in London and Berkshire would have been sold, as would her and John's London home, and the two brothers to whom she was closest would have died of TB.

During the war years the Big House household and the Ardkinglas Estate became more of an entity than at any time before or since. A sense of cohesion emerges: everyone was so dependent on each other. Lack of communication (telephone connection was intermittent and only at Ardkinglas House and the Post Office), and lack of transportation restricted everyone. Petrol rationing was imposed immediately; the fact that they had managed before that to have the Estate tank filled was a great relief – it would be so carefully managed that it lasted for years. They had little leisure to stand back and to reflect; but nonetheless, from time to time, they must have recognised that what they were doing was important for the locality, for those seeking refuge there and for the country. Despite this, Elizabeth was always haunted by a sense of inadequacy: the feeling that she wasn't doing enough or not doing it well enough.

John and Michael were not able to spend more than a few holiday days at Ardkinglas during the long war years. The pattern of the seasons was not embedded into their everyday lives as it was for Elizabeth, Daisy and Tasia. Their lives were distant from the day-to-day work at Ardkinglas, they would never experience that, nor would they have the experience of being so closely attuned to the lives of the people on the Estate.

There was anxiety on the Estate. Men between the ages of eighteen and forty-one were to be called up; Michael had a meeting with the men about what was likely to happen. Those employed in key industries, including agriculture, were to be exempted. Increasing the national food supply was crucial; pre-war, Britain had been importing 20 million tons of food a year, 70% of the total required. The imports included more than 50% of the meat, 70% of the cheese and sugar, nearly 80% of fruits and about 70% of cereals and fats. It was assumed that one of the principal strategies of the Germans would be to attack shipping bound for Britain, restricting industry and potentially starving the nation into submission.

Michael reported that the men had been very understanding. Tina Mac-Callum was anxious at the idea that Colin might have to go, as gamekeeping wasn't considered a national necessity. Elizabeth intervened: she suggested Colin could help on the farm, if he would, and thus be registered as a farm-worker. Bobby Johnstone was safe. There was concern about Dougie Shaw, driver and a man of essential helpfulness; could he be described as a tractor-driver and therefore be exempt? His wages were already calculated on an annual basis, as were agricultural wages, while Estate wages were calculated on a weekly basis, though they were actually paid monthly. Apprentices were also to be exempt from call-up.

Despite his elder brother's advice, by 23 Sept 1939 Michael had left Ardkinglas. Initially he went to work with his Uncle Harold Butler at the League of Nations. Later he joined the Royal Air Force Volunteers, and during most of the war he worked with their bomb-disposal teams.

Elizabeth's letters to John keep him posted with an account of each day. To an extent, autumn at Ardkinglas continued as normal. The details that Elizabeth described included the fact that Bobby Johnstone was pleased with the price for the lambs he sold and the ewes and tups he bought; that the Estate had registered with the coal merchant in Strachur for their allocation of coal costing 35 shillings a ton; that the Halloween party, for staff and evacuee children and everyone, had been fun with the usual bobbing for apples, sticky buns on strings and scattered hot pennies; and as in normal years, 'guisers' in fancy dress and masks went round the houses – their turnip lanterns escaped the blackout directives.

However the bad news, sent from Elizabeth to John, was that that Douglas Luke, Nicol's eldest son, had been called up and joined the Queen's Own Cameron Highlanders. This was a blow for everyone because Douglas played the accordion for the dances (after that Jake Speirs took on the role). Willie MacPherson, who had served his apprenticeship with Jimmy Stewart, was also called up, as was Ian MacLachlan, from Ardganavan croft, who joined

*Tea break at Achadunan Farm.*

the Royal Scots Fusiliers. He had been the Postie. He would pick up the mail from the Post Office in the village and cycle to deliver it to Ardno, Croitcho-nic, up Glen Kinglas to Butterbridge, back down and up Glen Fyne as far as Inverchorachan, then round the loch and back home. His duties as Postie were now taken on by young Mary Speirs, Jake's daughter, also on her cycle. She delivered to Glen Fyne, Butterbridge in Glen Kinglas and Ardno, but taking them in turn during the week on a rota.

During that autumn Elizabeth wrote to John almost daily, with the de-tailed news. We don't have his letters to her. Some of what she wrote may have been of importance to him, for instance news about the gamekeepers – Colin MacCallum (who so far had escaped call-up) had shot three pheasants, three snipe, and five rabbits. She was so sorry she wouldn't be posting John any of these as they badly needed them for their own larder. The cartridges ordered for Colin still hadn't arrived. Willie Manson was still in bed; the problem had been thought to be a strained leg muscle but now turned out to be an abscess. And the elderly keeper Bob Cameron was very ill, grey with pain in his foot and sleeplessness (the pain was from an old war wound). The doctor said amputation might be the only solution, and in the end the foot did have to be amputated.

However some of the detail in her letters, so vital to her everyday life, may have seemed petty to John. For instance: Dougie Shaw was meant to be helping Bobby Johnstone with the ploughing, but he hadn't done much.

Bobby was annoyed about that and was suffering from toothache. Some of the evacuee boys had caused serious trouble, chasing sheep, two of which had to be destroyed. They had been fiercely scolded; if it happened again the police would be called. And there was trouble in Ardkinglas kitchen. Laurie and Sybil were the Guyanese who had been John's and Elizabeth's cooks in London and who had been persuaded to come to Ardkinglas. Laurie and Bella Boyle, the kitchen-maid, had had a tiff and weren't talking to each other. And Laurie had shouted at Lilly Mackechnie (housekeeper and cook for the evacuees), who now complained vociferously to Elizabeth and threatened to leave.

These details perhaps seemed unimportant to John, in his other world in London, but for us the accounts of day-to-day life (particularly in Elizabeth's letters), contribute to a scrapbook of social history of Ardkinglas Estate during the war; and also to the wider picture of lives elsewhere in the Highlands at that time.

Elizabeth didn't complain to John, though many of these issues must have been trying to deal with. But she wrote always how much she missed him, always she reveals her lack of confidence, and sometimes she does complain about her companions, about the women's chatter. So far Sisi Noble and her children and Guiton Floor and her children were the only ones of friends and family at Ardkinglas during that autumn – the 'Phoney War' that lasted until the spring of 1940. (Most of the children – those who were to spend longest at Ardkinglas – didn't come until after the fall of France in June 1940.)

Elizabeth wrote:

It is very curious what strange ideas people have . . . it makes me long for your companionship when I hear this drivel going on. It is so difficult to know what to do and where to be. I do realise there is a lot of useful stuff to be done here – much of which I enjoy doing – but is it worthwhile? I think, almost know, it is, but there is always that great cloud of our not being together. There are of course the children – (ours not the evacs) and it is they who weigh the scales, along with duty and service and unselfishness! And admittedly the pleasure of being in such beauty and doing such happy things.

For much of the war she, like many women, was a single parent. She was also a mother to many. After it was over she wondered if in trying so hard not to favour her own children she had been too hard on them.

She always enjoyed children. On her rare absences visiting John in London some of the evacuce children wrote jokey, chatty letters to her from Ardkinglas.

Mrs John,
I hope you are keeping fine as all of us here is. Grace went home today as she got her letter and money yesterday. We made three snowmen yesterday but the snow is beginning to thaw. I saw Johnny bowing (*so low*) to Ethel and Bella just now and his nose nearly scraped the floor!!! ha! ha! There is a storm blowing just now, it is very wet.
    I must close now as I am going to play. See you later. From Sam (Mathieson)

Helen Hepburn's memories are a valuable contribution to the scrapbook. She illustrates the freedom for a nine- or ten-year old in those days, the distances walked and the responsibilities and daily chores expected. She remembered:

Many times I walked all the way to Achadunan Farm. I spent a lot of time with Amelia Lang & her sisters May & Betty, we played all kinds of games. I would help to muck out the byre & to churn the butter, then I walked all the way home.
    Mary Speirs was a very close friend of mine when she stayed at her Granny Stewart's house (Jimmy Stewart's mother) at Croitchonie, just up the Dunoon Road. Bobby, Billy Archie & Nigel Callander lived up there too. Granny MacPherson Donald & Willie were in same area. They had a cow & Donald showed me how to milk her. I walked up there from Granny's house to get the milk every other night.
    Betty Manson came a lot to Granny's to visit & play cards. She was newly married, aged only 17 or 18, & Willie had gone into the Forces, so my Granny took her under her wing. One of my good deeds was to walk Donald MacIntyre's dog (Post Office) at lunchtime, & I got a penny for doing it. I also picked up Miss Munro's paper & took it to her each morning (Teachers Pet!!)

# Winter

Reading about life without running water and depending for light, heat, and cooking on candles, paraffin, coal and firewood, I'm struck by the time-consuming work involved. Ian MacLachlan described how at Ardganavan they carried their water from the burn, and carried the contents of the dry toilet down to the low water line in the loch. With the cost of a ton of coal equivalent to a week's wages and its rationing from 1941, firewood was crucial. Ian said:

> Fallen trees and limbs from the oak woods also provided firewood for the house with its fire in each gable end. This was supplemented in winter as storm tides would regularly bring branches and trunks onto the shoreline in front of the house. Sometimes big timbers from boats or construction work would arrive to be dried out before being sawn and axed to size for the hungry fires.

Helen remembered how:

> Bath night meant a metal laundry tub to be filled by kettles of boiling water, in front of the fire. Oh! The toilet and the water!!! There just wasn't any! There was a tap outside which was piped down from the mountain and when that froze there was a long hike down to the river. A pail was brought in and placed under the table in the hallway for dishes, handwashing etc.
>
> The toilet was across the avenue, down a little curved path to an outhouse with a chemical toilet. Toilet paper was tissue paper squares and the tissue from mandarin oranges at Christmas!

So much time was spent every day washing and cooking, heating and lighting. Alice Beattie described how it was at Glaschoine:

> There was a black range in the living room on which all the cooking and baking was done. It had an oven on one side and a boiler to heat water on the other. The boiler had to be filled with a pail but it had a tap to empty it. A large, black, iron kettle always sat on the range to give more hot water. The range was black-leaded every day while the fender and the bits on the range were polished with emery paper every day.
>
> The living room was lit by an Aladdin lamp. Every day it had to be filled with paraffin, its wick trimmed, its globe cleaned and mantle checked to see that there were no holes in it. A candle or a double

burner lamp saw you out to the toilet or to bed, along with your stone hot-water bottle in the winter.

*Ella Luke at the mangle.*

At the Big House there was electricity (hydro-generated by the Gilkes turbine installed in Lorimer's time) and there was hot running water and central heating, but as winter weather began to set in there were complaints. Elizabeth writes that she had to have a bath at half-past seven in the morning, as it was hardly ever hot later. On 18 December Dougie Shaw said he changed the gearing on the system as the speed it was running at was wrong. It didn't help much. The radiators were still not warm, the house was freezing and it was so bitter cold outside it wasn't surprising that Sisi Noble and Guiton Floor complained about it all the time.

John and Paddy and family, and their sister Rosemary Montgomery were at Ardkinglas that Christmas, also Eva and Peter Rosenthal (the refugees from Germany whom Elizabeth had sponsored) and Harold Butler of the League of Nations – Uncle Harold, brother-in-law to Amie Noble.

Guiton Floor was a Belgian who had been a 'refugee' at Ardkinglas during the 14–18 war, and had remained a friend of the family. Her husband Ides (Idesbald) was at Ardkinglas for this Christmas. If seems that often Ardkinglas was host to those who were playing or would be playing important national roles. Ides worked for the Special Operations Executive, at the Ministry of Economic Warfare. The SOE's role was to carry out espionage, sabotage and reconnaissance in occupied Europe and to aid local resistance movements. It was highly secret: it is unlikely that those at Ardkinglas knew what he did.

Lotte and Heinz (later Henry) Grunfeld and their children also arrived for Christmas 1939. Henry had been arrested and briefly jailed by the Gestapo but managed to flee to London with his family. He had joined the New Trading Company. As mentioned earlier, this had been established in 1934 with Siegmund George Warburg who had just fled Germany, Harry Lucas (Elizabeth's brother) and John Noble, whose knowledge of German was useful. Siegmund had worked secretly for the 'Z' organisation, an offshoot of MI6, reporting from Switzerland. The New Trading Company was established to help refugees from Europe extract their money and invest it safely. In 1946 it was renamed as S.G. Warburg & Co. The value of the original or founding shares that John Noble had and that Harry Lucas owned against his original investment, were inherited by Elizabeth and later would contribute to Ardkinglas Estate's continued existence.

Far from the world of these 'high heid yins', Helen Hepburn scampered back up to East Lodge in time to shut up the hens and listen to the news. She remembered Miss Anastasia giving her a ride with the horse and sleigh, on a very snowy day. And that: 'My first Christmas was a very memorable one. Everyone was invited to Ardkinglas for the Christmas Party. I'd never seen such a magnificent tree in my life and we all got presents. I got candy-striped balls, wrapped in a silk hankie with the Empire Exhibition on it and this was in a Dutch wooden shoe. I still have it, here in Canada!'

The Christmas Tree Party was held for Estate tenants and employees, as it had been in previous years, and would be continuously until 1974. There is a Christmas Tree Party book with an orange cover which lists who was given what each year. The tree was candle-lit; Angus MacGillivray would be ready to snuff out a hazardous candle with a snuffer on a long bamboo pole. It is written in the Christmas Tree Party book, just as Helen remembered, that 'Helen from East Lodge was given a Dutch clog and an Empire Exhibition hankie'! Mr and Mrs Nicol Luke were given a tablecloth, Tina and Colin MacCallum a wooden cruet (this was the last year when adults were given presents), little Archie MacCallum a pistol and Janet an embroidery kit. The evacuee children had presents too – John Farrell and John Gilmour were given books, while for Sam Mathieson and others it was a penknife or pistol. Jack Taylor and Willie MacPherson, already called up, were not forgotten and were sent cheques, Jack's for 30 shillings and Willie's 10 shillings.

# Hunkered Down

January 1940 was bitterly cold. At Ardkinglas there was a sense of gloom and hunkering down; perhaps there had been hints from the high heid yins at Christmas that the future was grim.

Food rationing was introduced for the first time on 8 January, so far only for bacon, butter and sugar. What was called the 'Phoney War' was to drag on until May 1940 when Churchill replaced Chamberlain as Prime Minister. Still little was happening in Britain itself but the battles being fought in the Atlantic had already begun to threaten the food supply.

At Ardkinglas they would be relatively well supplied: they had home-grown vegetables and fruit, mutton, venison, eggs, chicken, milk, butter, salmon and sea trout. In March (always a poor month in the kitchen garden) Elizabeth was anxious that they only had celery and celeriac left and all the leeks were finished, though there was still a good supply of potatoes. Like everyone they had to buy flour, sugar, soap, vinegar, oil or fat, petrol, candles and lighting oil. Though Elizabeth often mentions how lucky they were to have access to home-grown fresh produce, as the months went on, masterminding the rations for the increasing and fluctuating numbers, between

*Tina MacCallum making pancakes at Glen Fyne.*

twenty and forty, in the household including staff, must have been a difficult task. Rationing for meat, fish, tea (2 ounces per person per week), jam, biscuits cereals, cheese, eggs, milk and canned fruit would be introduced in March.

Everyone's ration book had to be lodged with Coopers, the general grocers and suppliers in Glasgow. It is clear from the standing order for Saturdays and also for Wednesdays, the degree to which the nation depended on imported foods; and how precarious that dependence was with the U-boats patrolling the Atlantic. Among the items in the weekly order delivered by MacBryanes bus to be left at Ardkinglas drive gates were:

2 dozen imported eggs both on the Wednesday and on the Saturday
3½ lbs of New Zealand butter
5 lbs of Argentine steak and on Saturday 7 lbs of Argentine rolled rib with ½ lb extra fat
4 lbs imported ox liver
6 bananas (at that time still available) and a dozen on Saturdays

It is clear how fortunate were those who had their own cow and hens. Eggs were rationed; children and some invalids were allowed three a week and expectant mothers two. For most people the allocation was one egg per week or one packet of egg powder per month, which was said to 'make twelve eggs'. Game and venison weren't rationed, and offal and sausages were only rationed from 1942 to 1944. Vegetarians were allowed two eggs. Milk was supplied – three pints per person per week and 3½ pints for those under eighteen, with priority for expectant mothers and children under five. Each person got one tin of milk powder (equivalent to eight pints) every eight weeks.

Elizabeth was worried about whether they were being extravagant with imported food: should they be doing more for the war effort? She wondered if the household should be stricter with what they used, even if they had to go short. She wrote to John: 'And as we don't give the evacuees butter, we never have, only marge, I feel guilty about claiming their ration for it, as we are doing.'

Early in January 1940 two piglets were bought. They were the first pigs of some sixty years of pig-keeping at Ardkinglas, for home consumption. These ones cost £5 each, just under the price of three tons of coal. Elizabeth and Tasia had the idea of asking the Dougie Shaws, the Bobby Johnstones and the MacGillivrays to save their scraps for the pigs. And so began a ritual whereby Tasia, collecting the 'brock' for pigs and hens, would do the rounds at the Square, calling at everyone's house most evenings to chat and gossip, until she died in 2000.

Elizabeth's letter to John about the pigs shows the distance between their lives. He could dine at Claridge's and go to the ballet, while she was worried about the pigs. Despite the fact that he certainly would neither know about pig husbandry nor care about it, in her letter of 19 March, Elizabeth explained that Bobby Johnstone was saying that, if the pigs were his, they'd be up to their stomachs in mud, as mud is warm and the cement is cold. However she thinks she will just go on cleaning them out. It is an example of everyday detail so important to those at Ardkinglas but remote and insignificant to John.

All through that early spring there is a lengthy correspondence about Elizabeth's Irish setter, Jester, culminating in a heart-breaking letter from her to John of 5 March. She is haunted at the prospect that he is to be put down, at John's directive. But as usual she defers to his judgement: 'It was a lovely surprise your telephoning tonight. I am only sorry I was so gloomy. I feel unhappy – it is inevitable that I do and I can't help feeling that it is unnecessary . . .'

Her beloved Jester was her only continuation from her Berkshire home and family. The letters and the anguish about him had gone on for months. For some reason Daisy and Tasia had taken against the dog and John wrote to Elizabeth that it was 'silly to be making a fuss over a dog, and upsetting other people'. In the letter of 5 March Elizabeth went on:

> Nowadays he is no worry to anyone but the Camerons [he was living in Bob Cameron's kennel] and me and they are devoted to him. However there it is.
>
> I've put your rug safely upstairs. I hope you find your stud box all right . . .
>
> They said on the news tonight [in their correspondence the news is rarely mentioned – though this shows they did listen regularly to the wireless] that the council set up by the Prime Minister has announced that the consumer at home must go short and perhaps go without. Do you think we should go without more? Oranges for instance, we needn't have them in the dining room – are they things it's useful to go without? . . . I think we should have less scones made. I have ordered less bread. Is there anything else we can do?

In her letter of 19 March she asks if he would send another football for the boys. Then she says, always apologetic for her frailty:

> I am trying to be patient and tolerant and sensible, Johnnie, and not let any one aspect of 'a body', as Bob Cameron would say, outbalance another . . .
>
> I must go to bed now, goodnight again. It did all look lovely tonight, such a beautiful sky and light. One is lucky – I am, I mean – to have all the beauty of the country and the joy of it, the interest – the absorbing 'worth while' feeling to feed and satisfy one – me, I mean. *It is sad that so many otherwise quite intelligent people should despise the land and growing things and despise thoughts and conversation about growing things, and that they only 'admire' the country and not feel it and feed on it.*

This, instinctively and vehemently felt, was fundamental to her lifelong devotion to Ardkinglas. The importance she gave to domestic, horticultural and agricultural day-to-day work, was intrinsic to her perception of the place and her role in it.

That letter – the one of 19 March – is unfortunately the last of Elizabeth's letters to survive. After John died she burnt letters in a bonfire at the end of the terraces. Perhaps the fire consumed her letters that followed on from March 1940.

The war was going badly. Holland and Belgium fell to the Germans. On 10 May 1940 Churchill moved in to No 10 as Prime Minister of a coalition government and as Minister of Defence, First Lord of the Treasury and head of the War Cabinet. France began to submit to the German invasion, and ultimately British troops had to be evacuated from Dunkirk. Paris was taken by the Germans on 14 June and the French Government fled to Bordeaux, where on 25 June they announced France's surrender.

After the fall of France, Ardkinglas increasingly filled with children; children of friends and family sent away from the expected bombing of cities to the safety of the Highlands of Scotland. The Battle of Britain raged during July, August and September. The bad news wasn't mentioned much; perhaps it wasn't broadcast much, but those hunkered down at Ardkinglas must have felt the gloom and fear. What did they listen to? Tommy Handley, the comedian who cheered the troops and BBC listeners with 'It's That Man Again', better known as ITMA? Or J.B. Priestley? He was a regular broadcaster on the BBC in the early years of the war, and it's probable Elizabeth would have listened, if she could. There was only one wireless, in the billiard room. Priestley's 'The Postscript' was broadcast on Sunday nights through 1940, and then in 1941 he was taken off air; it was said he was considered too socialist. There were no weather forecasts during the war, presumably in case they were useful information to the enemy.

After the fall of France, during the autumn of 1940 and until well into 1943, the increasing numbers of people escaping the Blitz and the endless bombings of cities necessitated increasing numbers of staff. The total of evacuees at the Big House fluctuated between thirty and forty, and at times there were twelve household staff. Staffing was a continuous problem. It might be gardeners – they were trying, without success, to get a second gardener and Dobbie's in Glasgow hadn't been able to help. Or it was trying to find housemaids, or cooks: Laurie, one of the two Guyanese cooks who had come with Elizabeth from London and of whom she was very fond, gave two weeks' notice; she had had 'a letter' and had to go to London. That meant that Sybil would go too. Staff came and went. There was a Mrs MacFarlane recommended by the Employment Agency as 'aged 48. Church of England. Scotch and very nice-looking. She had to leave her previous job owing to the death of the proprietor. She is an excellent cook, sober, honest and well conducted'. She was hired that July, left in October 1941, but came back from time to time. In February 1941, Poyner, who had been the butler in the 1920s, was back working at Ardkinglas (Sarah says he was frightening and strict with the children). Lily Mackechnie, who cooked for the evacuees, squabbled all too often with the kitchen staff who cooked for the dining room.

During the war years the Big House and the Estate became more interdependent than at any time before or since. Day to day, Elizabeth, Daisy and Tasia were closely involved with what was happening to everyone. Health was precarious in those pre-National Health Service days. As the only telephones were at the Post Office and at the Big House, the latter became a natural hub. From inside the house to the outside and from the outside to the inside there was a mutual expectation of support. Nellie Shaw, sister of Mrs Alice Sinclair, had gone into labour at Glaschoine, had a terrible time and the baby died. The next day Elizabeth went to visit and commiserate. The doctor said that Bashie, Jimmy Stewart's wife, had to go to Glasgow and stay there until her baby was born. She cried and cried at the prospect. Jimmy was allowed take the van to Arrochar and then they would go on to Glasgow by train, where he would have to leave her. (Jimmy was in the Home Guards at the time but later was sent to the National Fire Service in Glasgow.) Poor Betty Manson, Willie's wife who had been befriended by the elderly Ures, was in poor health and unhappy; she had miscarried twice. She was living at Strone Cottage with her little son Peter. Daisy said the nurse was going to go and see her again and would also get the doctor to go. Soon after this her husband Willie was called up and Betty and little Peter went back home to Dundee, where she worked in the Valentine's postcard factory until after the war.

Lack of petrol, uncertainty of travel arrangements and little leisure meant that people were confined most of the time to their homes and to their work. Elizabeth, and sometimes Tasia, made an occasional journey to London; otherwise there is little mention of travel, either short or longer distances. In today's motorised world it is hard to imagine such a constricted life. One June day Daisy and Sarah and Johnny and Elizabeth made a rare trip up the Glen taking the school van. They went to see Tina and Colin MacCallum; unfortunately the MacCallums had gone on up the Glen to the Camerons at Inverchorachan for milk, as both the MacCallum cows were dry. The diary records that it was a shame to miss Colin and Tina, but old Archie was at home, sitting by the range. And they had a nice chat.

From the autumn of 1940 onwards, as the Big House was filled with those escaping the Blitz, the war began to have a direct impact at Ardkinglas. Alice Beattie remembers how, when her father opened the back door one morning, a soldier fell in. A Combined Operations Invasion Training Centre had been established down the loch at Inveraray and there were camps on Rhumore too. This fellow must have been a weary soldier on an exercise, overcome by sleep. Sometimes the soldiers gave excited children a lift in their jeeps and gave them comics or threw sweets and chewing gum to them. In June 1941, Churchill came across from Inveraray on a landing craft to watch the exercises, just along from Maggie Luke's. The stub of cigar that he chucked down by the slipway became a treasured object in the Post Office at St Catherines. The spot is still referred to as Churchill's cigar bay.

From now on there were three types of school at Ardkinglas. A governess, Miss Ross, was hired to teach the children of family and friends in the Big House. What had been Aunt Lilly's sitting room became their schoolroom.

In the village Miss Munro taught the local children in Kilmorich School, all in one room as she had done since 1914. On the way to school John Mirrlees would join up with the Speirs boys, in the earlier years walking, then on their bikes, but, he said, 'in the war there was a job getting tyres, rubber was scarce. There was virtually no traffic on the road then, we used to amuse ourselves with cycling in and out of the white lines.'

They would bring a jam 'piece' with them for their dinner and would be given cocoa in the middle of the day made by Mrs Archie MacVicar, who lived next to the school. Miss Munro would set the older ones to do a task while she attended to the younger ones. Peter Manson recalled: 'To strap us we used to have to take out an old box for her, she was only a small lady, so she needed to stand on the box to strap us.'

The third school was for the evacuees: it was in the Village Hall, where a succession of teachers from Glasgow came and went. From April until the end of June 1941 there was a drama over the teacher, a Miss Parker. A letter from Elizabeth complains to the Director of Education, Dunoon. Miss Parker had constantly been heard speaking against Great Britain and for the Nazis and Hitler. She discouraged children from buying Savings Stamps because she condemned the National Savings movement. She knew that the French would give in, and she would be delighted if Great Britain did the same.

Elizabeth's letter explains that Miss Parker's outlook could be summed up in her own words, 'The Nazi system should be introduced to Great Britain and Hitler is the man for me'.

John entered the correspondence, asserting that it was not a matter for the Argyll or Glasgow Education authorities to investigate, but the police.

From time to time the evacuees themselves caused trouble. Eddie Dibble and another boy ran off and walked all the way to Arrochar, where a lorry driver gave them money for the bus fare to Glasgow. Mrs Dibble saw Eddie coming along the street and took him to the police station. There he was made to telephone Mrs John (i.e. Elizabeth). He got a row from the police, his mother and Mrs John and he was soon back at Ardkinglas.

His sister Elizabeth, who came to visit us in Cairndow in 2010, gave us an insight into the evacuees' life at Ardkinglas. She described the playroom with a wind-up gramophone; they had toys and bikes and the boys as well as the girls were taught to knit. There is a photo of them holding up a blanket that they had knitted. They played cards and little Elizabeth was allowed to go to whist drives, held in the 'back passage' along from the store cupboard at Ardkinglas. They would go for nature study walks up the hill with Mrs John, and fish for Loch Fyne herring off the pier. Elizabeth said, 'Mrs John always tried to do something for us and she would give us our cod liver oil every day. We always had plenty of food. I had cheeks like roses and a blown-out face.'

*Evacuees and a blanket they made, at Laundry Cottage, The Square.*

*Ardkinglas, end of term, July 1941.*

It was in July 1940 that John had begun with the decoders at Bletchley Park; his role was as a German translator, as he had spent time in Germany in the early 1930s. This was about the period that they were beginning to crack the Enigma code, though they didn't succeed in making a significant break through for another year or two. John, like all who worked there, was sworn to secrecy, a secrecy not lifted until after his death. However his pessimism about the course the war was taking must have been felt by Elizabeth and the others.

At Christmas 1940 Hugh Dalton, another national figure, was at Ardkinglas. Before the war he had been an anti-appeasement Labour Party economist. Now he was in the War Cabinet and in the Ministry of Economic Warfare, and therefore a colleague of Harry Lucas's. There is no record of who else was at Ardkinglas that Christmas, surely a gloomy time. Was there the candlelit crib at the top of the front stairs, and did they sing, from 'Oh Little Town of Bethlehem', 'The hopes and fears of all the years/Are met in thee tonight'? I remember how Elizabeth, a non-believer, in much later years, used to give a little shiver at that line. I wonder if it took her back to those gloomy wartime Christmases? However Hugh Dalton's 'bread and butter' letter thanks Elizabeth for his Christmas visit: 'The war fell away like a garment I have come back to it now as across a great distance, far fitter for the fight.'

During the post-war Attlee government, among many other things, Hugh Dalton instigated the Correspondence Tuition System (forerunner of the Open University), as well as putting in place the first funding for school milk and significant subsidies to encourage food production. He also established the National Land Fund which enabled many heritage areas to be purchased for the nation. He saw this as 'socialism in action'.

## Memorable Events and the Everyday

The snippets from wartime diaries and letters and recent recordings provide some detail of everyday life at Ardkinglas and of what was important at the time to those who lived it.

The word 'self-sufficiency' wasn't mentioned, but at Ardkinglas people's dependence on their own food supply would have been so described at a later date. All diaries and letters mention the daily weather and an awareness of the seasons, which were crucial to their daily working life and to their food supplies. One of the pigs was killed around Christmas time every year. There was brawn from its head, sausages – the fat and the lean had to be minced separately – and sides of bacon and legs of ham which were pickled and cured for the months ahead. Hay was made on the terraces for the dairy cows. A new churn was bought, and every week pounds of butter were churned to augment the rationed butter and fat.

*Johnny haymaking on Ardkinglas terraces.*

Hens were even more important than the pigs. Kale was planted for the hens at the end of the wall garden, beyond the flowers. When the hens were laying well eggs would be stored away in 'water-glass' (isinglass). The water-glass preserved the eggs by coating the shell with an air-proof gelatinous liquid. The eggs were put in layered wire trays, submerged in the liquid and kept in large galvanised tubs. In spring 1942 they had 34 dozen eggs in water-glass, and more about to go in. But it was becoming difficult to get hen food. Daisy had managed to order a hundredweight of biscuit meal from the Farmers' Supply as well as lime flour, to be mixed into the hens' mash at the proportion of 5%. (Some 35 years later, in Loch Fyne Oyster marketing days, Johnny would explain that he had known about the local oysters for years, as during the war he would be asked to gather shells from the shore and bash them up for the hens' grit.) Hens were so important that young Vanessa Jebb, not really a rural girl, could tell one breed of hen from another, as she commented in a letter home: 'A surprise today! A Rhode Island Red came marching along with ten Ancona chicks. We are happy as it looks as if only 2 or 3 of them will turn out to be cockerels.'

Tasia may have been registered with the Land Army as a Land Girl; she certainly worked as one during, and also after, the war. At the time she was learning to milk, first of all on Nancy the Shorthorn who had calved the previous week. They baked 'beestie pudding' with the first milk after the calving. This was rich and yellow with colostrum and, when made into the pudding, orange and slightly rubbery.

John Mirrlees remembered:

During the war we always had potatoes and milk and the hens. The hens used to clock, maybe three hens. They hatched out and came back with chickens. What happened was when they grew up you killed and ate the cockerels, during the winter. And maybe killed off a few old hens and made soup, that's what we done with them. Always plenty rabbits, snaring rabbits. That was my job. Then you made rabbit stew. To skin the rabbits, hang them up to get hard, then skin them and make rabbit stew. The old tinker wife used to come round to collect the rabbit skins. I think they went into furs, rabbit furs for fancy decorated jackets and furry gloves.

Perhaps because one day followed another with little variation (except for the weather and the seasons) there is little reflection, little mention of what it was really like. Post-war almost the only wartime events mentioned were the landmines and the fire in the linen room.

In April 1941 two landmines fell, one on the East Lodge drive by the dam, and one in Dalligate field in front of Ardkinglas. The night the bombs fell Bin (Cynthia) Jebb (John's cousin) was staying, visiting her children Miles, Vanessa and Stella. The two girls were living at Ardkinglas and Miles was there for the school holidays. On 9 April Bin wrote to her father, Saxton Noble:

Two landmines dropped practically on the house at 3 in the morning. We have had a miraculous escape. The noise was terrific; fortunately I and the children sleep on the other side of the house, facing the loch, so we didn't get the full effect of the blast which broke a great many windows, and blew in and broke the back door. The Ford van in the garage had its petrol tank pierced by breaking glass. The craters are enormous. Sappers came over from Inveraray and boarded up broken windows and cleared away broken glass . . .

Miles didn't wake up and was very annoyed when he realised it had been an air raid he had missed. Johnny thought it was a paper bag bursting. As it was such a moonlit night the German pilot saw the enormous house and thought it was an important target.

Of course Inveraray is bound to be an objective soon as such important work is being done there. It is all very worrying as this place seemed so safe up till now. Should it happen again at Ardkinglas I think we should send all the children up the Glen to the Lodge.

There were various theories as to why the bombs were dropped here. Miles believed it was a deliberate attack. There was a rumour that someone at Ardkinglas (a nanny, or Miss Parker the ex-teacher?) had guided in the German pilot. However, the more generally accepted view was that the pilot was getting rid of unused bombs on his way back from bombing the Clyde shipyards in Glasgow and Greenock.

Tasia salvaged the parachute material from one of the landmines, and made use of the fine-quality, cream-coloured silk for many years. My sister Sarah and I had party dresses with a scarlet trim made from it, and the mine's crater in Dalligate was useful for decades after as landfill for bits of broken machinery and dead cows.

Two days after the bombs, Bin and family drove in to Glasgow to see off her husband Gladwyn Jebb (as Assistant Under-Secretary to the Ministry of Economic Warfare, perhaps he had a preferential petrol ration). On the way back, so they could listen to Churchill on the wireless, they stopped in Alexandria at the house of a friend of the driver. There they were given tea and biscuits, 'being grocers I suppose it is easy for them to get biscuits, for there was a plentiful supply on the plates' (was this a dig at a possible under-the-counter source of biscuits?). What Churchill said doesn't get a mention.

At the time of the bomb, in the spring of 1941, some Ardkinglas men hadn't yet been called up. Jimmy Stewart was there to help, and also Archie MacVicar, who was too old to be called up (though he was to go to Tiree as Air Raid Precaution officer at the airport). Then in November that year all men between 18 and 50 were called up, and also unmarried, childless women and widows between 20 and 30. Honey MacLachlan from Ardganavan, sister of Ian, the ex-Postie, was the only woman from Cairndow to go. She signed up with the Women's Auxiliary Force.

In November 1941 we now know the war was going badly on all fronts. The Germans were menacing Moscow, Japan was becoming a threat in the Far East, and Rommel in Egypt. Then on 7 December the Japanese bombed the American fleet at Pearl Harbour, with the result that Roosevelt declared the USA to be at war with Japan, and soon after with Germany and Italy; however the American intervention did not have a significant impact on Europe for some time. The Germans had cracked the British codes and until the end of 1943 their U-boats were causing havoc and destroying the Atlantic convoys of food and supplies. During the spring of 1943 the heavy losses to the supply convoys in the Atlantic meant that national food supplies were low.

How much did people know? How much did the newspapers and the wireless tell? What were people at Ardkinglas thinking? We lack Elizabeth's letters. They might have given some indication: was she, were people afraid? One evening Elizabeth, Daisy, and the others were listening to the news on the wireless in the billiard room when the door opened and there appeared three soldiers in unfamiliar uniform. They assumed they were Germans and were frightened. However the friendly soldiers soon managed to explain they were Poles from the prison camp at Inveraray, who had got lost.

Alice's family had a wireless at Glaschoine. It was kept up on the bookshelf. 'When Churchill came on, it would be brought down onto the table. Grannie liked Churchill because she came from Blenheim. Her father had been a cattleman there. She had come to Cairndow as a laundry maid with the Strutts [the fishing tenants] and met my grandfather, a roadman. On a Sunday she would sing along to the hymns and so would Mum. And we would listen to the dance music. There was an accumulator and a dry battery that had to go to Inveraray to be charged up. It would be taken by the milk van.'

The MacCallums in Glen Fyne were able to send their wireless battery down to the garage at the Square to be charged; being Estate employees the MacCallums had access to Estate facilities, while the Sinclairs, being tenants, had to go elsewhere.

Among the home news, Kilmorich School received a 'much appreciated gift', via the Director of Education, of seventeen assorted varieties of vegetable seeds from the British War Relief Society, Fifth Avenue, New York City. Later the school received 64 lb of sugar under the Jam Making Schools Allocation. £4 per head was allocated for jam for pupils who brought a jam piece from home, as they couldn't go home for lunch.

I was born on 10 June 1942 (Elizabeth wondered if my birthday should really have been the 9th, as it would have been had it not been for the double summer-time introduced during the war). Nicol Luke came to Ardkinglas to register my birth, and had a dram to drink my health. I was the first (and so far the only) baby to be born in Ardkinglas. It wasn't until nearly a month later, on 7 July, that John came for a brief visit to see me. On 26 September I was christened in the chapel in Ardkinglas. After the christening there was a party at the house for all employees. Five guineas had been collected for me and a lucky sixpence, which, according to Elizabeth, Nicol presented to me, along with a 'sweet' speech.

In July 1942 there hadn't been any communication from Douglas, Nicol's son, the accordionist, for some time. John (Noble) said he hoped that this was because he had been taken prisoner rather than killed, because 'we can so ill afford to lose any of those young lives from good stock'. On Armistice Day, Johnny Luke (son of John, nephew of Douglas and grandson of Nicol) placed the school wreath on the War Monument; by then it was known that Douglas wasn't dead but a prisoner in Italy.

Alice remembered the occasion: 'We all marched along from the school to the monument, with Johnny at the head of procession, carrying the wreath. He and I would have been nine years old at the time.'

The second historic wartime event, in Ardkinglas terms, was the fire in the linen room. Daisy's account to Michael begins: 'Isn't it too melancholy and miserable about the fire in the linen room?' (At the very same time, though Daisy couldn't have known, considerably more miserable things were happening: the Nazis were liquidating the Jewish ghetto in Krakow and Kharkov was about to fall to the Germans.)

Her letter gives a vivid description of the Ardkinglas drama.

It was on Friday afternoon between 4 o'clock and 5.15. Nurse was ironing and came down to see Christina who was crying. (Elizabeth was in bed with a slight temperature: and I had begged her to have a day in bed to rest that poison toe of hers that has been giving her trouble) and I had to go to up to Strone. I must have left Strone at 5.20 and met Mamie [daughter of old Bob Cameron] on the bridge in the drive. She called out that the house was on fire, she was running to fetch Nicol and John Luke. I knew at once what had happened – that awful electric iron. (Laila's kilt and Vanessa and Stella's dresses were being pressed) I ran across the field as hard as I could, and saw to my horror what looked like a mountain of flames rising up the house from the linen room window.

Mrs MacFarlane had discovered it. She had sent Vanessa running over to the Square to fetch Bobbie [Johnstone] and Dougie [Shaw]. They got to the house by 5.20 followed by Angus MacGillivray and Tasia. They had the hose playing on the flames by the time I got up there.

Bobbie was quite marvellous and crept on his stomach with head and mouth covered with wet towels, he was able to locate the centre of the fire. Dougie followed him in but had to come back out twice, while Angus was completely done in by the smoke and fumes. Tasia was wonderful, calm and cheerful, though eyes scarlet and stinging with the smoke. Miss Ross [the governess] and I tried to keep the water from going onto the front landing with rolled up sheets, we were able to keep the water flowing down the back stairs like a huge waterfall.

The insurance assessor was to come from Glasgow the next day so the linen was all laid out on the lawn for him to see the damage: all the fine lace too, with blades of grass poking through it. Dickson the electrician was sent for as the water had poured down through the lights and wiring. Daisy continued her letter to Michael:

What I would like is for John and you to write to Bobbie, Dougie, Angus and Nicol and John [Luke]. They were all splendid, what would we do without men like them? And nothing would please them more than to get letters from you both of thanks and appreciation.

Churchill visited a second time, this time with King George in early 1944 when the Allied troops were practising for the Normandy landings. My sister Sarah remembers: 'The King's visit was meant to be secret, but everyone knew. We cycled down to Ardno to see him arrive from a landing craft which had come over from Inveraray. I was disappointed he didn't look very king-like, small, and no crown.'

Ian Stewart (Jimmy's son) remembers waking up one morning:

It was when the Americans were here, I'm not sure which fleet it was, but I woke up one morning, and Loch Fyne had battleships and destroyers anchored off in the water. And at night-time they had live landings with barges. The troops would land on shore on the Ardkinglas Estate at Rhumore and Ardno. And they just knocked the fences down and had night fires and fired blanks. I can always recall the noise at night. The American fleet had all the food. We got given oranges, we had never seen so many oranges. They just had so much to give us.

# Lairds' Thoughts

There is a letter from John to Elizabeth dated 9 May 1942. He is having a day off sitting in a summerhouse beside a waterfall, in a relaxed mood in the warm sunshine, letting his mind dream of a future. Perhaps the intelligence information he had access to allowed him to think that the war really might end and that Hitler and the Japanese would be defeated. He pontificates on the importance of recreation, as well as hard work, and decides that he is justified to continue bathing himself in sunshine, and to continue day dreaming about a future.

The letter is the first evidence we have that he and Michael have decided to run the Estate. In passing he mentions the idea of taking over the Cairndow Inn, in terms of its income to help run the Estate. At the time Tommy Jones was still the inn-keeper, as he had been for many years. If Tommy retired, John thought the Estate could make it into a profitable fishing inn. He was also wondering maybe he should try to keep on Noble and Co, the insurance underwriting firm he had begun, as, even if it was going to be possible to keep on Ardkinglas they would need outside income. 'If the same prejudice continues against landowners as a class one's existence may be at the mercy of political shibboleths.'

Then he goes on with, in terms of this book, an interesting paragraph:

There will be personal peacetime problems to solve, mine will be between the competing interests of the city, which in many ways I like, and Ardkinglas, which in many ways I like much more and think more important . . . Ardkinglas would have to become a more living thing and more developed, more productive and less of a decoration to a rich man's existence. I don't mean that it has been no more than that in the past. It has indeed provided a reasonable and decent livelihood for a considerable number of people. However the aim would have to be to do more. With ability and some capital we might be able to do quite a lot, farming being the backbone, fruit growing and jam making, tweed manufacture and maybe making furniture out of our own timber.

As already mentioned, John and Michael sold some of the silver they had inherited from Sir John, towards paying Paddy what they still owed him for his share of Ardkinglas. John wrote (from Bletchley) to Michael on 25

*Sisi, Tasia, Anne, Michael and Elizabeth Noble in 1944.*

November 1943 about the sale at Christies. The prices were good (who, one wonders, was buying collectable silver in the middle of the war years?). The first day of the sale made £15,000; there isn't a record of the amount on the next day.

> I think we may consider ourselves pretty lucky. At least we can comfort ourselves that we have cashed in to a substantial extent while the going was good, and still have a good bit of the silver to fall back on in case of need. When we have sold the next lot, over which we need not hurry we can rest easily with what we finally keep as our treasures.

The second sale was in December of the following year, again at Christies. It too went well, totalling £14,109. The post-war sale of the house in Portland Place also contributed to paying off their debts to Paddy. These were substantial assets.

The laird in *Strathalder, a Highland Estate* inherited an estate a few years later. He explained that, as he sees it, though he is the laird, he isn't different from any of his workers. He supposes that the majority of people who live on the estate do see him as a wealthy man, but it is relative:

> Certainly I have a fine house, with large gardens and privacy, thousands of acres of land, salmon fishing, deer stalking, grouse shooting, all manner of leisurely pursuits at my elbow whenever I wish to take them up.

He goes on to explain how nowadays a laird has to operate an estate on a very strict budget, and estate duties and capital gains taxes take their toll. He says the death duties he has to find were simply enormous, even by the standards of the 1940s. For these lairds, who inherited physical assets and also attitudes of mind, it was extremely difficult to see themselves as their employees might see them; as in Burns's *To a Louse*

> O wad some Pow'r the giftie gie us
> To see oursels as others see us
> It wad frae mony a blunder free us
> And foolish notion.

The disparity both in assets and also in the perception of each other's assets, between an employee and a laird and a laird and his employee, continues to this day.

# Hopes and Fears

Early in 1944, John decoding at Bletchley must surely have begun to believe that there were real hopes for the war's end. On 6 June, 'D-Day', the Allies landed on the Normandy coast and by late August 1944 Northern France had been liberated. John wrote that he thought the war would be over by the end of the year.

Now his thoughts of the future were no longer just daydreams. He had been thinking about Scotland and Ardkinglas, reading *The Future of Scotland* by J.A. Bowie and was interested in the Saltire Society.

In October he sent a booklet *Ardkinglas and the Future* written by Michael and himself, from which I have already quoted, to Davidson and Syme, the Edinburgh solicitors, to be printed. He had written to the Scottish Unionist Association, in no uncertain terms, rebuking it for not taking Scotland seriously enough. 'I think it is right to express one's views quite plainly. One dare not return to pre-war lethargy about politics.' In June 1943 Tom Johnston, Secretary of State for Scotland, had visited Argyll for a few days. It was he who was to be responsible for driving forward the hydroelectric schemes of the 1950s across the Highlands – 'Power from the Glens!'. John also aired his views on the Hydro-Electric Board, that they should abide by their charter of giving the first consideration to the Highlands and he would fight to see that they did. What they ought to be able to do would be to take a reasonably long view, longer than any ordinary commercial company could do. 'I think the Board is important and must be guided with reasonable, and when necessary, sharp criticism. It will become too jittery to do anything if it is bombarded with an excess of politics.'

While John was dwelling on post-war strategy for Ardkinglas Estate and national issues, as usual Elizabeth was pre-occupied by the immediate. She wrote in the household diary: 'Thank goodness . . . We managed to finish getting the potatoes in at Clachan, we took all the children and they did quite a lot of planting too. Christina had a blissful time and looked like a potato by the end, so earth covered.'

And in May 1945 blossom was good and the promise of fruit promising, 'if only we could get enough sugar. Everything is looking lovely, the avenue

*Planting potatoes at Clachan.*

of pink cherries by the greenhouses has never looked better'. Sugar was for-ever in short supply and jam and bottling were the only way of preserving the bountiful fruit.

Illness, lack of companionship from those they loved and needed, limited food, hard work and hard winters took an accumulated toll on everyone. People were often in bed for days, even weeks. Poisoned fingers and toes, boils and infected chests were common. Elizabeth had to be in Glasgow, for a whole week, with a poisoned hand.

Elizabeth regularly posted off parcels of eggs (packed with brown paper and string in reused biscuit tins) and venison to friends and relations, and flowers – snowdrops and daffodils. Postie would come up the back stairs to the pantry where she would be rushing to finish. He would wait patiently, chatting, while Elizabeth completed the task. She posted butter, and some-times even salmon, to her beloved brother Harry, hoping her love and the nutritious food would restore his health. (His flair wasn't only for finance, before the war he had worked on innovative ideas for social security similar to William Beveridge's, which he put aside during the war.) Before the war he had been in a Swiss TB sanatorium. Now his hard work at the Ministry of Economic Warfare and the Political Intelligence Department at the Foreign Office meant the lurking TB was defeating him. Despite the butter and egg parcels he died just before the war's end. His obituarist, Sir Bruce Lockhart, wrote in *The Times* that 'He killed himself by overwork as surely as if he had made the supreme sacrifice as a soldier.'

# The Longed-for Peace Wasn't Easy

Husbands, wives and loved ones had lived such separate lives and in such different circumstances that inevitably, when the longed-for day came, it wasn't always easy. This, as Michael pointed out in an affectionate letter to Elizabeth, was all too common. 'The war has created physical barriers like the separation of families but also imposed mental strains which have added to the burden.'

We can't overhear the conversations between John and Elizabeth on his brief holidays at home. What was said may have been different from the tone of the correspondence. In the correspondence that I have found there is little explicit appreciation or encouragement: and surely he needn't have mentioned that for a short while he had a girlfriend on the side. A letter of late 1944 suggests a lack of understanding of the day-to-day life for those running Ardkinglas:

> If time hangs heavy with you, which I doubt [is this meant as a joke?], one trifling thing which would give me a disproportionate amount of pleasure would be if you cleared the smoking-room desk. It is always a mild irritation that if I want to write there is a large and unsightly cardboard box with receipts on one side and a heap of miscellanea on the other and the blotter is pregnant with a collection of scrap paper and old bills and letters. If you want a place for receipts they would probably fit quite well into that funny little egg cabinet affair down beyond the billiard table.

Knowing Elizabeth and their relationship, she probably apologised and cleared the smoking room desk for him.

Neither John nor Michael were at Ardkinglas for Christmas 1944, and by this time it was clear that the war with the Germans was nearly over. A copy of the booklet *Ardkinglas and the Future*, which John mentioned had been sent for printing back in October, was now sent to all tenants and employees on the Estate along with a covering letter: 'As its title suggests, the enclosed booklet gives some of our ideas about the future of the Ardkinglas Estate. We hope it may interest you.'

The authors explained that putting these ideas in print was rather stiff and formal, but they had had little opportunity of discussing things in any other way. By presenting their thoughts in written form people could read them at leisure and discuss them among themselves, 'then when peace comes you can tell us what you think and we can make a start with our plans'.

We have no record of what anyone thought of this booklet – but in terms of this book it is of great interest, as will be explained in the next section.

Before the war was officially over there were hard decisions to be made for the Nobles at Ardkinglas – with long-term impacts for them and for everyone on the estate. On 19 April 1945 Michael wrote to Elizabeth, from address SHAEF Main Air (RAF 22) SHAEF FPO BLA. He was treading carefully.

I expect John told you that I had a short chat with him about the Ardkinglas position generally. I have felt fairly certain for some time that it wasn't going to work as originally planned and am now absolutely convinced of it. [We don't know when that original plan was made – Michael and Anne were married towards the end of 1940 when she was only 17, and by 1945 they had two daughters.]

As I see the position, the weak spot in the planning was that we had the idea that two families could share the same house. For sundry reasons which are mostly beyond our control, like fundamental character, it is clear to me that if we try we will run the risk of letting our emotional strains become so aggregated that everything else will go up in smoke.

I therefore, asked Anne to consider carefully whether she liked the idea of living at Ardkinglas purely as a place, whether she liked the estate as a whole and was interested in promoting its welfare as a job. I didn't feel that it was fair to ask her to stay on and live there unless she was really able to say that as a general life it would appeal to her. She says it does and that is one problem settled. I therefore suggested to John that the first thing we should do as soon as war conditions permit is to make arrangements for us to have separate houses. I suggested we are prepared to go and live at Strone, with a young family the only possible house, Dunderave not being suitable for young children. Then I feel we could have a good chance of cooperating smoothly on the problems of the estate without the risks of friction from living on top of each other. Please think things over and see how it appeals to you?

On 1 May, there is another letter from Michael to Elizabeth. She must have already responded to his, and he now writes a warm, appreciative and sensitive response:

It was very sweet of you to write so fully and openly. I know how hard these things are to do and how very much worthwhile they are. You must not blame yourself for the situation, I know how hard you have tried . . . we all have equal parts of blame.

. . . It is true that I am very devoted to Ardkinglas as a house but I am really very much more devoted to the estate as a whole. [This is interesting in view of correspondence some twenty years later.] I feel therefore it is best to give up the pleasure of living at Ardkinglas in order to make more certain the greater pleasure – and I hope benefit to others too – of being able to keep on the place and run it well.

Both John and Michael were aware of the difficulties between their wives. Michael continues his letter to Elizabeth with endearing candour:

To blame yourself isn't at all fair, as you have had a tremendous job to do at Ardkinglas with the added strain of having John so little with you. Both Anne and I, after our comparatively short period of separation, can feel very vividly what it means. You have achieved the main task of making Ardkinglas a refuge for so many children from the many horrors of the war with tremendous success but only at the cost of tremendous personal effort with its attendant weariness. Just as I plead youth for some of Anne's tactlessness, so I freely admit, though you don't claim it, that if at times you were a bit intolerant it was because you had your hands very full and your war job in full swing, while Anne was only there from time to time always more or less on holiday.

PS – The wireless has just announced that Hitler is dead!

The longed-for peace had almost arrived (in the East war still raged and Japan did not surrender until August) but locally, nationally and internationally there were difficulties to be faced.

The *Daily Record* of 9 May, the day after VE day (Victory in Europe Day), carried an advertisement: 'Thousands of helpers are needed to bring in the victory harvests. Fix your holidays for mid-August or September and help to harvest Scotland's grain crops.' The advertisement included a quote from Tom Johnston, Secretary of State for Scotland – 'Famine and starvation, such as the world has not known since the Black Death, faces Europe. The outlook is grim and calls for the most active and sympathetic co-operation of all sections and classes of this land.'

Clothes rationing didn't end until 1949 (we had shirts made out of dusters) and petrol rationing not until 1950. Sweets and sugar weren't de-rationed until 1953, and meat not until 1954. There was no famine at Ardkinglas, but there were adjustments to be made and disappointments. Early in 1946 Elizabeth was delighted to be pregnant, but then at the end of February had a miscarriage. Suggested reasons were that it was it because she had been sawing logs, or driving the school van; more probably, as Michael appreciated, the war's mental strains of separation and anxiety, added to her tremendous personal effort looking after everyone else, meant she was exhausted and run down. She had another miscarriage in September.

*Mary Speirs, the postie, with Roddy, Colin and Alastair Mac-Callum and Christina Noble.*

But in sickness or health she was now devoted to Ardkinglas, the house, the place, the people. It was almost as if she was a 'convert', her loyalty was here; there would be no return to her pre-war life. It was similar for Tasia, but she had always known Ardkinglas, though in combination with a London home. She had devoted the war years to farm work that was now to continue – latterly more with horses (hackneys) and deerhounds at Ardkinglas – until the end of her life.

On 8 May 1945, VE Day, neither John nor Michael was at Ardkinglas. Alice remembers a huge bonfire at Strone and all the cars facing into each other with their headlights on, celebrating the end of the blackout.

Three days later John wrote to Elizabeth with a hint of complaint:

I quite see it was nice for you to have been at Ardkinglas for VE day, it would have been a pity for the children if you had not been there. But had you come here it would have been a fitting counterbalance for that inexpressibly miserable evening when you left London to prepare for the war.

In June Douglas Luke came home from being a prisoner of war in Italy, and was given £5 by John as a welcome home present.

I don't remember VE day but I do remember VJ Day (Victory over Japan Day) on 15 August. There was a huge bonfire by the loch, on the point beyond the bathing hut. It was decided that it was too late for a three-year-old and I wasn't allowed to go. I remember being angry, it wasn't fair. Everyone else was there, but instead I had to watch standing on the chest of drawers in the Myrtle Room, looking out of the window. I don't know who with – Daisy perhaps.

I also remember what I assume was my father's 'coming home' in 1946. I was waiting, standing up in the North East Window at East Lodge (it was old Mrs MacPherson's house then) looking out for him driving down from the Bendarroch Bridge in an ex-army jeep which the Estate had bought.

There is a letter from PO Box 500 (illegible signature) in Whitehall dated April, thanking him for his work and 'for staying on so long'. I don't know why he did.

# Aspiration and Improvements: 1946 to 1960

## The *Ardkinglas and the Future* booklet

Whatever thoughts John and Michael Noble may have once had about inheriting Ardkinglas Estate, before the war was over they had come to terms with it. In the spring of 1946, aged 37 and 34, they came 'home' to take over the Estate from the interim regime of the women and the scratch team. It is clear that much earlier they had given thought to what they wanted to do; witness the letter that John had written to Elizabeth while sunning himself by the waterfall in May 1942: 'With ability and some capital we might be able to do quite a lot, farming being the backbone, fruit growing and jam making, tweed manufacture and maybe making furniture out of our own timber.'

And then there was the *Ardkinglas and The Future* booklet. It is a 16-page printed and bound booklet, dated November 1944. A copy was sent to all households on the estate with the covering letter already quoted, dated 1 January 1945, and saying 'Since, unfortunately, we are unlikely to be able to say it by word of mouth, we send you now all good wishes for the New Year.' Many copies of the booklet still exist but no one remembers receiving it. Did anyone read it?

When I first read it, years ago, I found it embarrassing, patronising, pompous and condescending. I now realise that, though it is all of these things, in both the context of the time and, perhaps even more, in the wider context of twentieth-century Highland estate owners' thinking, it is unusual and interesting. And in terms of what I remember my father and my uncle to be like, it is very surprising.

Sir William Beveridge's report had been published in late 1942. It recommended to the Government various measures to tackle the five giants of Want, Disease, Ignorance, Squalor and Idleness. The recommendations were adopted by the Liberal Party, the Conservative Party and the Labour Party and were to become the basis of the Welfare State. The Labour Party manifesto for the 1945 election was called 'Let Us Face the Future', and after Labour's victory many of Beveridge's reforms were implemented through a series of Acts of Parliament. What John and Michael envisaged might happen, in a minor way, on the Estate involved similar aspirations. In the booklet they explain that they are making proposals, only aims and hopes because plans couldn't be made for unforeseeable years ahead. 'Ardkinglas will have to fit into plans that will be made for the nation . . . which will be designed to fit the state of the world as it develops after the war.'

The outline of their aims is:

That employees should have the reasonable security of employment that they have had up to now.

That there should be a better standard of life – this meaning not just higher wages but improved housing, better living conditions generally and more interest in work.

That there should be opportunity for more people to enjoy those better conditions.

What they write is based on the hope and belief that it would be possible for them to continue to own Ardkinglas.

The section 'Finance and Occupation' is the most surprising in terms of what has, or rather what never, happened on the Estate. 'It is within your knowledge that the income of the estate has fallen far short of the outgoings.'

I don't think any employees or tenants knew this. If they did know, would they have considered it significant, considering they could see the scale of the assets around the Estate? The explanation continued:

Thus the capital locked up in the estate returns no income. On the contrary it is necessary to use the income from other capital to balance the account. The same is true of most other Highland estates . . . This is not a complaint . . . Happiness or success are not to be measured exactly in money. Neither we nor our predecessors have regrets. On the contrary, our affection for all of you and for the place has firm roots and we are determined to remain at Ardkinglas, if we are able to do so.

It was not that they wanted the Estate to become a commercial concern with employment and a standard of living dependent on the success or failure of the enterprise because, they explained, 'That would take away from the feeling that we are part of a large family. For our part we believe that all rights and privileges carry corresponding duties and that our responsibility is to do what we can to maintain and increase welfare of all who live here and increase their number.'

They suggest that what will have to be done is to develop the production on the Estate, the income, in order to provide for the better life for everyone. The challenge is to close the gap between the outgoings and the income. They explain that in the past the solution had been to reduce the outgoings, but in the long term that is not a good solution. In the long term outgoings should bring a return. Farming would be the most potentially productive activity, but there might also be market gardening, furniture-making, forestry, tweed-making, wool-dying, fishing and shooting etc. The people involved in this production wouldn't be the only important ones:

> No less important will be the people who provide services rather than goods . . . masons, plumbers, joiners, drivers and the like . . .
>
> When, as we hope, the point is reached when we can give you all a direct interest in the estate by means of some profit-sharing scheme, these people will rank for their share of the increased prosperity of the community on the same basis as those more directly engaged in production.

A *profit-sharing* scheme? As far as I am aware this is the first, and also the last, that has ever been heard of such a scheme on Ardkinglas Estate. What happened? Why were these Fabian ideas so short-lived?

My parents really did value manual labour and craftsmanship, but perhaps the following was not the most persuasive way of explaining it:

> In this country there has grown the view that manual labour is below brain work. This has led to the idea that it is better and more 're-spectable' to earn a wage as a schoolteacher, doctor or minister than to earn by other ways. The truth is that mason, school teacher, shepherd, minister, gamekeeper, etc are all of importance to the community and certainly manual work is very well worth doing for itself and not merely as a means to obtain a livelihood. We hope you will think of this and take pride in work well done, getting the pleasure and satisfaction out of it which you ought to get.

The next section is headed 'Housing Health and General'; in it they refer to the Beveridge Report. They explain that after the war, depending on how the Government proposals will work out, decisions would be made as to what more might be needed at Ardkinglas in terms of sickness benefits, pensions and life insurance, and what these might cost.

They say that though a lot had been done in terms of improving housing on the Estate in the past, it was not enough: the houses were not as good as they should be. Prices for building work had been high and were likely to be so for some time after the war, so improvements would have to be done gradually. If and when the Hydro-Electric Scheme came into operation there would be electric power for heat, light and cooking. If, as they hoped, there were more people employed on the Estate and more prosperity, then more houses would be needed and more would have to be built.

The thoughts about welfare included the suggestion that there might be a nurse on the Estate. They wanted to provide information on food and nutrition, health, maternity and child welfare. Their aim was that everyone might have a life less troubled by illness. Perhaps (a kibbutz-like idea?) the older people, who lived alone, might earn a small sum by minding the children of younger women who could then do active part-time work.

The booklet now moves into a style somewhere between the Civil Service and the pulpit. If any employee or tenant did read it that New Year, it is hard to imagine what they would have made of this section:

> In the world there are nations, and there are communities and individuals, the main concern here is with the individual and the community. We need to increase the feeling of community to give it a more definite purpose, sense of direction. Not because a sense of community is the only aim in life, but more because the community is part of the life of the nation. All of us are aware of our own existence.

> What does that mean?

> We live in a democracy. What is a democracy, we should not be fobbed off with catchwords, nor be unthinking . . . we should seek truth and pursue it. It is not always enough to accept without question someone else's opinion. Personal advantage is less important than the common good.
> *Let us* not give rash promises.
> *Let us* give value for what we receive, cooperation.

*Let us* have the same attitude to the nation that we have the right to expect that others will do their duty by us.

If we make a success in our small community – we will be an example to others.

The conclusion raises interesting issues:

We have a lively interest in the future of the Highlands as a whole. They have a great tradition behind them and have perhaps lived too much on that . . . In the last hundred years they have withered and have in some respects lived an artificial life . . .

The aim must be to preserve what's good in the past and present but to infuse new life and vigour into the Highlands . . . Only thus can we hope to attract back some who have wandered away because they have not had a chance of a reasonable life in the land of their birth.

The section concludes with a homily: 'We should endeavour together . . . We hope to help you and that you will help us.'

And then, in terms of the father and the uncle that I remember, come the most surprising paragraphs. Michael went on to serve many years in Tory cabinets and John, though not a political Conservative, would hardly have been considered a reformer. The following sentiments would be surprising from a Highland laird today, let alone over seventy years ago:

We believe that it will be possible to arrange matters in the future so that you will have a direct interest and will share with us as success is achieved.

As we have already said, we want you to have a direct share in the increased prosperity of the estate when it is achieved, and will in due course discuss that matter with you so as to see how best to bring it about. We also want to arrange things so that we can more often and regularly discuss matters of common interest. In this way you may have a larger share in directing your lives than you have had up to now, while we will have the benefit of your advice.

Finally all the employees were thanked for their steady and constant work on the Estate during the difficulties of the war – 'We knew it would be safe in your care.'

I wish I knew if anyone read the booklet and what they thought of it. Alice Sinclair, born in 1933, so nearly twelve in January 1945, was my best hope. The Sinclairs lived at Glaschoine, a relatively large property, perhaps once the manse, rented from the Estate. Alice's mother began an archiving tradition, continued with remarkable acumen by Alice herself and now by her daughter Dot Chalmers. So Alice has a copy of the booklet, but has no memory of its contents ever having been being discussed.

It was a year or more after the circulation of the booklet when John and Michael came 'home'. Thereafter, for John, it was to be 26 years as laird (he died in 1972) and for Michael 38 (he died in 1984). I don't remember what they were like together, but we have to assume that until the early 1960s, perhaps when Michael's political career as a Tory minister really took off, they worked collaboratively and congenially (despite their wives never getting on). As I remember them they were not alike. John was spare and meticulous; he wore a tie and jacket and tweed trousers, a lighter jacket in summer perhaps. He had Turkish cigarettes in a silver cigarette case, and a classic cigarette lighter in his pocket, large cotton handkerchief in his top pocket. He was shy, certainly reserved; Alice said 'He was aloof, but he was a gentleman of that era, I looked up to him, he was a gentleman.' Michael was not portly until towards the end, but was more loosely built and less meticulously dressed. He was more flamboyant, more a man of the people, more approachable, and despite in later years spending time at Westminster, he was the one with rural interests. They both drank fine wine (kept in commodious cellars at Ardkinglas) played bridge at their St James's Street clubs and travelled first class; men born with silver spoons in their mouths.

## Now that People Had Come Home, How Was It on the Estate?

So, back home in Cairndow, was it a time of expectation and aspiration for employees and tenants on the Estate?

Not every family had fathers, sons, daughters who had been away during the war, but almost every household had been disrupted. Now the war was over, but for most of Britain the late 1940s were austere times: wages were low and houses in short supply, as was coal; gas had reduced pressure, food, clothes and furniture were scarce, rationing was hard. The diaries kept by the 'Mass Observation' participants that year reflect how tough things were for many people.

In April 1947 Maggie Joy Blunt, living near Windsor, wrote:

Though we won the war, the battle against the cold during this long winter, the continual Government crises and blunders, the delayed spring, and the everlasting austerity has exhausted us all to the bone. Our nerves are on edge, our anxieties and depressions enormous.

And later the same year George Taylor, an accountant in the Midlands, wrote:

Potato rationing is not an unexpected blow, but after two years of peace, this continuous taking in of the belt is becoming very discouraging. At 3 lb each we shall have difficulty managing as we are very fond of potatoes. [The potato crop had been severely damaged by frost that winter.]

In the 1940s and early 1950s Ardkinglas owned all of the 78 houses in Cairndow. Nobles lived in Strone House and Ardkinglas House and they still owned Dunderave Castle (which was sold for £7,000 in 1947). The Hotel, the Post Office, the School and the Village Hall were all still Estate owned. Though there was no change in ownership of the houses from 1905, there was a change in occupancy – a sizeable increase in employee occupancy. Estate employees now lived in 36 of the houses, so 50% of the total. The remaining houses were rented from the Estate: Ardganavan and Upper Glaschoine were crofts, Achadunan and Ardno were farms with arable land and sheep hirsels, and several others, like Cuil Cottage, Cuil Beag, Laglingarten and Glaschoine, were smallholdings on long lets. For instance the Sinclair family had been at Glaschoine since 1902 and Maggie Luke's (now Policy Gate) had been her family's rented home for over 100 years. When Sir Andrew bought the Estate the total rental received was £1,174, equivalent to about £67,500 today. The total rental received by the Estate for dwellings, farms and land for the year 1949 was £1,277 or about £29,000 today. In 1949 Clachan Farm, which had represented some 17% of the 1906 rental, had been 'taken back in'; even so this is a large fall in income, reflecting the significant drop in land values and land revenue, compared with the period before the First World War.

Life in the rented farms, rented houses and 'tied' houses would not have been easy, but the accounts I have of those years don't mention hardship.

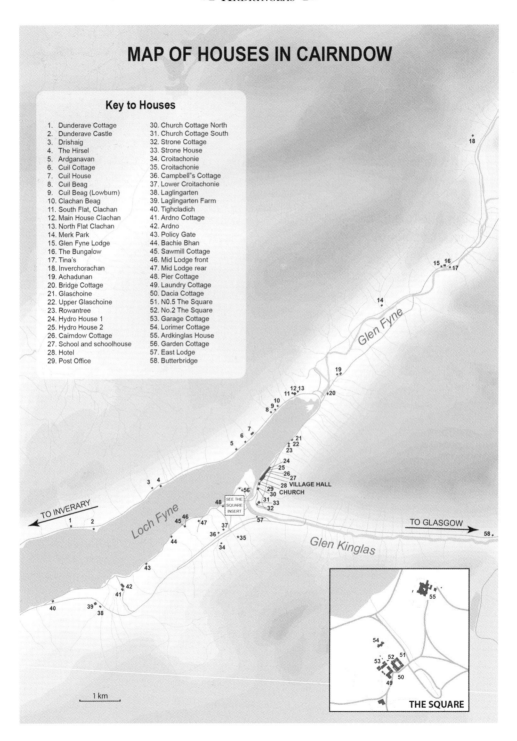

# MAP OF HOUSES IN CAIRNDOW

### Key to Houses

1. Dunderave Cottage
2. Dunderave Castle
3. Drishaig
4. The Hirsel
5. Ardganavan
6. Cuil Cottage
7. Cuil House
8. Cuil Beag
9. Cuil Beag (Lowburn)
10. Clachan Beag
11. South Flat, Clachan
12. Main House Clachan
13. North Flat Clachan
14. Merk Park
15. Glen Fyne Lodge
16. The Bungalow
17. Tina's
18. Inverchorachan
19. Achadunan
20. Bridge Cottage
21. Glaschoine
22. Upper Glaschoine
23. Rowantree
24. Hydro House 1
25. Hydro House 2
26. Cairndow Cottage
27. School and schoolhouse
28. Hotel
29. Post Office

30. Church Cottage North
31. Church Cottage South
32. Strone Cottage
33. Strone House
34. Croitachonie
35. Croitachonie
36. Campbell"s Cottage
37. Lower Croitachonie
38. Laglingarten
39. Laglingarten Farm
40. Tighcladich
41. Ardno Cottage
42. Ardno
43. Policy Gate
44. Bachie Bhan
45. Sawmill Cottage
46. Mid Lodge front
47. Mid Lodge rear
48. Pier Cottage
49. Laundry Cottage
50. Dacia Cottage
51. N0.5 The Square
52. No.2 The Square
53. Garage Cottage
54. Lorimer Cottage
55. Ardkinglas House
56. Garden Cottage
57. East Lodge
58. Butterbridge

THE SQUARE

1 km

Maybe hardship is not mentioned in the first-hand accounts of these years because most of the descriptions we have are from people who were young then. And, as Jim Brodie put it:

> Growing up in Cairndow was a very happy experience for my brother and I. Though our father was away for long spells in the Navy we had a secure and fun-filled family life. Perhaps we look back through the mists of time and certainly with longing for the folks who shared our early years, but while life was physically hard in the forties, and fifties, and sixties, at Cuil Cottage there was a great deal of fun and laughter and it will always be a special place for our family.

*Alan, Jim and Jim Brodie Senior, Cuil Beag.*

Many years later Jim's wife Elizabeth wrote a poem entitled 'Cuil Cottage':

It had simple charm, so homely,
That at once you'd feel at ease,
Sitting out among the daffodils
That fluttered in the breeze.
There were fresh eggs with the bacon,
Girdle scones that were a treat,
Mince and dumplings and rice pudding,
Always plenty food to eat!
We had fun and laughter plenty,
Children played beside the burn,
Home of Conways, Lukes and Brodies,
How we wish we could return!
See the same familiar faces.
Hear the voices heard before,
Yes, we always will remember
Cuil Cottage by the shore.

Ian MacLachlan, once the Cairndow postie and now demobbed from the Royal Scots Fusiliers, was back home on the Ardganavan croft, just along the Loch from the Brodies at Cuil Cottage. What he described were young men's escapades, when he and Willie MacPherson would go 'winching'. They cycled to dances in Lochgoilhead, Arrochar, Strachur, ten or fifteen miles, and even to Colintraive, which was thirty miles and up a steep hill before going down into Glendaruel – 'we seemed to be able to see in the dark better in those days'. Ian told us, not long before he died, aged 87, that they danced quadrilles, waltzes, military two steps and Eva three steps and then had had 'a bit of a long push back over the hill in the morning'. Ian was the youngest of seven siblings. He did not mention hardship but he did explain that eventually, after the war, he and his sister Honey were the only ones left in the locality. The others were spread out across the UK and beyond the Atlantic: Glasgow, Hull, Dumbarton, Aberdeen and Canada. He said that 'the Second World War began to shape relationships which eventually took most of the family away from Cairndow.' For a while Ian had gone back to Post Office duties in Dunoon. But then, like some other young men, he got the opportunity to start with the contractor Balfour Beatty, putting up poles for the Hydro Board, and was soon employed by the North of Scotland Hydro-Electric Board itself on the Sloy scheme, which provided a house at Inveruglas. He was to remain a Hydro Board employee for the rest of his working life.

The MacLachlans' home was a croft; the Brodies' and the Sinclairs', though not crofts, were properties leased over several generations. Alice's grandmother Alice Mayo had come as laundry-maid to the Strutts, who had rented Ardkinglas, for its fishing and stalking, before Sir Andrew Noble bought it. She had married Archie MacNair in Glasgow in 1895 and in 1902 moved to Glaschoine, taking on the lease of the house in her own name. Their daughter, Alice, was born there and when she married Lachie Sinclair, a County Council roadman, he came to live there too. Glaschoine was a substantial house; its rent (in 1906) was more than that of old Strone House, where the Callander brothers had been shifted when Ardkinglas was sold. Had the Strutts helped Alice MacNair with the rent? It was to be home to the MacNairs from 1902 until 1972 when old Alice MacNair died and Alice Sinclair gave up the tenancy.

My friend Alice Sinclair (later Beattie) has been an inexhaustible source of information for this book. I have known her since she came to work as a kitchen maid at Ardkinglas in 1948. I remember the teasing and the dancing in the kitchen then with Janet and Alice. In the photos of the time she is a lanky teenager, Janet already more of a young woman. But it is in more recent years that I have fully appreciated her wisdom, her knowledge and her intelligence. She has been a lynchpin of Here We Are, the community organisation I work with; without her it could hardly have existed.

Among her valuable contributions about day-to-day life in the 1940s are her vivid and fond memories of her home and her childhood. Her daughter Dot recorded her describing life at Glaschoine:

*Alice Sinclair on her way to work in Ardkinglas kitchen, 1949.*

The garden was quite big. There was a lawn which had bulbs in it, daffodils and crocus and snowdrops. Behind the house was the washing green. Round the sides was a flower garden and in the middle was the garden that had all the usual things.

Dot asked 'what are the usual things?' Alice was irritated with Dot for not knowing what the usual things were.

Peas and cabbage and kale, whatever you get in a normal country garden. There were fruit bushes and raspberries and strawberries and apple trees, plum trees; we made jam with them in a good year.

The byre and the hayshed were out at the side. The hayshed was just a great big wooden shed that was tarred. The hay was brought in and packed into it in the summer. Another wee lean-to off of that was the stick shed, where my father had all his tools, and the sticks and kindling were kept in there. Above the byre was the barn. You had to go up a ramp to get to the barn, which my grandfather had lined with wood. In the summertime we used to move out of the house to live in the barn and let out the house to people from Glasgow who came for their holidays, for a fortnight, or a week or maybe a month. Lots of people used to let out their house in the summer.

In the later years when we all moved out Grannie never did, she was getting too old then, so she just stayed in the main house with the other people.

There was a burn right down the side of our field to the loch. That was where the cow grazed. She could graze on the hill too; we paid for her grazing there. The far field was the hay field, which the cow wasn't allowed into; part of that field was ploughed and potatoes were planted. Then they were lifted and stored in the barn for the winter, laid on the floor and turned and dried and stacked.

My father cut the hay with a scythe. At Glasgow Fair time he had his holidays and he started the hay. Mum, she worked the hay and spread it and turned it and coiled it and spread it and turned it and put it into rucks. The ploughing for the potatoes was done by the Estate. I don't know if we had to pay for it or if it was just a Saturday afternoon job for someone.

My father carried a 'piece' to his work because being a roadman he was never home during the day. He left at half seven in the morning and wasn't home till night. Our tea was called dinner. Everybody sat down together, everybody waited for everybody else and we all sat down at the table in the living room. For dinner we had soup and stew or mince or something like that and potatoes. And if it was soup we would sometimes have the piece of meat that the soup had been made with. Sunday we usually had a pudding, it would be meat and then the pudding; we didn't have soup on a Sunday.

We made butter. It was made in a wee round churn with a handle that turned it. The milk was left to stand in big bowls in the dairy and then you skimmed off the cream. It was put in a jar to be saved to make the butter, maybe once a week, when there was plenty of milk, but then when the cow was going dry, we didn't have any butter.

We always had hens, the odd duck, but we always had hens. Mum sold eggs; she'd roll them up in newspaper. Sometimes she would send a boiling hen to her sister Kitty in Cumbernauld and put eggs inside the carcase to send safely.

We fished, we always had a rowing boat – flounders and saithe and the odd wee dog fish; dog fish were boiled up for the hens. We did trawling as well – that was good fun, you could catch half a dozen mackerel at one time, you had a darrow with all those hooks on. We fished off the shore sometimes, we caught wee sprats, we used to stand out on the sewerage pipe, it had concrete bits on it, you could stand on them and that took you further out into the loch.

We had snail races, sometimes John Mirrlees and I, and also Nigel my cousin. He and I had snail races, on the steps going down to the shore. Auntie Lizzie and Nigel and his brothers used to come up and have Sunday dinner with Grannie. Auntie Lizzie was a widow and had four boys to bring up. Her husband had been killed in a motorbike accident. They went home after tea; they lived at the Square at that time.

The shopping was all done by vans. The grocer's van came round, the butcher's van came round, there was a van every day of the week . . .

Nothing much happened for Christmas at home. We got in holly and had paper decorations, but I was quite old before we got a Christmas tree, in the 1950s maybe. But we had presents and the stocking. All my children [she was to have six] were born before we had a big Christmas dinner at Glaschoine.

New Year you were supposed to clean all last year's dirt out before the new year came in, everything had to be cleaned, and the ashes taken out before midnight. Then you got a drink at New Year, the men would get whisky and the women would get port or sherry, never anything more than that. I had left school before I was old enough to be allowed to stay up for the New Year.

## The Ardkinglas Household Diary for 1947 and the Pattern of the Year at the Big House

The Diary (I have been able only to find the 1947 one) is a two-day-to-a-page Collins Diary. I don't think it had a particular purpose: in the past diary-keeping used to be a daily activity for many people. It is mostly written by Daisy, in her green ink, but sometimes by Tasia or Elizabeth. Tasia continued her Land-Girl style life, often dressed in jackets and breeches, or airtex shirts and well-patched trousers, smelling a bit of cows and dogs and always late for meals. In those everyday clothes she would seem very much the Land Girl, but when dressed for London or an occasion, she was handsome, beautiful even. Daisy too continued her wartime roles – gardening, butter-making and bread-making. She was far from pretty, but tall and always well turned out; she liked good clothes. Her white hair was in a neat bun, and with a freshly laundered long white apron at the bread-making board, she was a striking figure. Neither she nor the third diarist – Elizabeth – ever wore trousers. They gardened in tweed skirts, stockings and suspenders, cotton skirts and espadrilles for summer. Elizabeth was short, always thin, never confident of her appearance (she complained particularly about her wiry hair) or her clothes. She was always energetic, on the run; I would tease her that one day she would have used up her quota of energy (dying in her early seventies I think she did). I could tell who was who of those three, and of many others, by their footfall on the parquet floor of Ardkinglas corridors.

To an extent I was brought up by these three women, and as my sister Sarah was seven years older than me and Johnny five years older, and both by now were at boarding school, in a way, within the household I was an only child.

The Diary has an entry for every day of 1947. As Alice's account of her childhood days gave a picture of the domestic year at Glaschoine, so this Diary tells us something about the year for the Big House; though it is a shame that so much of each entry is devoted to describing the day's weather. Weather was important for them because everyone spent so much time working outdoors – they are out in the mornings, in the afternoons and, in the

*Tasia at Jake Speirs' stack.*

summer, in the evenings after dinner as well. However, luckily for us, 1947 was a year of dramatic weather. There was a very long and very hard winter (the frost was so hard that the water for the turbine on the Kinglas river froze – so no power at the Big House), and there was a long, hot, dry summer – 'never has there been such a spell'.

Many people's health was depleted after the war. So often the Diary mentions people ill, in bed and for days, even weeks. Houses, the large and small, were cold, so ill people were kept warm in bed. John's nephew Iain (son of Paddy) was ill at New Year, so he could not get up for the celebrations. John himself went to bed on New Year's Day and by 6 January Sarah and Johnny were in bed too. John didn't get up until the 8th, and then only for lunch. A couple of days later Christina was in bed and Sarah had a poisoned finger. The war had taken its toll on health and there were still no antibiotics. I remember bacon poultices, bread poultices and kaolin poultices, and the pungent smell of Friars' Balsam, being under a towel inhaling it while being read to, and also the delicious butter rolled in brown sugar to soothe a sore throat.

There is much of interest in the Diary including some curious snippets, for instance recording the post-war scarcity of matches – 'Fortunately Bryant and May [the match manufacturers] came to discuss buying timber, for matches, and gave John a dozen boxes. Most welcome, as we are very short at the moment.' And the fact that the 'double summer time', imposed during the war to make more use of daylight hours, went on until the night of 10 August 1947 when it went back to being the 'normal' summer time of one hour ahead of GMT. Occasionally, suddenly, there is something in the Diary that jogs the memory of a forgotten moment. I can just remember sitting high up on Charlie, the Clydesdale, as he was led out of the stable and through the gate by the midden, into the stable field. It must have been during old Charlie's last days, as don't think there were any draught horses after 1947.

That winter was not only exceptionally cold, it was also exceptionally long. Curling matches on the Caspian, the artificial lake below Ardkinglas that predated Lorimer's design, continued regularly from mid-February. On the 21st John paid the wages on the ice (presumably most of the wage-earners were players) while the Cairndow team challenged Dunoon, Strachur and Inveraray, 'and more than held its own'.

For those at the Big House their lot was not as dire as it had been for Maggie Joy Blunt, who described in her Mass Observation diary how the battle against the cold and the austerity had exhausted them all to the bone. But nevertheless at Ardkinglas they were clearly thirsting for light and warmth.

On 9 March – 'marvellous sun, really hot and enjoyable'. But it was not to last: on the 12th there was more snow, a gale and blizzards, and yet more on the 13th and again: '18th The Rest and Be Thankful was blocked, the mail van had to go via Dunoon and the first goose egg was found; it was frozen on the hard snow near the midden.'

The war years over, little by little there is a sense of a return to the familiar. The drawing room, used as a furniture store during the war, was brought back into use, and on '7th April, Archie MacVicar and Douglas Luke cleared and cleaned the mermaid pond to make the fountain go once more.'

At this period, as in the war years, the employers' family and employees worked together in the garden and on the farm. On 3 April the diary records that I went to help plant potatoes with Tasia on her pushbike. Tasia's bike was a man's one with a cross bar, which she would pad up with a sack, tied with twine, so it was like a saddle. I would hold onto the handlebars, her hands each side of mine, and we cycled round the head of the loch to Clachan. At lunchtime we brought back the message that everyone was needed to help with the planting. It must have been Johnny Bell, the newly arrived ploughman from Mull, who was to be on Clachan Farm for many years, driving the tractor with the cultivator, while a long line of workers planted by hand.

As well as the reassurance of returning to the more 'normal' life, the Diary reflects a sense of excitement about the new and the wider world. For instance there were visitors to do with the proposed hydroelectric schemes. A Mr Williamson from the Hydro Board and John Berry, their piscatologist, came to assess the impact of the hydro schemes on salmon in the Fyne and

*Sarah, Johnny and Christina Noble in their Sunday best, 1950.*

the Kinglas rivers. Ian Lindsey, an architect, came to discuss the proposed two new Hydro Board houses, which were to be built in the village by Estate joiners and masons. Jim Reid, editor of *The Bulletin* who had become a friend, brought the editor of the *Glasgow Herald* to lunch, and Saltire Society members, including academics from Glasgow and Edinburgh, would come to stay; over dinner there were lively discussions about Scotland and the future.

On 16 April, late because of 1947's cold winter, for the first time they began to pick daffodils for the market. Despite the cold, so painful on the endlessly chilblained hands, they picked 225 bunches, of a dozen each, and early the next morning John drove them off to Glasgow. The record day for that year was 336 dozen, picked on 15 May. The daffodils picked for market grew alongside the front drive, on the slopes beyond what was called the old tennis court, towards the Square from Ardkinglas, and in the beds in the Ladies Garden, outside the wall garden. I don't know when these had been planted, and I don't remember any others being planted. A few gentian plants were sold by post, but daffodils were the major commercial crop with a first year's total of 1,708 dozen sold. From the initial selling of daffodils the plan was that the market garden enterprise was to grow into a viable business. The fruit and vegetables currently sold by the Gardens to Ardkinglas and Strone Houses would develop and there would be a commercial demand. This was how John was to explain it to the Tax Department.

In the middle of May of 1947 the first compost heap was constructed, according to the recommendations of Lady Balfour, the founder of the Soil Association; John and Elizabeth were early Soil Association members. During the early summer much time was spent putting bracken on the azaleas as mulch, and leaf-mould, carted and stacked by John, Elizabeth and Daisy in the autumn, on the flowerbeds.

Then, when summer did arrive, it was as hot as the winter had been cold and equally memorably long: it didn't rain for five weeks. Daisy writes:

> Hot again. Picked sweet peas in afternoon and in the evening, the house is exquisite with them, a big bowl of white ones in the tea hall particularly good.
>
> The most divine evening with moon, after dinner sat out on the loggia for coffee; entranced with the beauty of it.

Then it came to haymaking: on 16 July the Irishmen (seasonal workers who came to do bracken-cutting and other jobs) started scything the hay on the terraces (in pre-war days the terraces were landscaped lawns that extended down towards the Loch). The 'Park', the field in front of the house, had already been cut with tractor and reaper. By 19 July they had half the field up into ten ricks. On the morning of 20 July the coils on the terraces were spread, and by the evening they put up four and a half ricks. The next day they moved on to the Rhumore garden area: 'Turned the hay on Rhumore, picked raspberries for jam, and went up to Glen Fyne Lodge to have tea with the fishing tenants there.'

At the Big House it was busy, especially in the summer with friends to stay. The friends were rarely entertained with trips and expeditions; it was assumed they would help with whatever was the main activity at the time – fruit-picking, weeding, carting leaves or wood.

1st August picked red currants and bottled them and made jelly from them. Finished Rhumore garden hay, picked glorious sweet peas, and then at nine in the evening, after dinner, went to turn the hay at the end of the tennis court.

2nd August picked raspberries and filled 15 bottles [these were large bottles, maybe 2 lbs of fruit in each, sterilised in a big can on the range]. Then picked 7 lbs of red currants for bottles and 5 lbs more for jelly.

*Haymaking at Dallegate in 1947: Christina, Johnny Bell, Charlie Boyle and his brothers.*

*The harvesting at Dallegate. Michael Noble is to the right of the tractor.*

By 9 August all the hay was finished – 240 ricks of it. And by the end of August the harvest was finished too: it was reckoned to be a record.

On 15 August there were fifty ('society') guests for the Sheep Dog Trial lunch; it was laid out, with place names, on tables in the dining room. Huge bowls of sweet peas decorated the tables and 26 lbs of raspberries had been picked for the pudding and the 'wine cup'. This was the first Sheep Dog Trial lunch since the one in August 1939 on the eve of war, when they packed away the china in the dining-room cupboard and locked it up.

Sugar was rationed until 1953, so as the fruit began to ripen the continuous sugar scarcity caused concern. Because of the market garden enterprise, all fruit used by the Ardkinglas and Strone households now had to be carefully weighed and recorded; also any fruit that was sold locally. On one August day Betty Manson, wife of Willie the gamekeeper and mother of Peter and Willie, bought 30 lbs of blackcurrants. The wife of Bobby Johnston, the farm manager, bought 14 lbs of blackcurrants and the postman bought 15 lbs of gooseberries. The household diarists kept a rough record of fruit picked that summer; though more must have been picked than was recorded, as the Diary often says 'we picked fruit', without detailing the quantity picked. According to the Diary entries the totals were:

| | |
|---|---|
| Gooseberries | 59 lbs |
| Raspberries | 257 lbs |
| Blackcurrants | 250 lbs |
| Plums | 275 lbs |
| Brambles (wild) | 62 lbs |

In the Ardkinglas jam larder by the end of the summer there would be rows of jars of jam and jelly, and in the store cupboard there were shelves of bottled gooseberries, red, white and black currants, raspberries, plums and brambles. In 1947, by the end of August, there were 37 bottles of raspberries – this in addition to the pounds that had been consumed during the summer. The bottled fruit would be used for puddings during the winter (there was no deep-freeze at Ardkinglas until after Elizabeth's death). In the plans for the market garden there was increased sale of fruits and vegetables, but no mention of plans for jam or bottling for sale; in any case, at this time it wouldn't have been possible due to the sugar scarcity.

The Diary describes the first nettles picked, the first cuckoo heard, the first salmon caught, flowers and fruits, potato-planting, haymaking and harvesting. It also highlights the events that interrupted the routine – the Sheep Dog Trials, the shinty final, the coal boat (there were two that year), the fancy dress party; in 1947 the fancy dress was judged by John and Elizabeth's friend Anthony Blunt, later revealed to be a spy. (Roddy MacCallum won, dressed as a penguin.) There was a jumble sale – clothes were still rationed and most children wore hand-me-downs or clothes bought from the jumble sale. Towards the end of the summer there were the Cowal Games in Dunoon (for some reason considered to be for the hoi polloi), and the Oban Games and Oban Ball for the gentry.

Otherwise outings and picnics were rare, and it was very rare that younger children were allowed to stay up late. When I read in the Diary that on Sunday, 17 August, 'We went up the Glen for a supper picnic with all the children. Walked nearly to the ruined cottage at the head of the Glen before supper. The picnic was tremendous: there was grouse pasty, cheese, raspberries, cake – a tremendous feast' I had a flash of memory, not of the feast, nor of the walk, but a crystal-clear sensation of excitement as we came out of the turn by the Achadunan Bridge, by the (now fallen) beech tree. Perhaps it was because the car picked up speed there – speeding in a car was not part of my everyday experience. Speed was exciting, and it was exciting to be out on a trip and out so late that it was dark, though it was summertime.

Early October was the tattie-picking school holiday. Alice Sinclair and John Speirs got two days' pay (16 shillings) for potato-lifting, Peggy Taylor and Margaret Robertson got one and a half days (12 shillings). Then there was the Halloween party in the Village Hall, with ducking for apples, picking up the hot pennies thrown on the floor for us (rather less pleasant) and struggling to eat stodgy mashed potato to find the sixpences buried in it. 'Guising' was for both children and adults; everyone dressed up and walked from house to house in the dark with their flickering turnip lanterns (the half-cooking turnip had a distinctive smell), laughing and squealing. Once inside a house the hosts had to guess who was who behind the disguises, and the visitors had to do a turn – sing a song or tell a joke. Then, pocketing apples and sweeties (I don't remember money), we would set off into the night.

> '27th November the herring boats were up again at tea time, but they
> headed off down the loch soon after, not many herring about.'

I remember looking out from behind the heavy dining-room curtains through the glass doors; even now in my mind's eye I can see the lights of the herring boats and the moon on the millpond-still and smooth Loch. The herring fleet coming up to the head of Loch Fyne was soon to be something of the past.

As the year drew to a close there was venison to be butchered. Every employee was given a piece of venison for Christmas – meat was still rationed. Elizabeth sawed and sliced in the cold deer larder, selecting the size of cuts appropriate to the size of family, and choosing the best cuts for the families she liked best.

At the Big House there were Christmas preparations. 1947 was the first Christmas since the war that the Christmas tree was put up in the drawing room. During the war the drawing room had been used to store furniture from Noble homes in London – Portland Place, and Palace Gardens Terrace. Now, on 13 and 14 December, everyone, helped by the joiners, cleared and reinstated it. Its huge carpet had come from Portland Place, with a section cut out for the hearth in that town-house.

21 December, paper-white narcissus have been brought in from the greenhouse (by Angus), they smell delicious.

24 December Christmas tree decorating etc – it is so lovely to have the drawing room once again for all the children.

On Christmas Day (there were sixteen Nobles staying in the house; Elizabeth must have been missing her own family) 'there was a most lovely Christmas feast, everything perfect. Mike and family to tea, and Mike to supper, Anne too tired after midnight mass. We played games.'

On 30 December, 'More snow today, Johnny and Iain tobogganed. Preparation for the Christmas Tree Party – a great turn out of people and children, lovely party.'

The Christmas Tree Party book listed each child and what he or she was given from 1937 until the final party in 1974. The scribbled lists of the later war years reveal the wear and tear on time and energy. But by 1947 order had returned, and the list (in John's writing) shows fifty-six children were given a present. Alice Sinclair was given a book, her cousin Nigel a top and Jim Brodie a car. As Alice remembers:

At the Big House there was a party always between Christmas and New Year. The party was for the whole village. Early in the afternoon they sent the lorry round to collect people, we all climbed into the back. It took you back home again at six in the evening.

The children had tea down in the back passage, along from the kitchen. The tea was all set out there on white cloths. The adults and toddlers were upstairs in the dining room. When we'd eaten we were taken up to the drawing room. There was a big tree with candles on it, proper candles, and there was one of those snuffers on a stick that you put over the top of candles to put them out. And everybody used to go round the tree to see what you were going to get, to see their name on a ticket. Then presents were all taken down off the tree and Mr John called out your name and you went up and got your present. And at the end all the men were given an envelope with money in it.

At the end of the present-giving, my father or Michael would call out 'If there is a child who hasn't got a present please come forward.' I remember the feeling of being left out, being one who hadn't got a present and the awkwardness of knowing that I wasn't meant to go forward and say so.

Alice continues: 'You played games like the Grand Old Duke of York, musical bumps, musical arms, pass the parcel. Douglas Luke played the box. It was very good fun.'

Ian Stewart, perhaps through the misty eyes of the expatriate, remembered:

> The special occasion to dress up for was the Christmas tree in Ardkinglas House at Christmas. I always recall, as a young child, everyone got a present. I remember the big tree in the drawing room. The beautiful drawing room at Ardkinglas House, which has got a wonderful ceiling on it. And, let's hope it stays like that for years and years to come. So that was a special occasion as a child.

The Diary completes 1947 with a matter-of-fact note on 4 January that all the children dashed off to the Square when the news came of the annual pig-killing (with the humane killer pistol). Not a thought as to whether this was suitable entertainment for children.

# Idealism

The booklet's view that manual work was well worth doing for itself, was a view certainly shared by Elizabeth. Sawing firewood on the sawing-horse was a daily activity; valued for keeping the home fires burning, also as itself a way of getting warm. The foresters would bring a load of branches. Each load would be recorded and the Household Account would owe the Estate Account for it. From time to time the foresters brought a load of sawn logs, to be paid for at a higher rate. Jack Taylor ensured the transaction was cross-referenced from the Household Account books to the Estate Account book.

What you grew, cooked and ate was important. It was not just John and Elizabeth who valued this; Tasia and Daisy too were advocates. I don't know where their radical ideas originated from: what had led them to determine to create a progressive or idealistic way of life? Maybe their experience of home produce and 'self-sustainability' during the war contributed to their views. And also perhaps it was because this post-war period was fertile with optimism and aspiration. They were enthusiasts initially for Leopold Kohr, the economist who inspired the Small is Beautiful movement, and then Schumacher, who popularised it. In many ways they were ahead of their time. They did not participate in the consumer society. The wooden washing tub in

*Christina Noble and Invergarry Flossie at the 1951 Ayr Show.*

the Ardkinglas pantry sink must have pre-dated the war and was in everyday use until after Elizabeth's death. Tasia had an unusual method of repairing leaky pails. She applied an Elastoplast strip to the hole and then covered it over with paint. The repairs lasted for years.

In many ways their progressive idealism embraced a traditional rural life with everyone lending a hand on the land. By this stage Tasia was involved full-time with the farm side and her deerhounds, and Daisy was busy bread-making for the household, with stoneground flour, two or three times a week. She also masterminded the butter-making, skimming the wide pans of creamy Jersey milk standing on the marble shelves in the dairy, and churning it in a wooden churn on a pedestal. In summer there would be crowdie, made from hanging soured milk in a butter muslin bag.

There was also enthusiasm for new projects, like the compost heaps and the idea of making 'hams' pickled from venison, and they began to experiment with cheese. This may have been part of the reason for the beginning of a Jersey herd. The first Jersey cow, Flossie, was bought from the Goodbody herd from Invergarry. Daisy said, 'She was a sweet creature, rather on the thin side we thought. Her grandmother beat all records for butter fat content so we have great hopes for Invergarry Flossie.'

Two more heifers were soon added and later, for a short while, the Ardkinglas herd even boasted its own Jersey bull. On 19 June Daisy wrote, 'Very exciting, we made our first cheese, it was made with 3 gallons of milk.' And on 30 July they made the second. The next day they turned the cheese twice, and it seemed good.

# John's Estate Journal

From 1 November 1949 until mid-July 1951, John Noble kept a daily estate journal. This is along the lines of poor old Ballingal's and then Winton's in the 1920s and early 1930s. Presumably its purpose was simply to keep a record of what happened when, in case it needed to be referred back to. It is dull, repetitive, not coloured by joy or sorrow.

The foremost new venture was the 'market garden', and considerable space in the Journal is devoted to recording numbers of bunches and prices.

The first daffodil consignment of 1950 was on 5 April, a fortnight earlier than 1947's late spring start. John would set off early to reach the Glasgow market by 8 am. I was sometimes allowed to go with him, wrapped in a silky fur blanket and clutching an electrically powered hot-water bottle, which was hard and blue, more like a thermos flask than a hot-water bottle. On 8 April John's journal note for the consignment is cheerful:

> The sales note came from McCaig and Webb for daffodils with satisfactory prices. Average was 10½d a bunch. Large yellow 2/3d. 'Ardkinglas' and smaller yellow, of which there were 108 bunches, 8d, narcissus 2/-, Golden Spur 5d.

There were at least five consignments taken to the market that April. You get the feel of the ups and downs of a cottage industry; they were apprehensive, anxious. On 12 April Elizabeth, Daisy, Michael, Ann and John picked 22 boxes, 292 dozen daffodils – 'They were rather damaged by the bad weather and picking was not easy'. Those sold quite well, the gross amount being about £15.10.0d (though unfortunately some adjustments had to be made because McCaig and Webb credited a few bunches that were half-dozens as dozens). But after that, spirits were low: the 20th April daffodils sold less well, totalling only £7.3.3d, 'though Wednesday is never so good a day'. The last consignment for the year sold very disappointingly at a total of £3.18.9d, 'though there were two or three excellent boxes for which top price was only 6d a bunch'.

Was it worth the price of the petrol, and indeed of petrol coupons (petrol-rationing didn't end until May of that year)? No doubt it was considered valuable as an experiment and as experience in the early stages of the new commercial venture, with some tax advantages.

In the wall garden, where the fruit and vegetables were grown, there were also long, wide borders of herbaceous flowers. For the wall garden and the greenhouses there were three gardeners, two full time: Angus MacGillivray (a gardener on the estate since 1919 when he started, aged twenty) who was being paid £4 a week, T. Pow who was paid £3.10s and part-timer W. Davidson on £1.15s. (When Elizabeth and I went to London in October that year, sharing a first-class sleeper – which was uncharacteristic: she never usually went first-class – it cost £14, or three and a half weeks of Angus's wages, about £340 in today's money.) The 'amenity gardens' (as John was to term them to the Inspector of Taxes), were the azalea gardens and the gardens around the house, which were tended by Elizabeth, John, Daisy and helpers, and not by the gardeners.

Early in 1950 the Inspector of Taxes in Dunoon had written questioning whether the proposed market garden was a bona-fide business. John recorded in the Journal that he had written to the Estate solicitors, Davidson and Syme, about this:

> I went and had a discussion with him [i.e. the tax inspector in Dunoon] and explained that we were anxious to make as much as we could of the garden but that so far lack of housing and other things had rather held us up. All the same we have done quite a lot in sending daffodils to market, buying azalea seedlings from Holland for resale and so on. He proposed a new basis whereby profits or losses should be assessed for tax according to the ratio which sales to Ardkinglas and Strone bore to total sales.

Davidson and Syme must have written to the Inspector as John's next comment is that:

> He [the tax inspector] seems neither to have accepted nor rejected our offer but rather to have reiterated his first view. I suggested to D and S that they should get the inspector to look more closely at our proposals.

The figures that Davidson and Syme had for the Garden Account to 8 January 1950 showed a loss of some £600. Sales to Strone and Ardkinglas houses were £150 and the 'outside' sales totalled some £170. Not surprisingly the inspector questioned the business. At the end of July Mr Russell, the Inspector, came to Ardkinglas himself. It would be interesting to have Mr Russell's account of the meeting. He was the tax inspector, thus in a position of authority; the Labour Government was in power, taxation was an issue; it is likely Mr Russell was of the opinion that right was on his side. But John's authoritative manner when dealing with a relatively minor civil servant is likely to have given him the upper hand.

> I showed him the garden and demonstrated that gardeners did practically no 'amenity' gardening . . .
>
> I drove home the point that if he persisted in his opinion that our market gardening was not a business undertaking we might hold him to it, since the Revenue's position could not swither from year to year, and having obtained the position, we might develop the garden as a most profitable tax-free venture. We agreed more or less on the basis that we had discussed before, i.e. that for taxation purposes a fixed amount of £175 should be taken as the produce delivered to Ardkinglas and Strone. Assessments would be made on profit or losses in the proportion that £175 bore to outside sales . . . As things are at present it means that about half the garden loss can be set off against income and if profits begin to be earned we will at least have £175 of tax-free supplies.

Realistically the market garden (even with its potential tax advantage), compared with the income from sporting lets and sales of game, was an insignificant contributor to the Estate coffers. For the year 1949 the accounts to Martinmas record the fruit and vegetable sales totalling £234.14s.10d, and bulbs and flowers £129.18s.4d, a total of £364. The rental of Glen Fyne Lodge (for fishing) was £155, and the stalking rentals brought in £337.10s. The sale of game (salmon and venison) brought in an amazing £483.14s.8d (about £11,000 today); no wonder there were poachers around. In September 1947, with the river low after the long dry summer, Colin, Willie and Archie retrieved fourteen poached salmon from above Inverchorachan but they didn't get the poachers. The threat of poachers was real: Colin, Willie and Archie took turns to watch the river every night.

❧

What was everyday news in the 1940s and 1950s seems of another world to us today. In the household diary it was the shortage of matches and how often and for how long people were ill off work. In John's Journal there are rats and rat-catchers. I remember excited and noisy dogs, men and children running round the feed shed and the yard brandishing sticks. The Journal records the saga of some 'rascally rat catchers from Killapest'. Something made John suspicious; he stopped the cheque he had given them and contacted the police. It was discovered that they had been up before the Sheriff Court in Dunoon thirty-three times on charges of defrauding farmers. After that there was a deal agreed with a Mr Stewart of 'Ratin': for 80 guineas (the best part of £2,000 today) over twelve months they would guarantee to clear Ardkinglas, the Square, Strone and Clachan of all rats. Rats must have been doing significant damage to merit paying such a hefty sum to be rid of them.

Another signpost to times past is the endless references to vehicle breakdowns – the lorries, the jeep, the Humber (the school van) and the Rolls are all endlessly in need of the mechanic's attention and spare parts. Many of the vehicles were old; during the war years and immediately after there was no chance of buying replacements. The old lorry was off the road awaiting new boarding, or 'the joiners were shoring up the cab of the lorry which has a bracket rusted through – no shame on it after 16 years hard work'.

## 'Power from the Glens'

The North of Scotland Hydro-Electric Board had been founded in 1943 to design and construct projects in the Highlands. John Noble was an early enthusiast: in a letter to Elizabeth of 1 February 1945, when he was still in London, he mentioned that a Mr Lawrie, Secretary of the North of Scotland Hydro Board, had come to lunch. Lawrie had said he thought the plans for the Loch Sloy Scheme would be decided in the Hydro Board's favour, and that they hoped to start work in the summer.

John had suggested the importance of training some local boys so that they could eventually be employed in the power stations and associated businesses. Lawrie responded enthusiastically and said that they would also be looking for less technical people to look after sluices, canals etc., when the schemes were built.

A year earlier, in August 1944, in a letter to *The Times* John had written stridently in the Hydro Board's support, it seems in answer to correspondence from Lord Lovat:

> The right development of our water power is of the greatest importance to the Highlands. It will be a misfortune if the really important points are obscured by fashionable catchwords like fascism, profit motive, bureaucracy, and the like.
>
> It is the legal duty of the Board to develop the water resources of the Highlands and in doing so, to give first consideration to the interests of the Highlands . . . It will be for all who live in the Highlands to see to it that the Board fulfills that duty. The interests of tourists, sportsmen and others are not negligible. [But] far more important is securing a vigorous prosperity for the Highlanders so that emigration may be checked and the population increased. Unwise industrial schemes would destroy the special virtue of the Highlands. A continuance of the recent steady if picturesque decay will be equally fatal.

He continues with a side swipe at Lord Lovat by speculating facetiously on what the soldiers under Lovat's 'gallant leadership' might think about electricity coming to the glens. He concludes that those who fear for the beauties of Loch Lomondside should remember that its beauties overcame the building of the railway and will overcome the building of a power station and a pipeline.

> In this connection it should be emphasised that progress is not an enemy of peace and beauty. Neither the Hydro-Electric Boards nor anyone else should be allowed to excuse their proposals under that pretence.

(This was an argument reiterated by Donald Dewar, Scotland's first First Minister in 1999: 'There must be ways of integrating the economic, the social and the environmental and the desire to live 21st-century lives while still maintaining Scotland's beauty.')

In *The Times* of 17 August, Patrick Smollet, of Cameron House, Loch Lomond, hits back at John:

> It is all very well for Sir [!] John to say that 'the railway built 50 years ago has done no harm'. The southern end of the loch has already been spoilt beyond repair. The power house which it is proposed to build

opposite Ben Lomond on the edge of the Loch, may not do much harm. But what it may bring in development is the danger. A further death knell to Loch Lomondside is the proposed widening of the road up the west bank. People have come from all over the world to see Loch Lomond as it is, and not to be able to roar past it on, what from the plans suggest, is little better than a race track.

(Not many motorists nose to tail on the west bank Loch Lomond road today would consider it a 'race track'!)

Tom Johnston had become Chairman of the North of Scotland Hydro-Electric Board in 1945. He had been Secretary of State for Scotland, appointed by Churchill, since 1941.

Johnston was a giant figure in Scottish politics and is revered to this day as the greatest Scottish Secretary of the century. His Chairmanship came to be regarded as one of the major achievements of a very remarkable man. He was a committed socialist and a man of the times in his determination to address the very strong popular sentiment of the immediate post-war period for a more equitable distribution of the resources and benefits of a modern economy. (T. M. Devine, *The Scottish Nation*, 1999)

Johnston worked relentlessly to win over all interested parties – not least the recalcitrant lairds. In the end:

The Hydro Board's teams of planners, engineers, architects and labourers succeeded in creating an epic succession of electricity generation and distribution schemes that were world-renowned not only for successfully achieving their technical aims in very demanding terrain but for often doing so in an aesthetically inspiring manner. The economic and social benefits thus brought to all the people of Scotland, and especially those in rural areas, were immense and long-lasting. (T. M. Devine, *op. cit.*)

Tom Johnston and John seem to have been on friendly enough terms. On 3 October 1950 the Journal notes:

Wrote to Tom Johnston about the suggestion that the Hydro Board's road from Inveruglas to Sloy dam and from Butterbridge to Abyssinia should be linked up to make a toll road for tourists. I discussed this with him, not for the first time, last week in Glasgow . . . He said there was a demand for it and, if it were to be turned down, he would prefer that it were not turned down by the Board or us . . . We would not object to the road as long as there was protection for our sheep and sport . . . if the scheme showed promise of being self-supporting, if the road was only open in daylight hours from April to Oct and was only open to pedestrians, cyclists, motor cyclists and motorists. [The road never happened, I don't know why.]

Ardkinglas House and some of the Square had had the benefit of the electricity generated from Kinglas Water by the Gilkes turbine installed in 1907. There was no mains supply in Cairndow. The only other electrically lit house was Mid Lodge, where the imaginative and enterprising Jimmy Stewart had built and installed his own turbine powered by the burn that ran past his house. His son Ian described it:

The lighting had been the old Tilley lamp. Then later my father made a water wheel and a chute at Mid Lodge. He made a chute and decided that he was going to put an old car generator on a drive from the water wheel shaft. He had the chute go in below the bridge at Mid Lodge from a wee dam he made just above the bridge. And he made the water wheel out of two marker disks that the landing craft had used. They were brown disks probably about 4 feet diameter around. They were used by the landing craft at night and the Americans left them around the shore and my father got two of these disks. He made paddles in between the disks and put a shaft in. There were batteries to store the power. It was only 6 volt, and it was enough to give lighting in the house. The water wheel was going most of the time as there was plenty water in the burn.

Butterbridge Cottage, in Glen Kinglas, beside the huge camp of workers on the Sloy hydro scheme, was the first Cairndow house to be connected to 'the mains'. The camp itself was well illuminated, or so it seemed to us, a great splash of light just beyond Butterbridge; for us it was exciting and daunting as, so we were told, it was full of wild, drunken men. The Hydro Board's Sloy scheme was completed, with amazing speed, in 1949.

The early electric bulbs may not have been thought to be as bright or as warm as the Tilley lamps, but the arrival of electricity changed everyone's lives. In November hydro men laid a cable and installed a switchboard at the Square to supply it, the Big House, Garden Cottage, Lorimer Cottage and all the houses along the loch to Bachie Bhan. So on the evening of 21 December 1949, 'mains' light was switched on to Garden Cottage, Pier Cottage, Mid Lodge and Sawmill Cottage (though on Boxing Day it failed!).

It was not only domestic houses that were benefitting from being able to click on a switch. May MacGillivray in the laundry had an electric iron and there were plans for additional labour-saving devices; the plan was to install electric boilers and an immerser to replace the old copper boiler. They also wanted to try an 'industrial heater', which had a fan behind a heating element and would be good for airing clothes. On a larger scale, estimates were being discussed for electrifying the recently 'improved' farm steading at Clachan and also the sawmill. For years, like many estate sawmills, it had been driven by a water wheel from a little dam in the wood above. An estimate had also been requested for a 'thermostatically controlled apparatus' to heat the garage where the Rolls was kept!

The Estate began to benefit from the Hydro Board, not only as a source of power, but also of income. Now timber sales were not just war compensation for timber used, or to Bryant and May for matches, but, more lucratively, were sales to the Hydro Board for construction and shuttering.

Most communication with the Hydro Board was now with Mr Lawrie or his underlings. There was a long-running discussion with him about compensation for water diverted from the Kinglas watershed back towards the Sloy dam. On 28 November 1949 John wrote 'to Lawrie of the Hydro Board about our Power House, suggesting that we should receive compensation in kind for the loss of units generated as a result of water being abstracted from the Kinglas river for the Sloy scheme.'

Lawrie replied that they did not favour that kind of arrangement. John climbed onto his high horse. ' I said any financial settlement fair to us must be very extravagant for the Board owing to the tax position, since we need 2/- gross income to be able to purchase our 6d unit of electricity.'

The dispute rumbled on. On 7 March 1950:

In the afternoon our Mr Guthrie [it isn't clear who he is] came to discuss the future of our power station, as regards compensation payable by Hydro Board for the loss of generating capacity. He reported that the Hydro Board had put the loss at 3000 units p.a. Guthrie thought this might be all right, but might not allow enough for fact that the water taken off to Sloy may represent a much larger proportion of total flow when river is low. This is the important time since when there is a spate there is a big surplus of water. He suggested we could agree to 3000 units as a basis for discussion if we had the right to ask for measurement if, when the Sloy scheme is finished, we are dissatisfied. I said I would write to Lawrie in this matter.

23 June 1950:

Lawrie of Hydro Board wrote to say that the Board has agreed to give us 3000 units p.a. free as compensation for the water they are taking from Kinglas for Sloy Scheme. This seems to me to be on the low side, but this, in the end was what was agreed.

Soon Mr Lawrie must have been finding his relationship with Ardkinglas Estate's owner was testing his patience. The difference of opinion over fire damage is indicative of a landowner's attitude. It's not the question of who was or was not in the right, it's the patrician haughtiness of tone. 13 May 1950:

Colin MacCallum came to report a big fire burning on Cruach. He had seen it during the night. Michael went up by Hydro Board road to back of Achadunan and organised a fire squad. It was quite plain that the hill had been set on fire by Hydro Board's contractor's men, though some attempt was made to deny it.

John wrote to Lawrie to warn him that he would claim for the fire. In October John went to Butterbridge to meet a Mr Robertson, the Hydro Board's evaluator, and Mr Inglis, who was acting for the Estate, to discuss the settlement.

I was very angry to find that Mr Rolls of Balfour Beatty [the contractors], and also the Board's resident engineer Mailer, were both once more denying liability or at least refusing to admit it, supporting themselves with puerile arguments. I asked for the camp policeman who took statements at the time, but he said he could not produce the statements; applications must be made to the Chief Constable. I am not certain that there wasn't some attempt at conspiracy. Anyway I made it plain to all concerned that the incident left a very unpleasant taste in the mouth and that we would claim as much as we possibly could.

On 29 January 1951 there was a letter to Inglis which detailed the Estate claims, totalling nearly £600, including £275 for 'disturbance to stalking'. Then John adds, without much care for 'seeing ourselves as others see us', an additional claim for a £5 for 'the theft of holly and rabbit poaching'!

On 18 October 1950, the Queen came to open the Sloy Scheme at the huge turbine house on Loch Lomond. It was a big event. John and Elizabeth were invited to the lunch with the Queen and the 'high heidyins' at the Tarbet Hotel. Forty estate employees and wives and all the children went over in a bus to watch.

Electricity brought light at the flick of a switch. Now the wireless could be on day and evening and soon there would be electric cookers installed in kitchenettes and there would be immersion heaters for hot water at the turn of a tap. But in the meantime it is clear from John's 1950 Journal that there continued to be a constant shortage of fuel for heat, both in the cottages and in the Big House. In 1950 there were two coal boats, the first on 31 May with 65 tons of ordinary coal and 20 tons of anthracite, the second on 29 June with 85 tons of coal. The Estate allowance for most of its employees was 5 tons. But with coal still rationed, they had only been allowed to receive 3½ tons for the year 1949 to 1950. For this reason their May wage packet included a cash payment in lieu of the balance. The allowance was based on a figure of 75 shillings a ton (which must have been a subsidised rate).

Ian Stewart remembers:

Our house was heated by a Triplex range, the heat went through to the rest of the house. It was an open fire but it had an oven at the side. And you could put coal or wood on it, and of course every year we got supplied with a ton or two ton of coal from the Ardkinglas Estate. That came in by a puffer that berthed at high tide. There were tractor-trailers and lorries and that took the coal around and dumped it at the Big House and all the different houses of the people who worked on the Estate (sometimes they were good enough to take us children for the ride). So most of our heating was from coal in the wintertime and a bit of wood to supplement. That was the heating we had.

Apart from driftwood people were not meant to gather wood for their own use, even fallen timber: not then and not now. Most people burnt coal in the range and also in the 'good' room.

# Improvements

The greater part of the entries in John's Journal for 1949 to 1951 is devoted to improvements. There was substantial work taking place at Clachan; the old steading and byres were undergoing major renovation. The Hill Farming Acts of 1946 and 1947 had provided some grants for improvements, and then in 1950 it was planned to spend a sum totalling £24,000 (some £500,000 today) on farm improvements over 10 years. It was to be subsidised at the rate of 50% grant funding: a substantial sum. The work was to be done by the estate joiners and masons, while the foresters would be supplying the timber. So to an extent, the estate was acting as a building contractor to the farm, and accordingly the farm would be charged for the materials and the labour.

In December 1949 John and Michael went with Archie (MacVicar, head mason) and Jimmy Stewart (head joiner) to the camp by the castle at Inveraray to look at army huts that were being dismantled. They bought four Nissen huts at £30 each, an asbestos hut with a good deal of sanitary ware in it for £17 and a larger asbestos hut for £23 (note, there were no worries then about the asbestos!). Those Nissen huts stood into the twenty-first century.

There were also the 'improvements' being undertaken for dwelling houses; for these there were Government standards that had to be adhered to. This was part of the post-war Labour Government's legislation aimed at improving the comfort and health of ordinary people. This involved landowners having to improve employees' dwellings, in terms of running water and indoor toilets. There were County Council grants to assist landowners with this. In *Yesterday Was Summer: The Marion Campbell Story*, Marian Pallister and David Adams McGilp explain that some landlords sold cottages and farms rather than incur (even when subsided) the expense of installing WCs, bathrooms and kitchens. Some of the estates would not have had the advantage of resident squads of joiners and plumbers. At Ardkinglas: 'When possible our aim will be to have running water, bath, sink and

*The joiners: Hamish Speirs, Willie MacPherson, Nigel Callander and Jimmy Stewart.*

modern sanitation in all cottages, and make alterations as needed to bring them up to a good standard – gradually.'

In 1949 a bedroom, a bathroom and a scullery was added to old Archie MacVicar's cottage at a cost of £593 (£13,500 today). Clachan Farmhouse was to be made into three flats; this required permission from the County Planning Office. Laundry Cottage was improved, the joiners putting false ceilings into the living room and two bedrooms (it had been converted out of the cart shed and still retained the old high ceilings); the walls of the living room were lined with plasterboard.

Some comments in the Journal (though all too few) correlate with accounts which have been recorded recently from people who lived in the houses at the time. In September 1950 work was to start on Willie and Patsy MacPherson's house at Croitchonie (this was the Willie who, with Ian MacLachlan, had cycled to faraway dances before the war). John (Noble) went up with Jimmy Stewart and Archie MacVicar to look at the work. John noted:

There is the byre at the back which if a little extended can provide a bathroom and scullery without much difficulty. The water would come from the burn which supplies Ardkinglas. Archie suggested recovering the copper pipe from the Strone supply no longer needed. There is some difficulty over a septic tank since it cannot flow into the burn which comes down by the old joiner's shop since that burn provides Pier Cottage with its water supply. It will have to go to the burn nearer East Lodge, past Lizzie Callander's cottage. That being so we might take the water to her cottage at the same time and provide her with a WC.

In 2010 Dot Chalmers (Alice's daughter) recorded the memories of Patsy MacPherson, Willie's widow, who was 87 at the time. She had been born in 1923 in Inveraray, one of six children of Mr MacLaren the butcher. Patsy had left school at 13 to help at home, and then in 1939, aged 16, married Willie MacPherson.

Willie had been at the school in Cairndow. He had lived at Croitchonie, with his mum and dad and the two brothers Dougie and Donald. Then he went to apprenticeship at the joinery at Ardkinglas, then he went to the war.

He came home from the war and he started working with Jimmy Carmichael [the contractor on many of the Hydro schemes] in Inveraray, then Mr John came and asked him to come back to Cairndow.

So I came to lower Croitchonie House in 1948. It was a wreck. There had been workmen in it; they were working in the forestry. There was no water in it. We had no water in the house and no toilet. There was a dry toilet, an Elsan.

We got the water from the burn, with a bucket, Lizzie Callander (next door) got her water at the burn too. I did my washing at the burn. And then Willie got a boiler and a big beer barrel – for rainwater. And then I did my washing in the house.

There was a living room and the 'big room' [i.e. best room] downstairs. When you came in the front to the right you went to the living room and to the left to the 'big room', we used that as a bedroom. And we had two wee rooms up the stair and skylights. And it was a ladder we had to go up the stair, the ladder was out straight of the lobby as you came in the door.

There was candles, the Tilley and the wee oil double burners. They put the power in 1950 ['they' means the Estate].

We had the black range to cook on in the living room, for coal or sticks. There was a fireplace in the 'big room'. Nothing for heat upstairs. When you went through the living room you went to the back door to the outside, no kitchen, just a wee cupboard, a larder, in the living room.

I had a big garden and the byre. Later they had a bathroom and a kitchenette built on there. They put in a Triplex that heated the water. And we got two new windows out the back and they put in a proper stair then.

My daughter May was born at Croitchonie in 1952. We had no telephones; to contact them you had to go down to the telephone box at the Post Office. Archie Callander from next door, he went down to the phone. He had a car. Then Nurse Shearer and Doctor Dougie came. Willie was away playing at a shinty match. He didn't get back till evening.

That was the Saturday afternoon and it was the Sunday morning before she was born. She was born in the big room. When the doctor came up he said 'Oh you'll be a long time yet, I'm away out for a walk'. You know Dr Dougie.

By the time he came back she was born. And then he had her all rolled up in a bit of blanket and he went away out to the living room and Elma [Mrs Keith, sister-in-law and wife of the head forester] were out there. And Mrs Keith was shouting 'the wean'll get the cauld.'

Oh it's changed days now.

*The MacPherson family at Colintraive in about 1950, Mrs MacPherson and baby Greta on the left.*

Then I was in bed about 3 weeks. My leg all swelled up, she thought I was going to take one of those white legs. [Also called 'milk leg', a thrombosis that can set in after childbirth.]

When Granny MacPherson (my mother-in-law) gave up the wee East Lodge house she stayed in the Big House. That was after Grandpa Dougal MacPherson died. She stayed in the Big House because she used to milk the cows. She used to come up to us every afternoon and then she would go back down at night to do the milking.

Then when she retired she stayed up with me, till she died. One time she ran away, mind the night she ran away? Oh God. She was out nearly all blooming night. Yes, the police were sent for. She was found a way down the wood above Pier Cottage, sitting below a big tree.

[Dot asked – 'What took her to do that?']

Just she was minded.

['So you think it was a hard life in those days?']

Oh, I would far rather then than what it is now. The neighbours were neighbours. It was more village life then. Oh I just had to shout if I needed help with Granny and Lizzie would be over like a shot.

Jack Taylor masterminded the account books, separated for the different departments, in neat figures and copperplate script. Indeed, with the exception of the war years, he had done so since 1928 when he came to Ardkinglas from Motherwell as a clerk. Because he had kept the books in Sir John Noble's day, and would continue to do so into Johnny Noble's era, it isn't easy to place him chronologically. It is equally hard to know where to place him in terms of his role: book-keeping was by no means all that he did; he was a man of many talents and with a thirst for expertise in all of them. But I doubt if he would have ever expressed views on what was happening – on the future of the market-gardening or which timber to use for fencing.

Jack (John) Taylor was born in 1902. In 1920 he had joined the RAF and served in Malta and Mesopotamia, when the RAF were bombing the Kurds, though he was an 'observer', not a pilot. While in the RAF he joined a band and played violin, banjo and guitar. (This was, presumably, when he acquired his expertise at the Charleston dance; only very occasionally would he

*Jack Taylor.*

demonstrate it and dazzle us at an event in the Village Hall.) He had arrived at Ardkinglas during the doldrums of the late 1920s.

In 1939, being an RAF reservist, he had been called up: he spent most of the war as a sergeant in Yorkshire. When he came back in 1946, he and his wife and four children lived in Pier Cottage.

He was a spare man, no surplus fat, neatly dressed, grey flannel trousers with a jacket and cycle clips – not for him trousers tucked into socks. His cycle, lit with a dynamo, was immaculate. He was unassuming, you wouldn't pick him out in a crowd. He kept his head down and went on with his tasks – which he took pains to learn.

The extracts below are from a small ordinary notebook; inside the fly leaf is written 'Legal notes etc'. He kept the 'books', double entry, handwritten, and masterminded the rents and wages – in those days the bank van came once a week delivering money. In 1947 Jack was paid £3.15s per week, less than Johnny Bell, the newly employed tractor man from Mull who was paid £3.17s. Jack checked the maintenance of the 'power house', the hydro-electric scheme installed in Lorimer's day. Mid-morning every day he cycled off along the Ladies Walk to collect the 'second mail' from the Post Office. He

120

painted the wrought-iron gates. He even painted the lorries. He wound all the clocks in the Big House. Every week he changed the paper on the barometer and checked the ink. He recorded the daily rainfall, from a gauge out on the terraces. He drew out electrical and drainage plans for any building alterations. He sat at an old fashioned clerk's desk in the 'porch-room', on an orange buttoned-leather swivel chair. We all would be in and out of there, putting on our gumboots and coats, chatting and using the telephone. (There was a book in which you had to detail the calls you had made, and for months afterwards poor Jack would have to chase you up with your phone bill.) While he was out collecting the mail, or on one of his innumerable tasks, we would burl each other round and round on his swivel chair and when he came back in he would have to re-adjust it.

In his 'spare time'? He made beautifully turned wooden buttons out of estate birch and yew. And, most memorably of all, he made wooden toys, lorries, tractors (David Browns and Fergusons) with trailers, painted with authentic colours; but they were not just models to put on a shelf, you could play with them, tip the trailers and roll them along the passages. He made models too: we are proud to have a coal boat, *The Starlight*, in the 'Here We Are' centre today, and his six-foot model of the SS *United States* is in the Glasgow Transport Museum.

By the late 1940s and early 1950s Jack's ledgers began to expand – 'Ardkinglas and the Future' began to bud if not to blossom. We have the Wage Book from 1943 to 1958, at first in Daisy's green fountain-pen ink, then in John's handwriting, and latterly typed by Jack. In June 1947 there were 16 men on the Estate payroll and seven on the farming side, including a manager. By April 1951 there were 18 employees on the Estate and 14 on the farm (not including a manager).

Farming was looking promising. In March 1951 Davidson and Syme, the solicitors, sent the confirmation at last from the Hill Farming Scheme. It brought the good news that a total of £24,000 could be spent on farm improvements over the next ten years with the anticipated 50% subsidy.

Davidson and Syme also sent the new farm-workers' rates. The Government regularly issued details of the approved level of agricultural wages and allowances; these varied depending on the standard of accommodation provided. The higher the standard of accommodation the greater was the wage reduction. In addition there were wage deductions for cows and followers, and for coal. Malcolm MacDonald, shepherd, had arrived at the Whit term in 1951. In June he had £9.10s deducted from his pay packet, all of a six month coal deduction in one go; subsequently it would be deducted month by month, but for now he and his family had to survive on £13.11s for the month.

Shepherds were to have 7 shillings a month allowance for two dogs. There were also allowances for potatoes. The Agricultural Wages Regulations Scotland Act (1949) order of December 1957 stated: '"Dressed" potatoes shall mean sound potatoes in accordance with the definition applied for the purpose of the Government guarantee.'

But it was not just a question of 'dressed' or 'undressed' that affected the value, it was also the variety, making it clear that Highland farm workers knew their spuds. The rate for up to but not exceeding one ton of potatoes was:

Dressed, Grade A, rate 13/3d per cwt and Grade B dressed 11/3d
Undressed, Grade A, rate 11/3d per cwt and Grade B 9/3d per cwt

In Grade A were Golden Wonder, King Edward, Red Kings, Gladstone, Kerr's Pink and Redskin; in Grade B were any other varieties, i.e. the inferior varieties.

Farm wages at Ardkinglas in 1951 were (before deductions for potatoes, coal etc):

Shepherds:

| | |
|---|---|
| Gilbert Livingstone & Donald Morrison per week | £6-10/- |
| Neil Aitchison, Donald MacPherson, Roddie MacDiarmid & Donald Robertson | £6-0 |
| John Spalding & Hughie Nicolson | £5-11d. |

Tractor drivers:

| | |
|---|---|
| John Brown & Johnny Bell | £5-15/- & £6. |

In the mid-1950s the overall number of employees on the Estate was probably at its all-time peak, with about 17 employees on the farm side and 17 on the Estate. Though the actual numbers on the farm side and the Estate were now similar, the farm wage bill overtook the Estate's; this was because the Farm Wages acts of 1949 and 1951 and again of 1953 stipulated minimum rates. So whereas in 1947 the 16 Estate employees had been paid a monthly total of £198 and the 7 farm employees £99, by 1953 the Estate wage bill (for 17 of them) was £270 a month and the farm (for 16) was £338

*Callum MacDonald, Duncan Robertson, John Spalding, Colin Mac-
Callum and Gilbert Livingstone, dipping at Inverchorachan in the
early 1950s.*

per month, with a total annual wage bill for Estate and farm of £7,296. Numbers of farm employees grew throughout the 1950s.

The sheer number of people must have had an impact on the life on the Estate. Perhaps when people look back to an era of halcyon days – if they do and if there was one – it was during the 1950s. The worst of poverty and austerity was behind them, they didn't have to light the range to make a cup of tea and there was some opportunity for fun and relative social cohesion.

## In the 1950s on the Estate What Was Life Like?

Nigel Callander recalled, 'Oh yes, there was fun and good tares in those days'. One autumn Janet's uncle Roddy, from Laglingarten, decided that upstairs at

Maggie Luke's would be a good place to create the horse for the fancy-dress dance. 'He was a fancy-dress enthusiast. The horse had one person in its back, one in its front and another who led it. It was a good laugh. And then we had to carry it all up to the Hall.'

Donald MacIntyre and his sister Julie had run the Post Office for thirty years. At the end of March 1950 Donald died and Julie didn't want to carry on without him. The Estate owned the building. The Post Office pay was £400 pa, with rent to the Estate and staff wages to be paid out of it. When the vacant Post Office post was advertised John wanted to go through the shortlist and interview the applicants, along with the PO officials. He was keen to make sure the right kind of person was appointed, so that it would be maintained as a 'decent shop'. In these ways the Estate had control over much that happened in the village of Cairndow. It was a similar situation when the Jones's retired from the Hotel, John and Michael vetted all the applicants; finally a Mr and Mrs Foulger were given the lease, and the hotel was to be a licensed premises once more. This was clearly a big event. John Mirrlees remembered it: 'I mind when Cairndow Hotel bar opened, it was 1953 I think, when Willy Foulger came. He opened up the Hotel and got a licence. That evening three or four of us walked from Tighnabruaich, where I was working at the time, some 30 miles, to the opening of the Hotel. There was a good dance in the hall that night.'

The welfare and the vitality of the community were close to Elizabeth's heart. She was without class snobbery: her friends in Cairndow were friends by any yardstick. She had friends, and she also had those she was less fond of. She took trouble to know people, and their children; when she went shopping for toys for the Christmas Tree party, the children she was most fond of would be in her mind's eye, and she would think what present they would like. It was to widen and encourage women's interests that led her to found a local SWRI (Scottish Women's Rural Institute). Its official role was to 'promote the preservation of Scotland's traditions and rural heritage, particularly in the sphere of household activities'. The inaugural meeting was held in the newly electrified Village Hall. Through the winters 'the Rural', as it came to be called, met regularly once a month. In its heyday it had a membership of twenty-five. Alice said she joined not long after it started: 'It was one of the things to go to. The talks would be quite interesting and it showed you how to make things and do things.'

Elizabeth also founded Scouts, Guides, Cubs and Brownies. Alice Sinclair and her friend May Lang were among the six Guides, and Nigel Callander and Hamish Speirs, who would become apprentice joiners together, among

*Looking up Loch Fyne from Laglingarten. Policy Gate is the white house by the Loch, middle foreground.*

*Lorimer Cottage, The Stables and Ardkinglas House in the 1930s.*

*Ardno Farm in the 1950s.*

*Gilbert Livingstone and an old ewe.*

*Jean MacDiarmid and Janet Callander with a plucked hen at Ardkinglas in 1956.*

*Tasia and her deerhounds on the front drive at Ardkinglas.*

*Tasia (Anastasia) and Johnny Noble at Sarah's wedding in 1957.*

*View across Loch Fyne from above Kilmorich Church, 1963.*

The coalboat unloading on Ardkinglas foreshore in 1969. In the foreground
are Lucy Sumsion, Alice, John and Dot Beattiee.

Donnie MacDonald, John Beattie and Colin Callander watching as the
coalboat is unloaded.

*Jimmy Waddell and Donald MacPherson with 'improver' tups in front of Achadunan in 1975.*

*Cairndow Estate shepherds at Butterbridge in 1975. From left, Donald MacPherson, Archie Campbell, Callum MacDonald, Donald Beaton, Kit Reid, Jim Wilson, Ernie MacPherson, Malkie MacDonald and Jimmy Waddell.*

*The Phantom 1 Rolls Royce at the Square. Betty Manson, Elizabeth Noble
and Alice Beattie are by the garage arch.*

*George Knight with a crop of his onions in the bicycle shed.*

*Morag Keith and Greta Cameron.*

*Christina at Mossariach, above the head of Glen Fyne, 2016.*

the six Scouts. There were eight Brownies (including me) and about the same number of Cubs. She organised these and led the groups herself.

As already mentioned, electric light came to the Village Hall in November 1949. Until then it had been lit by candles and oil lamps, and in the winter there were two coal fires, one at each end. In those early post-war years, everyone was ready for an opportunity to enjoy him or herself. The Hall was run by the Cairndow Recreation Club, and there were dances every other Saturday night. There were fortnightly whist drives and basket whists too (when each 'table' brought its own tea, with tablecloth, fine crockery and even tea-stands), and there were weekly carpet bowls on the bowling tables. There would be frequent ceilidhs to raise funds for the Curling Club or the Bowls or the Recreation Club itself.

John Mirrlees remembers being a young man in those days.

Dances, oh aye, you went to everything that was on, whist, badminton and a dance on a Saturday night in the Hall. I tended to keep this side of the loch – St Catherines, Strachur, and Strathlachlan. Somehow or other I never went to Inveraray, always kept this side of the loch.

I'd go on a bike, down the shore road, and on to Strachur. No hills along the shore road and quite a good road in those days. Saturday night dances always strictly stopped at a quarter to 12. No alcohol in the hall: you'd go outside between dances with your quarter bottle in your inside pocket.

And Alice, at a similar age to John Mirrlees, described it from a young girl's view:

I went to dances not long after I left school and started work. At first I was only allowed to go to ones in Cairndow, but that petered out and we went to ones anywhere, Strachur and Inveraray and St Catherines. Sometimes there would be three in a week, Thursday, Friday, and Saturday. Local people played at some, and sometimes there were brought-in bands, an accordionist and a drummer. Twice we had Jimmy Shand at Cairndow. We wore evening dresses to it. It was a big affair, in 1948 or 49 I think.

Dot, interviewing her mother, asked if men wore kilts for the Jimmy Shand occasion. Alice laughed at the idea.

*Alice Sinclair, Janet MacCallum and May McIlwain, on the way to a*
*Jimmy Shand dance at Cairndow.*

Kilts weren't something that grown-up men wore much. They wore
suits probably. No, there wasn't a bar, definitely not. At Cairndow,
and most of the halls, there was a rule that there was no drinking in
the hall. There used to be something called the 'broom dance'. When
the music stopped the woman in the middle, who had been dancing
alone with the broom, dropped it and picked a partner, forcing the
displaced woman to pick up the broom. 'Poochie', Archie McVicar's
wife, was good fun with it.

We always had tea half way through at the big dances but not at
the regular Saturday night ones because there wasn't time before the
quarter to twelve end.

To go to dances in other places we usually went with May Lang's
sister, Amelia, she had the use of the Langs' car: she drove, and we all
piled in and went to wherever.

When the electric light came to the Hall, and illuminated the dances and
the whist drives, it also enabled a fortnightly film night. The Highlands and
Islands Film Guild had been established in 1946. It was non-profit and 'founded to improve the educational, cultural, and recreational amenities for rural
communities'. There was a fleet of vans and drivers/projectionists. It showed
a Pathé newsreel, a cartoon and the main film. There would be a break in the
middle while the projectionist changed the reels, and there would also be an

interruption while Alex Drummond, who lived alone in a hut at the bottom of Glen Kinglas, stumped out in his tackety boots to relieve himself. The Highlands and Islands films continued for many years and for me would become the every-other-Saturday-night highlight of my teenage years. After it we would cycle home along the Ladies Walk in the dark, dreaming of Marlon Brando.

Electricity also came to the school, the only light previously being an oil lamp on a pulley. At the end of the 1949 summer term there were 29 pupils on the school roll. These would be children between five and twelve years old. This number would more or less accord with the total in the Ardkinglas Christmas Tree book, which then listed a total of 63 children's names (including babies and high-school-age children).

Miss Anna Munro, the teacher, had a long-term influence on the Cairndow community. After 40 years teaching there, 'Wee Annie' retired in 1955, when the school roll was probably at its peak. She had certainly taught two generations of the same family, perhaps even three. She was born in 1890 at Achnagoul, by Inveraray. Her father was a gamekeeper on the Duke of Argyll's estate. Achnagoul was known as 'the college' because (unusually for Argyll at the time) so many from that hamlet went off to college in Glasgow (taking a bag of potatoes and one of oatmeal as their rations). She had a MA from Glasgow University and trained as a teacher at Jordanhill College.

She taught at Kilmorich School initially, in 1914-15, then she went to teach in London. The story was that the Zeppelins so terrified her that she had some sort of breakdown and returned to Cairndow.

Peter Manson, born 1939, remembers Wee Annie.

My brother Willy and I were taught by the same teacher who taught my father. She was an old lady. Because she had about 30 children in the school, all different classes, she would set the older ones a job to do, while she tended to the younger ones. And that's how she kept control. To strap us we used to have to take out an old box for her. She was only a small lady, and she used to stand on the box so she could strap us!

Ian, born 1937, son of Jimmy, visiting from New Zealand, remembered his schooldays here:

We walked to school most of the time. Later on we had bikes; we made our own bicycles. But going to school we just walked. We called

*Miss Munro.*

in at the Square and went to school with the Taylors and the Mansons and all, just went along and had mud fights, and scrapes, and got told off by different parents. And our schoolteacher, of course the one I had right through, was Miss Munro.

The subjects that I remember were arithmetic, which I was quite good at, and woodworking. I did study a bit, learned a lot about the history of New Zealand, as it happened, in the geography, as you did study more about the Commonwealth in those days.

We played shinty, rounders, and kicked the ball around, played cockeroostie [a game involving kidnapping and releasing prisoners]. We all joined in: a team on each side. And we got told off if we got too muddy going into the classroom. I think back on a few bad things that happened, not a whole lot. Everyone misbehaves, and if we misbehaved we got told off by the parents of the other child when we were on the way home.

The event remembered by all, if in varying versions, was the fire in the school. It was remembered for years as a beacon of interruption in their unchanging everyday lives (just as the landmine had been). Ian's version was:

I was there when the school was burned down. We didn't have a phone in the school, and I ran down to the Post Office and Mary Speirs [his cousin and the postie at the time] happened to be in the Post Office. I said to her 'The school's on fire, can you ring the Fire Brigade?' And she looked at me and said: 'I don't believe you' [Ian was known as a bit of a tease], but reluctantly she did go out onto the road to have a look and then she saw the smoke. The Fire Brigade arrived from Lochgoilhead. We tried to start the water-pump and it wouldn't start. Then the Inveraray Fire Brigade arrived, and duly put the fire out. After that we had to have school in the hall.

Peter Manson had a different version:

The year I was going to leave to go to Dunoon Grammar School, was the year the school burnt down. We were in the school at the time, and I was the oldest boy. I said 'Miss! Miss!' She was a right little tartar and she told me 'Manson sit down! Manson sit down!' I said 'But Miss!' All the little ones were getting panicky because we could see the smoke coming out from behind her desk. I went up to her. She said: 'Why did you come up here?' Then she said: 'March the kids out,' and she took the books, and the school registers.

John Noble's version of the incident in his Journal for 13 December 1949 is less dramatic, more matter-of-fact:

During the morning a fire started in the kitchen of the Schoolhouse and got a good hold before it was noticed. At the time a good many estate employees were back home for their dinner and went to help, and the Inveraray brigade came but were ineffective, being mostly not the regular crew. A good deal of Miss Munro's property was saved but the inside of the building was gutted. School will continue in the Village Hall meantime.

Recently the famous fire was the subject of lively discussion in the pub in February 2015, some 65 years after the event! The version of events that came out of this was:

Peter Manson had been naughty, so, though one of the oldest in the school, Miss Munro had put him to sit with the little ones up at the head of the schoolroom. He raised up his hand, clicked his fingers many times, and called 'Miss! Miss!' Wee Annie was moving around the back of the room and kept telling him to be quiet. Finally she asked what it was 'Miss – have you left a pot of soup on the range? There's smoke coming up between the floorboards' (The schoolroom was above the schoolteacher's house). She said she hadn't left the soup on and anyway Mr Fergusson (her cousin who lodged with her, for some reason called 'Stoochie Stalachar' by the children) was at home. 'Oh no, he's not,' someone yelled from the back, 'we saw him get on the Inveraray bus!' Wee Annie took Peter by the hand and went out and down and opened the door to her house – then there was a whoosh and the place was in flames. Peter was sent running down to the Post Office to get them to phone for the fire engine. Wee Annie told everyone to gather their books and their coats and shoes and march out. Outside, Netta MacPherson began to howl because somehow her shoes (which were new) had been left inside, and wee Alastair MacCallum was sobbing because his coat had also been left. Peter gallantly went back in for them. Clothes-rationing had just ended, but children knew shoes and a warm coat were expensive and precious items.

From her first schooldays the records show Alice's early scholastic promise and what an enthusiastic pupil she was:

March 6th 1942 [Alice was nine] – Unusually severe snowstorm. Alice Mary Sinclair and Mary Cameron Speirs [later to be the postie] are the only pupils at the school today. They were dismissed at lunchtime as the snowstorm showed no sign of abating.

January 30th 1945 – Only one child (Alice Mary Sinclair) reached school, she travelled alone over extremely difficult roads to attend school. In the afternoon the child was safely escorted home by the recorder.

Miss Munro was a highly professional teacher: all ten Kilmorich School pupils who sat the Qualifying Exam in 1945 passed it. The Correspondence Tuition scheme ('CT'), also called the Dalton Plan, after Hugh Dalton, had come into being in 1939. Rather than going to the grammar school at Dunoon 30 miles away, pupils who had passed their Qualifying Exam could be sent their 'CT' lessons from Dunoon. Two weeks of lessons were sent at a time. Argyll was the only county to take on the scheme; it turned out that it was not a great success and after a number of years it was scrapped.

Alice explains how it was for her:

After primary school, at twelve years old we sat 'The Qualifying' and if you had good enough marks you could go to Dunoon Grammar

School, but there was no transport to get there, and no hostel; you had to live in lodgings. I could have gone and lived with my uncle and aunt; they offered to take me but I didn't want to go. Miss Munro was desperate I should go to Dunoon School but I didn't want to.

So I was for the 'CT'. There were several of us that did it. We were sent a fortnight's work at a time; we rushed through the work and we would have it all done it in a week. Then Miss Munro would have to find us other things to do.

Miss Munro was still determined I should go to Dunoon because I had quite good marks, so eventually I did go, though by now, being 14, I could have left school. Mum and Dad were also determined I should go. It was a disaster – at Dunoon they were doing completely different things to what we had been doing in CT. For one thing they were doing a foreign language, which we hadn't done. They were doing science and we hadn't. I went at Easter till the summer holidays and then for the full year. I would have been better staying here and getting the CT Certificate than going to Dunoon and getting nothing because of my lack of foreign language and science.

Peggy Taylor, a contemporary of Alice's, and also a CT student, later went on to nursing school, and Johnny Luke went on to Glasgow University and became a teacher. But for decades few Cairndow youngsters would take up the idea of further education; the majority left school and went to work as soon as they could.

In February 1946 Janet MacCallum, aged fifteen (daughter of Tina and Colin, and granddaughter of old Archie, the stalker), had begun to work as kitchen maid at Ardkinglas on a wage of £52 p.a. Cooks' and kitchen maids' wages were quoted at a yearly rate, though they were paid monthly; everyone else's at a monthly rate. By August 1948 Janet had been promoted to cook and Alice, who had just left school at fifteen, was taken on as kitchen maid. Janet lived at Ardkinglas as her home in the Glen was too far to travel every day. When Alice came, though she lived much closer, she too stayed at Ardkinglas. She, looking like the teenager she was, cycled home for her afternoon off, and on Sunday afternoon. Janet and Alice became, and still are, good friends.

Janet left Ardkinglas (though she came back at various periods) in July 1949. Alice stayed on for a year or so with a pay increase to £72. She described why she left the Ardkinglas kitchen:

A Swiss couple came. He was the cook. I fell out with them, or they fell out with me. It was during the time of the rationing and the land girl, she was always later coming in for her breakfast. We only had our own wee bit of butter. And the Swiss man he said I was saving the butter for her, which wasn't right because we all had our own bits of butter. I couldn't understand French and he couldn't understand English, which wasn't a very good combination. And this one day he was laying on in French and the next thing he hit me in the face with the butter. So that was the end of that, I decided I wasn't staying. So I gave in my notice and left and I went to Ardbrecknish Hotel over at Loch Awe. I worked at Ardbrecknish for a year, then went to the 'Dough School' in Glasgow for three months. I stayed with relatives there. I liked the School and I would have gone back, but I didn't go back because I got married.

It was 1952: she was nineteen. She married Walter Beattie, tractor-man working at Cladich some ten miles over the hill from Inveraray, later trac-tor-man at Ardkinglas. In those days some people got married in church in white wedding dresses, but for many weddings were not elaborate affairs: Alice, like many others, was married by the Minister in the hotel. Close friends and family would be invited for the meal there, with speeches and the reading

*Bobby Callander and Anne Donald's wedding in 1950, Douglas Luke*
*with the accordion.*

of telegrams – 'May all your spuds be Golden Wonders' etc. – some unambig-uously risqué. Afterwards everyone went up to the Hall for the dance. This wasn't by invitation: a notice would be put up in the Post Office announcing the wedding dance and that everyone was welcome.

Wedding parties, as always everywhere, were looked forward to as an opportunity to celebrate with family and community, even if they had to be arranged in a hurry. It was funerals that were more demanding in terms of expense: they required formal clothes and attending them could involve expensive travel. They were important occasions and Estate employees were always allowed time off for them.

# Reflections

The 'village life' that Patsy said she hankered after had advantages and dis-advantages. It depended on how you saw it. Everyone knew everyone and everyone knew each other's business. For the adventurous it could be claus-trophobic and constricting. This was the childhood world that Ian Stewart (now a champion sheep-shearer in Mastodon, New Zealand) looked back on with the expatriate's nostalgia, as did Helen recalling her war years in Cairn-dow from Canada. Ian remembered:

> Yes, I can recall my father came home just after five. We usually had dinner between five and six. In the summertime we went out and played afterwards. Or quite often we went out on the loch in the boat. As I got older I used to row across the loch to the other side especially to get hazelnuts off the trees there. Now that I think of it, it was very risky. I never had a life jacket on, never. And I would be out there as a 10, 11-year-old, even 9 years old, on my own in the boat pulling in nets and fish. Nowadays people would scream at you if you did that.
>
> I joined in for the whist drive evenings in the hall as I got older and was allowed to go out. And there was curling in the wintertime on the Caspian when it froze over or on the old tennis court at Ard-kinglas gardens. They used to flood that there. I used to enjoy going out at night and the floodlights. We just made our own fun playing rounders, playing shinty and football. And we didn't worry about how neat the grounds were. We put up our own goal posts, we made our own goal posts, we made our own jumping bar, we made our sand pit or sawdust pit for the long jump. We entertained ourselves.

Sunday was a day of rest. With a Sunday as a family of three boys we were dressed in a kilt when we went to church. Getting dressed up, well that was for church. But school we just wore old clothes, patched and what have you, you didn't have the choice that people have got today. There was darning and stitching. And as a pupil in primary school in them days you learned to knit and you learned to darn.

For the employees on Highland estates at the time so much depended on the character of the landowner. It was paternalistic but this was the 1950s; if all went well, you were looked after. 'They' improved your house and helped when you were sick. But most of the estate-owned houses were 'tied houses'; not surprisingly this was an underlying source of anxiety, particularly for those with young families. It has left a twinge of anxiety inherited from generations, even today. As John Jameson, chauffeur and lorry driver in Robert Grant's explained:

> The biggest millstone around any estate worker's neck is the tied house, if you fall ill for a long time you are dependent on the goodwill of the laird . . . you should pay a rent, it shouldn't be part of your wages.
>
> The happiest day of my life was when I heard I had been allocated a council house.
>
> I have no regrets at leaving estate work, I feel a free man, I am working again and have a boss but my new boss has no hold over me as the laird had when I was his chauffeur and driver . . . Only now I realise how independent I have become now as a result of getting away. The ways of a laird are not my ways. Good or bad, most lairds have too great a hold on the lives of those who work for them.

In 1944 the elderly Mr and Mrs Dougald MacPherson were living in East Lodge. (Mr and Mrs Ure, Helen's grandparents, must have moved by then.) At this time Mrs MacPherson milked the dairy cows. She also polished the parquet floors at Ardkinglas with a large leather thing like a leather curling-stone and sang Gaelic songs as she polished. Old Dougie, her husband, was chasing after their own cow when he collapsed and died. Daisy wrote that 'Dougie was going to be a great loss as he was doing the drives so awfully well and loving the work. Poor woman Mrs MacPherson is very anxious to stay on a little while at East Lodge until she can look around and make up her mind what to do.'

She would have been apprehensive because it was her husband's employment that entitled them to the 'tied' house. In fact Mrs MacPherson did stay on at East Lodge until well after the war, but at the time widows in particular would have felt the threat of losing their homes.

The story of Lizzie Callander, a widow with four sons, illustrates the tied house issue. Nigel Callander described his mother's predicament when the death of his father Willie left her a widow. Willie had gone to Glaschoine on his motorbike from where he worked as a gamekeeper near Tarbert. On his way back he had stopped for a drink with Lachie Sinclair, roadman, working on the other side of the loch. But Lachie, who would not have covered up for Willie, said that he was not drunk and that it was he, Lachie, who had finished the bottle. There was an accident and Willie was found dead. Nigel (who was only two at the time) told me his father had been found sitting on his motorbike with his neck broken. No one really knows what happened.

> We were at the Rogers of Achahoich, we were staying at the gamekeeper's cottage. Well, my mother had four boys to bring up. She had to leave the cottage where we were living because the Rogers got a new gamekeeper. She had to go out of that house. She used to cycle to Lochgilphead to see if she could get a place to work and to live. It was 1940. She must have been enquiring if there was any place here at Ardkinglas and it would be through Mrs John that she got the house. It was a small house. There was a bath with a lid in the living room. My mother helped cook in the Big House during the war. She often took me with her to work.

Another issue for employees was apt to be the transportation of their children to school, particularly for shepherds who often lived in remote houses. John Noble:

> On August 11th we sent to flit Roddie MacDiarmid's from Loch Eck. He is going to Butterbridge, [3 miles along the main road from the village] on the clear understanding that we are not to be responsible for getting his children to school.

(In the end they were fetched by the Estate-run school van, and went home by MacBrayne's bus.)

The MacCallum family were less lucky. In February 1950 John MacCallum, a shepherd, was living up at Inverchorachan in upper Glen Fyne, with wife, four children and his old mother. Bravely he came to the Big House to ask if the school van could pick up his children on wet mornings. Inverchorachan is two miles beyond the nearest dwelling. The mail was delivered to Inverchorachan three evenings a week by the Estate school/mail van. John responded:

> I said no, because we did not want the van to have extra running on the bad road nor the inevitable misunderstandings about 'wet mornings'. I pointed out to John that people on this side of the school walk both ways a longer distance. He feels aggrieved because he says Michael Noble said the children would be taken home on wet evenings when he was engaged. The poor man is not much use as a shepherd owing to fits, but he did not disclose that when he applied.

By 5 April of the same year John MacCallum was leaving.

> This is a good thing as the poor man suffers from epileptic fits and it is hardly safe for him to be on the hill. In addition it makes him an unreliable shepherd and we have paid him wages for a great many weeks when he has not worked.

Peter Beaton, who had been an Ardkinglas Estate employee briefly in his youth, looked back in 2015, and commented on the house issue:

> The tied house, that was always at the back of a married man's mind. I don't know if I could have hacked that. Some people must have had to take a lot. It was different if you were a single man but there must have been times of humiliation. If you misbehaved you could end up in the tight corner. It was as simple as that. It could be a worry but I suppose it was an accepted thing then: everyone was in a tied house.

There were still a few Ardkinglas-owned houses that were rented out to non-employees on long-term leases. During the 1920s and 1930s the farms were rented out, as were most of the houses, and the larger part of the Estate's income came from rents. This happened at Laglingarten. John's Journal comments:

MacVicar from Laglinagarten intends to pay out his two daughters (Mrs MacVicar died intestate) and take over the lease which was in his wife's name. I discussed this with his lawyer and said we would agree (we cannot refuse) but suggested the rent should be revised.

There was a similar situation at Glaschoine when Alice's Grannie died. The lease had always been in her name, perhaps since the Strutts' days when she was their laundry maid. John discussed the issue of renewing the lease with Lachie Sinclair, the old lady's son-in-law and Alice Beattie's father. He had worked all his life for the County Council as a roadman, and since his marriage, in 1930, he had lived at Glaschoine. John explained to him that either he could pay a higher rent for the house (and then pay for improvements himself) or he could pay no rent for the house (i.e. it would be a 'tied' house) and he would become an Estate employee (he would have to pay rent for the field for the cow's grazing). He decided on the latter deal (he had had enough of living off 'pieces' and being a roadman out at all times of night and day and in all weathers). He joined the foresters' squad on the Estate. Lachie could hardly be blamed for not being able to see into the future, but in retrospect it was a bad decision. Had he chosen differently, a decade or two later Alice and her sister Margaret might have been well-off householders.

# Disappointments

John's Estate Journal is pretty dry; only occasionally, between the lines, do you get an inkling of his feelings.

Just after the war gangs of Irishmen came to the Highlands as bracken-cutters (my brother Johnny used to give a rendition of the 'Bracken-cutters' Song'. That song, as well as bracken-cutting, is something of the past). Charlie Boyle had come from Ireland with his brother and brother-in-law to cut bracken for Willie Weir in 1946. The same year they had also cut bracken for Ardkinglas. There were bracken-cutting grants: in 1948 there was a Government bracken scheme, Charlie and his gang were paid £300. In 1964 it was 25 shillings per acre for 'double cut' (the second cut had to be within six weeks of the first). In addition Charlie took on a contract to repair the dry-stone dykes, which had been damaged by the Army during the war. The first section was from Strone Brae along the High Road from East Lodge to Ardno Quarry, and the second from there back along the shore road, in all a considerable distance. John comments: 'Charlie's father-in-law knew about dry stone dyking and had taught the others as they went along. Showing that it is not so difficult an art as is sometimes made out.' (Said John!)

Then Charlie and his brother gave a hand with the Estate masons, or on the farm or wherever they were needed. Charlie had brought over his wife and children and they were living at Sawmill Cottage. Then, on 24 April 1950:

> Charlie Boyle came to say he wanted to leave at the end of a month on account of the difficulty of getting his children to Mass. In between dyking the Irishmen had contracts with us for fencing and draining and sometimes stayed on and worked through the winter with the foresters. For the last year and more Charlie has stayed and worked almost entirely with the foresters. The others had gone back to Ireland or went to work for Carmichael on the Hydroelectric scheme at Clachan.

Then, a month later, in an uncharacteristically outspoken entry, John wrote: 'Went down [to Sawmill Cottage] to say goodbye to Charlie Boyle and his family. We are all very sorry to part with him as he was an unusually open, pleasant and hardworking man.'

Clearly John was sorry to be losing the Boyle family, but the departure of the Stewart family to New Zealand was a worse blow.

The Estate team of joiners and masons had secured the contract to build the two new houses for the Hydro Board, designed by Iain Lindsay. There is a photograph of Elizabeth laying the foundation stone with old Archie MacVicar, waxed moustaches sharpened, standing by. Completed in 1953, the commission must have been something of a coup for the Estate: an encouragement towards future expansion. Jimmy Stewart would have been in charge of the joiners.

Handsome Jimmy had been born on Ardkinglas Estate and was an employee since 1919. As a boy, John, a mere three years younger than Jimmy, would have known him or certainly would have known of him. Jimmy had featured in Amie Noble's 'Assess' of the early 1930s. 'J Stewart will interpret Mr Winton's wisdom for you as he is his A.D.C. and knows how much knowledge is contained in the grand old man's shining head. Naturally J Stewart, taught by this GOM, can turn his hand to any mortal thing on an estate.'

I think John admired and depended on Jimmy, much as Winton, the loyal employee, had been depended on in the past. I think he saw Jimmy as

*An outing to Perth. In the centre are crouched Jimmy Stewart, Donald MacPherson and Nigel Callander.*

a lynchpin for development at Ardkinglas. In *Ardkinglas and the Future* a stated aim was: 'to preserve what's good in the past and the present but to infuse new life and vigour . . . to attract back some who have wandered away because they have not had a chance of a reasonable life in the land of their birth.'

The recent electrification of the joiners' shop led to proposals for further improving Estate productivity:

> Mr Bell, local organiser of Scottish Country Industries Development Trust called and we had a talk about machinery for Jimmy at the joiners shop. I ordered a small electric sanding machine costing £19 and Mr Bell was to inquire whether we could obtain an electrical adaptation for the existing hand mortising machine.

And in October John wrote:

> Jimmy Stewart came in to Glasgow with me to see demonstration of the Elliott 'super wood worker' at exhibition at Kelvin Hall. It is a very neat machine which does planing, thicknessing, morticing, ripsaw, cross cut saw and various other operations. The cost is about £400 with attachments, but I think it might pay for itself over the years.

139

Recently Ian explained his father's motivation for emigrating to New Zealand, along with his wife and his three sons.

My grandfather was John Stewart, a shepherd at Croitchonie. And my father James was born in 1906. He was the head joiner. I think he left school when he was 14 or 15 and served his time as a joiner with the head carpenter at Ardkinglas, Winton was his name. Apart from the war years, my father spent all his life on the Ardkinglas Estate.

My mother, before she was married, was Charlotte Bashford, lady's maid for Lady Noble [Amie]. That's how she came to Cairndow from Croydon in England. And she went to London with Lady Noble and when she went to Paris she would go to Paris with her. And that's how my mother met my father at Ardkinglas Estate.

We never went about much from Cairndow. Well, it wasn't possible. That was partly the reason why we went to New Zealand. My father decided that for me to do an apprenticeship in Glasgow it would cost more for accommodation then you got paid. So that is why my father decided to head for New Zealand with us three boys; he thought there would be good opportunities for us there. That was in 1953.

Nigel Callander, who in turn served his apprenticeship with Jimmy, remembers:

Jimmy was a good tradesman, he kept young boys in line at that time. I always worked with Jimmy; Hamish [Speirs] worked with Willie [MacPherson]. We got on great. Jimmy and Willie were both good joiners, good tradesmen. We had just finished building the New Houses for the Hydro. Aye I couldn't understand at all why Jimmy went to New Zealand. I am always saying to that to Kate [Jimmy's niece] because he was at everything at Cairndow, important to the bowls, the shinty and everything.

He came here, one time when he was visiting from New Zealand and I was speaking to him and he was saying, 'It was for my family that I went for really'. He was 48 when he went, quite an old man.'

Reading between the lines I think their departure was a blow for Elizabeth, who was fond of Jimmy and his family, but it was particularly felt by John.

In 1953 Jimmy, fun and talented, set sail for New Zealand with his young family on an 'assisted passage' from the New Zealand government. They even took their car. John and Elizabeth and Daisy and Tasia too (to whom Bashie had sometimes been lady's maid) were all sorry on a personal level – after long years of shared times with a family who were lively members of the community.

For John I don't think the regret was just on the personal level. It was a blow to his aspirations for the future. His hope had been that the joiners' shop would be improved and modernised and become more productive, with the skilled Jimmy at the helm. And it was not just the loss of Jimmy but also the loss of those Stewart boys, who might have infused 'new life and vigour' and been examples to others, and 'to attract back some who have wandered away because they haven't had a chance of a reasonable life in the land of their birth.'

Instead the family – with the three sons, just the kind of family that was needed – like all too many of the preceding generations was turning its back on the Highlands and heading away across the seas.

I was eleven at the time; if the regret was aired, it wasn't in my hearing. But I remember the Stewarts coming to say goodbye. We were all in the Billiard room, downstairs. Presumably they were given a cup of tea, a dram, some cake, a handsome parting gift? I don't remember, but I do remember the atmosphere: everyone was brave, and sad.

# Ups and Downs: the Later 1950s to 1972

For some these years brought a change of focus and for some new opportunities. In 1957 Harold Macmillan, 'Supermac', famously told the country: 'Let us be frank about it – most of our people have never had it so good. Go around the country, go to the industrial towns, go to the farms and you will see a state of prosperity such as we have never had in my lifetime – nor indeed in the history of this country.'

The following year Michael Noble became a Unionist (Tory) MP for the first time. He was elected in the by-election caused by the death of Duncan McCallum, the longstanding MP in a safe Unionist constituency, Argyll.

Towards the end of the 1950s John and Michael's attention became less focused on Ardkinglas. Michael was increasingly involved with his political career. He became Secretary of State for Scotland under Macmillan and Douglas-Home from 1962 to 1964. Then, after the Labour governments of 1964 and 1965, with the return of the Tories under Heath, he was made Minister of Trade from 1970 to 1972. He retired in 1974 and was awarded a peerage, becoming Baron Glenkinglas.

John and Elizabeth's interests were directed more towards Scottish culture. She collected modern Scottish painting. As early as 1950 their enthusiasm for quality craftsmanship had taken them to Holland and also to Denmark, to look at the Danish Craft Centre. John became chief executive of the Scottish Craft Centre at Acheson House in the Canongate, Edinburgh, and on 21 April 1953 when it was opened by the Queen, I presented her with a bouquet of red roses. John and Elizabeth's political affinities, such as they were, were not Tory. In April 1950, John had gone to a meeting of the Scottish National Covenant Association to participate in a discussion on Home Rule. In the general election of that year he noted in his journal:

Home Rule, 2 candidates, % of seats in contested constituencies 2.05%
Scottish Nationalists, 4 candidates, 6.39%
Scots Self Government, 1 candidate, 2.31%

John and Elizabeth were not dedicated 'Nats', as the Scottish Nationalists were known then, but they were more 'Nat' than Tory. They were European in outlook, international even. John spoke fluent German, Elizabeth spoke French and some Italian. They considered international relations to be important. From the 1950s they had hosted visitors through the Victoria League, which arranged accommodation in people's homes for Commonwealth students. In addition to the Craft Centre, John became increasingly involved with the Saltire Society, the Dovecot Tapestry Company, the BBC, Scottish Opera and other musical initiatives.

Later Elizabeth and John jointly hosted 'musical weekends' at Ardkinglas; a chamber orchestra played in the drawing room and the weekend guests were treated to lunch and dinner with local, home-cooked food. Still later Elizabeth became involved in the Bridge, an Israeli-Scottish organisation that hosted groups of Israeli students. For Elizabeth it was always important to share a warm welcome and conversation round the dining-room table. Downstairs, to the right of the front door, the green baize door leading to the kitchen was never closed. The kitchen door was always open too, exuding smells of bread baking and raspberry-jam boiling (sometimes over-boiling). From there anyone coming in through the front door would get a 'coo-ee!' and a welcome.

From 1955 to 1958 I went to St Bride's girls school in Helensburgh. I went initially as a miserable boarder, then I lodged with a friend of my parents and was at home at weekends. During my teenage years my world was Ardkinglas. I would ride a pony or cycle through the village and along the main road (less of a main road then) and continue on up the glen. Or I would thumb a lift; in those days we thought nothing of it. I would head for wherever the farm-workers and shepherds were working – making the hay, bringing it in to sheds and lofts, gathering, clipping and packing wool. I learned to drive on tractors and old Land Rovers with wonky steering. In the evenings I could creep out through the dining-room window onto the outside staircase and, as soon as I could drive, I and my partner in these escapades, Maggie Paterson, taking my mother's old Morris without telling, would head off to dances – at St Catherines, Strachur and Inveraray. In those days women sat at one end of the hall, on wooden benches, and men at the other. The worry was that if some drunken lout asked you up for the Hesitation Waltz, you couldn't refuse him and then agree to the offer of the man you wanted, who had been too slow to cross the floor. Indeed if you did so misbehave, the MC would tell you to leave the floor. This was most crucial when it came to the last dance, and therefore the confirmation of who was 'going to see you home'.

Maggie, some ten years older than me, was an influential friend. She had been brought up with seven siblings, six older sisters and a younger brother, all of whom had lived in a two-room cottage on Cladich Hill above Inveraray. Her brother Angus was now a shepherd at Ardkinglas, and he, his mother, his wife, child and Maggie were living in Garden Cottage. In today's world she might have been thought a feminist. Slightly surprisingly, when she left Ard-kinglas she got married and had two sons. We stayed friends until she died, but were never as close or having such good times together as when I was sixteen and seventeen. She taught me, teasingly, never snidely, to recognise that I was the laird's daughter, but at the same time she treated me as a friend and an equal. She was the first close friend I had.

*Corn stack at Achadunan in 1956. In the picture are Donald MacPherson, Christina Noble, Jimmy Waddle, Walter Beattie, John Spalding, Donald Morrison and Callum MacDonald.*

*Hogmanay, 1959. Maggie Paterson is in the centre holding a bottle.*

Farm and estate affairs weren't discussed in the Big House: never a mention of wool or lamb prices, good or bad. And of course I didn't regale the dinner table with the local gossip I had picked up that afternoon.

## Good Times for Employees

In the later 1950s the country had begun to benefit from a post-war boom in the global economy. The Meat Marketing and Wool Marketing Boards had a beneficial impact, and at Ardkinglas the sheep and wool prices were good. The Hill Farm Subsidies for both cattle and sheep were generous: the government encouraged breeding quality hill-farm stock that would become store cattle and sheep on lowland pastures. Achadunan Farm was taken back in hand in 1957 (John Lang had died, gored by a bull). And then in 1961 when John Weir died, Ardno Farm, which had been tenanted by the Weirs from 1918, was also taken back in hand.

In 1957 there were 31 employees and the wage bill had grown. In 1949 Sam Keith was employed as a professional head forester on the high wage of £5.10s; at that time no one else was paid as much as £5. However by 1957 old Archie MacVicar, Sam Keith, and Angus MacGillivray, the head gardener, were all getting over £8 a week.

145

At Ardkinglas the number of employees and the August wage bill over the ten years (from the Estate records) was:

'47
Farm        7 employees    £107    per month
Estate      17             £211

'51
Farm        16             £360
Estate      18             £302

'52
Farm        16             £385
Estate      19             £379

'57
Farm        14             £421
Estate      17             £408

This represented a considerably increased wage bill for the employers. Over ten years the number of employees had gone up by some 30%, but the monthly wage bill (for August – it varied a little during the rest of the year) had gone up by over 160%. There were still more Estate employees than farm employees, but farm wages were higher and must have levered up Estate wages. Farm wages were dictated by the Agricultural Wages (Scotland) Act of 1953 (and then updated). Minimum agricultural wages were set district by district, for male and female, by age and by occupation: for shepherds, grieves, stockmen, horsemen, tractor-men, ploughmen etc. So over the ten years the average Estate employee's wage and the average farm employee's wage had gone from £15 to £30 (farm) and £12 to £24 (Estate). (However the figures listed above don't take into account allowances for house rates, cows, garden etc, and so may not be exact.)

In 2014 I asked Nigel Callander about his early years on the Estate (he married Janet MacCallum, daughter of Colin, the stalker of Glen Fyne).

I got married in 1956, I was 22, and tragedy happened to me. That was October and in January I landed in a sanatorium in Oban. I was there from January to October, nine months. When I had gone for

*Janet MacCallum and Nigel Callander's wedding, 1956.*

my army medical they found a spot on my lung, so I wasn't fit for service. While you were serving your time as an apprentice you were exempt from National Service. Your father would write to the MOD and tell them that so and so was an apprentice. But you had to go within a year after you were finished the apprenticeship.

Nigel Callander and Hamish Speirs had served their time with Ardkinglas joiners, including working with Jimmy Stewart on the construction of the New Houses. Then they had both left and seized an opportunity to work with Marples, the contractors on the Hydro Board's Lairig scheme. (I remember people murmuring about the 'ridiculous wages' paid by the contractors on the hydro schemes, which were enticing young men away.)

Nigel had worked with Marples for two years and then went on to J. and M. Carmichael's, the contractor on the Clachan-Shira scheme. He and another joiner did the 'shuttering' at a small dam up the hill there.

Everyone would go up the hill on the railway, 16 or 20 of us in the bogie, with one rope pulling us up. Then you had to walk across about a mile to get to the mouth of the tunnel. The tunnel was right through the hill. You had to walk through to the other side. I was only

147

21. On these schemes you worked eight in the morning till eight at night. And you worked Saturday and Sunday. 80 hours a week: two weeks in one week. It was too much for me, they found the TB and I had landed in the sanatorium. Janet had to go back up the Glen to live with her parents.

I came back home in October and then I went to see your father. It was old Archie MacVicar who had told me to ask Mr John for a job. Your father was at the front door when I went to ask. He was pulling on his wellingtons. 'Yes,' he said 'I'll consider it, Nigel, I'll think about it and let you know.' And he did. He said I could get started as a joiner again, and get Dacia Cottage at the Square, that was a great wee house at the Square that had been newly done up.

So Nigel, who used to play snail races with his cousin Alice Beattie, and who was one of the four sons of the widow Lizzie Callander (who had come looking for a house on the Estate in 1940) was back working on the Estate, where he has been for almost all of his, so far, 82 years. He and his wife Janet now live in half of Mid Lodge, and represent continuity from 1905, when Janet's grandfather, Old Archie, was already in Glen Fyne. Janet and Nigel's son Colin (a joiner-builder) and wife Margaret and their two sons now live at the front of Mid Lodge (where the Jimmy Stewart family once was).

Nigel described the roll-call at 8 am at the Square every morning. John Noble used to bicycle over. Everyone stood around in a semicircle in front of the arch into the garage yard.

Mr John would stay on his bike, one foot on the ground, and he had his light on, the dynamo, all the time. He was supposed to be telling us what to do, or was it that we were telling him what we were going to do?

I asked Nigel if John would say 'No, I don't want you to do that; I want you to do something else.'

Very seldom, mostly he was quite in agreement with what you were saying you were going to do. I must give him his due; in the morning he might say he wanted something done. And then you never see him till the next morning. He would never come prying round to see what you were doing. He never bothered; no, he never bothered. He was a gentleman. He never came near. [!]

I asked why Angus and any gardeners never had to turn up for the roll-call.

I don't know. Angus walked straight by at 8 o'clock; he never looked right or left, never greeted anyone. And there was Maggie Paterson, who worked in the garden with Angus at that time. We used to laugh – Maggie would be at a dance at St Catherines on a Friday and Maggie – without fail on the Saturday morning at 5 to 8 – she walked by; 'Morning' she would say. [Maggie and I might have been at the dance together, but unlike her I would probably not be up at 8 on the Saturday morning.]

I don't know how Maggie Paterson survived it with Angus. We would be in the greenhouse for our 10 o'clock tea. Someone once asked Angus 'What kind of machine have you got in the gardens?' 'That's the machine there – it's Maggie!' I don't know, he was an odd one. He went to his work without fail, and he turned out some wonderful stuff: it was a beautiful garden. We would be painting in the greenhouses, and Willie would say 'Could you open that window?' Angus would barely open the window and then close it right away. He had a mind of his own. He wasn't a sociable fellow.

Mrs John was frightened of him. One afternoon she was in the garden and Angus was coming along with the plough and he was coming to the end of the row to turn and she said 'Did you see his face, Nigel?' She was frightened.

You must have had good fun times, I said, knowing that Nigel was renowned as an instigator of nicknames which lasted across generations, often used by those who had no idea of what the name had once referred to.

We had great times. Some nonsense! Willie MacPherson was there with the joiners and Janet's brother Roddy MacCallum was there; he was serving his time. Ronnie Cameron was there; he was serving his time. Willie's son Bill MacPherson – he was there too. Willie was a joiner and I was a joiner, so we were a team of five – that was some gang . . .

As time went on it became more interesting for me as I got the job with the Land Rover taking all the kids to school and all that, and then your father told me I could maybe look after the cars and I said that suits me down to the ground, I'd love that . . .

No, I didn't give up the joinery, I still did the joinery. Peter MacLennan came as mechanic once a month for a week to look after your father's cars. Your father said – 'You go with Peter and you'll learn a lot about cars.' And I said that suited me great, so I was away from joiner work for a week at a time.

The Beaton family arrived at Ardkinglas in 1957. Kenny joined the foresters. He was originally from Lewis; he had been in the naval reserves and then joined the Royal Navy in 1939. His wife Rachel was also from Lewis, but brought up in Glasgow. They had two sons, Peter and Norman, and two daughters, Morag and Tina. Kenny and Rachel were a good-looking couple, Morag and Tina in their summer frocks with their hair done in ringlets were the prettiest little girls, and Peter and Norman good-looking young men. They lived at Sawmill Cottage at Bachie Bhan. The family soon became friends of mine – the bolshie 15-year-old that I was. Kenny would gently tease me about who I was, with a twinkle in his eye encouraged me to see myself as others saw me, and also to listen to others as they were. They were staunch Labour supporters, or rather old-fashioned principled socialists. I spent a lot of time at their house and they were to remain my good friends

*Rachel and Kenny Beaton at Sawmill Cottage in 1958.*

when they moved to Islay. Elizabeth became friends of theirs too, and her first visit away from home after the trauma of John's death was to the Beatons in Islay. Kenny, and then Rachel, died much too young. Peter and Norman now live in Ardrishaig, down Loch Fyne from Cairndow.

Peter talked recently about those far-off days.

> I remember when my father and I came down to be interviewed by your father, sitting out on the front green at Ardkinglas. It was a boiling hot day and I was burnt; my ears were red – I was eighteen – I was always getting burnt.

So the employment contract was with Kenny, as a forester on £7.15s. Since at the Kinlocheil Estate (their previous employment), Peter had been given vermin-control work and had been put in charge of the stalking pony, the factor there had given him a reference in that field: so at Ardkinglas he was taken on as a junior gamekeeper at £4.10s.

Peter explained that his family had left Glasgow in 1953 and had gone to work with the Forestry Commission at Farr, south of Inverness. Peter finished high school in Inverness and joined his father and the forestry squad. They were in a brand new house, but it was very cold. Kenny got £5 a week and Peter £2. It was a 5½-day week, and, even though it was the Forestry Commission, they had to buy their own firewood and there was no coal allocation. The forestry squad were ex-servicemen in a camp: 'It was quite an experience. They all had a story to tell. A lot of them men had been away in the war and also in the Korean war.'

The Beatons had gone from there to the Kinlocheil Estate, and then to Ardkinglas. At Ardkinglas:

> We were given Sawmill Cottage, Bachie Bhan; it was very small, two up and two down. We were six of a family. We just had to double up. The houses we had been in were bigger. But this had electricity, there had been none at Farr or at Kinlocheil; my mother had taken it badly being without electricity, because she had had it in Glasgow. Walter Beattie [Alice's husband, and at the time the estate tractor and lorry-driver] flitted us down from Lochaber, in the estate lorry. He must have spent the night up there with us.
>
> When we arrived at the house the fire had been put on for us, that was what was done when there was a flitting. A dram was given –

151

*Peter Beaton playing a salmon at the Falls in 1958.*

to Walter and to Sam Keith [head of the foresters' squad] and to Lachie Sinclair [Alice's father] and Bobby Callander, all foresters [so with Kenny there were four in the foresters' squad]. My father must have bought a half bottle.

Norman went to Inveraray School and then to Dunoon Grammar, and Morag and Tina to Cairndow. Bolek and Mamie Kobiela and family were just up the hill from us at Mid Lodge, Bobby Callander and family were just above us at Bachie Bhan; the Paterson family – Maggie who worked in the garden and her brother Angus, a shepherd – lived along the loch at Garden Cottage.

Looking back, Peter remembers his early days on the Estate. Perhaps after his travels far and wide since then, he recalls the Estate in those days more clearly than those who have remained closer to it.

I cycled and walked to work every day, right up to Abyssinia in Glen Kinglas and to Inverchorachan in Glen Fyne. I mostly worked by myself, left to my discretion. Your father was very trusting. Vermin control in those days was all through the year. For the foxes, maybe you got £2 for a brush, and you got quite a bit for the badger skins that were sent away for curing, and there were the hoodies [hooded crows]. In the summer I would be fishing – I was given a free hand – I could fish where and when I wanted, for salmon for the Big House.

On pay-day everyone stood outside the porch at Ardkinglas until your name was called; Jack Taylor and your father would be doing the wages. You would get a little brown envelope, with a bit of cash – not much! All my money went to my mother for the housekeeping. Well, occasionally I took something for the dances . . .

How my mother actually managed is mind-boggling. There was

no hunger or anything like that, but with the wages as they were I don't know how my mother did it, with a big family. She certainly never had any money, any surplus. No one had any money, everyone was much the same, unless you had a sideline of some sort. On an estate you were boosted a bit by the perks; the garden and the coal allocation helped a bit. Everyone was pretty much in the same boat.

My father said that in Lewis they had had a dresser, a table and some chairs. That was it. They were poor. They never had anything.

I asked if he remembered his parents ever being short.

No, well the hire purchase was a great thing. There was no other income than what came in your wages. A car was only a dream.

Funerals – they were costly. My father and I had been up to Lewis because his mother was ill. We had hardly been back (I was working and living in Arrochar by then); there was a knock on the door, there was a phone message: she had died. We had to go back up. My father had to borrow from the Foulgers at the hotel, he had no money and we had to pay for the train and ferry and of course the funeral itself. Lairs [in the graveyard] were very costly even then.

In those days a half-bottle of whisky was the thing. Even at Hogmanay, a bottle was a rarity. It was those little thimble glasses. You went around the houses with your half-bottle. Willie Manson's party recitation was 'MacAlastair'. 'Come on Willie!' we'd say, 'give us MacAlastair!' but he'd have to have another dram before he would heave himself up and give it to us.

There was a travelling library, old Captain Fraser at the Post Office – he had been a pilot on the Hooghly River in India – he was the librarian, he was very good to me and let me take books. I did a lot of reading in those days.

And we had the garden and we had a boat – my father was fond of the boat.

In a way we were incomers. There was acceptance on the surface but it took a long time to settle in. There was a chap of my age working at Ardno Farm along the loch. He must have been lonely, he had come from Acharacle, Morven – he would walk all the way along to us, just for a chat. Most of the time working I would be all day alone, left to my own devices.

Peter commented that when they were at Cairndow it was just the tail-end of the Hydro schemes, the Callander boys had worked on them and the Cameron boys and then most of them moved on elsewhere.

Roddy MacDiarmid, son of Roddie MacDiarmid the shepherd, joined the shepherds as soon as he left school.

I left Inveraray school in April 1959; I was 15.

I have no doubt that there were shepherds who went to work with Hydro schemes. At the time even non-skilled jobs on the Hydro schemes would get three or four times the money you got shepherding. You could not blame anyone, they were perfectly happy shepherding on the estates but money talks, always has and always will. They were bettering themselves. The same opportunity hadn't been in it, not until the Hydro schemes started and that's when people started leaving working on the land.

As Malcolm Mackay, shepherd and a contemporary of Roddy's, said:

On the Hydro schemes – oh, they were getting hundreds of pounds and we were only getting pennies, and we were working, away out at five in the morning and working till ten o'clock at night sometimes. Going to dances, those workers, they would have plenty of money and we were scrounging about for pennies; that was a bit off, a sore thing. I did think about going to the Hydro schemes right enough, but never got any further than that.

Roddy commented:

It wasn't for me. We, my parents and my seven brothers and sisters, were living up at Butterbridge at the time, in Glen Kinglas. My father Roddie had been a shepherd for the Nobles for years. When I started I was herding a hill away at the back of the Estate called Ben Vane. It was owned by Michael and John Noble. Donald Morrison asked me what I was going to do when I left school and I said I wanted to be a shepherd, and he said, well, there's a job here for you. He was the head shepherd. [He didn't get on with the newly appointed factor, Captain Ben Coutts.] I spoke to Michael Noble and he took me on.

*The Ardkinglas six-a-side shinty team, 1960: Stevie Fergusson, Charlie Bell, Ian Morrison, Roddy MacDiarmid, Donald MacPherson and Billy MacPherson.*

Roddy, in his early seventies, still very fit and still shepherding – from time to time – looks very much as he did in the six-a-side shinty team of 1960. These days he often has a thoughtful, quizzical look before he replies to a question. He recalled the things that had happened at that time that were new and exciting.

I remember clearly in Butterbridge when we got the telephone – it was the mid-1950s – it was just something like from the moon. We could not believe that you could pick up a phone and speak to someone two or three hundred miles away as if they were sitting next door to us . . .

The first television set that I ever saw in my life was after I left school . . . I was invited down to a house in Cairndow, Jimmy and May Wilsons', to watch a Scotland v. England football match one Saturday afternoon, and that, believe it or not, was the first television set that I had ever seen in my life.

In 1960 Mary Speirs and her parents came round the Loch from Cuil to Garden Cottage to watch Princess Margaret's wedding on Alice and Walter Beattie's TV because there was no reception at all on the Clachan side. On the Ardkinglas side of the Loch, whether it was a football match or a royal wedding, there was reception but the action was seen through a perpetual snowstorm.

Television would be blamed for destroying the social life of the Highlands and Islands, undermining neighbourliness and the 'ceilidh culture' of old.

I asked Peter Beaton why he left the Estate.

Well, old Willie Manson said to me that the keeper and his gun were getting done. That made me think, as a young fellow, 21 maybe at the time, where am I going?

I moved on to better wages and a line of work I took a fancy to. Overhead line work. I went and joined the squad at Arrochar, building pylons and overhead wiring. It was an entirely different world. I could have been there half my career. But then again I just said 'I'm going, I'm moving on'. I got a good reference; references were important in those days. I went to Uddingston and got a job there, learning about pylons and overhead wiring from the bottom up. It was an outdoor job and you had to be very fit. Yes, I had aspirations. I went all over – the Lake District and way beyond.

My father left Ardkinglas to a better-paid job: to be head forester on Islay on the Schroder Estate. Then he went to work in the distilleries. And he became a student: he went to night school in Bowmore and took A-level English literature.

And I travelled everywhere – Australia, Africa, Indonesia, Canada – with pylon work and then with the mines: the real money was with the mines. I always sent money home, for Tina's college and whatever. I wrote home all the time.

And I did a university correspondence course in English literature, it took me five years.

It was a time of freedom to work and to travel. I think the sixties was a wonderful time. There was freedom and opportunity: austerity was over.

## Times Were Changing – For Young Men New Opportunities: For the Proprietors?

For those who lived and worked at Ardkinglas in the late 1950s, had they 'never had it so good', or do they seem to have been halcyon days only in retrospect? Had there really been a sense of a stable status quo that would go on and on? We can't tell. The period ahead, from the late 1950s to the death of John Noble in 1972, was going to bring significant changes. Some of these changes, like the impact of television and the telephone, might have been foreseen: others, for the employees, were entirely unpredicted.

Into the 1960s, both on the Estate and on the farm, it was a time of expansion. The number of employees grew and, with the help of grants and subsidies, farm buildings as well as domestic ones were 'improved'. In 1960 the joiners spent months building a new shed at Inverchorachan and roofing a good part of the fank there. Similar work was done at the fank at Butterbridge. There were grants for improving agricultural infrastructure and land, for drainage and liming, and there were the generous hill-farm subsidies per head, even for wintering hoggs (in 1947 wintering the hoggs had cost £400, equivalent to £10,000 today).

In 1960 the income from sheep sales was £10,984, from wool £7,143, and from subsidies for sheep £1,640 (this didn't yet include the Ardno stock). 1964 was the first year of a 'home' sheep sale at the covered yard at Clachan; rather than taking the sheep to Dalmally or Perth, the auctioneer and the 'mart' come to Clachan. With the Ardno stock included, the sale totalled £12,493 (the breeding ewe flock was about 8,500 at the time), wool sales were £6,170, and subsidies £7,041. Whether or not it is true, it is often heard said that around this time the blackface wool cheque was so large that it covered the shepherds' wages. The wool was bought by the Wool Marketing Board and the big wool bags were supplied by the Board. Malcolm MacKay recalled:

The fleeces had to be sorted and rolled and packed into them, then the Estate lorry would transport them to Paisley where it was graded – different grades, different prices. Mostly in those days it was sold to the mattress trade and carpet trade in Italy. Quite a bit in the sixties and even the seventies it was used for textiles, then nylon and suchlike came in and put the price of it down a bit.

From our figures it is difficult to substantiate whether the wool cheque did cover the shepherds' wages, as the wage bill included tractor and lorry drivers. But the message of the time was that hill sheep were relatively lucrative.

The Highland Panel was an advisory body which had been set up by the Labour government to plan development for the Highlands and Islands. Its members included illustrious figures like Neil Gunn and Naomi Mitchison. It was now reporting to the Tory government and its Secretary State for Scotland – Michael Noble.

Its report of 1964 favoured land redistribution, and declared: 'There is a good deal of underused, and in some cases grossly underused, land in the

*John and Michael Noble at the first 'home' sheep sale at Clachan, 1962.*

Highlands.' Reay Clarke, who was on the Panel, commented: 'The report had to be watered down to get it past the Scottish Office's agricultural people [i.e. Michael Noble] but we managed to get over some of our points all the same.' (From James Hunter and Annie Tindley's Foreword to *Two Hundred Years of Farming in Sutherland, The Story of my Family* by Reay D.G. Clarke, The Islands Book Trust, 2014.)

Then, that October, Labour won a narrow majority (which it increased in 1966), and Willie Ross became Secretary of State for Scotland. He was instrumental in replacing the Highland Panel with the Highlands and Islands Development Board, created in 1965, which was to encourage industry rather than agriculture.

≈

In 1959 Captain Ben Coutts was appointed as farm factor, perhaps because Michael now had to spend time away being a politician. Despite a war-damaged face Ben was flamboyant, even in the pulpit (he occasionally took the service) and he conveyed bonhomie; that may have accounted for him being regarded by some as a bit plausible. Ben was more of a farmer than an estate man, and interested more in cattle than sheep. He would be factor until 1964.

By 1965 or 1966 the farm overdraft with the National Commercial Bank of Scotland was £23,400 and the Estate overdraft was £31,000, thus totalling £54,400 (equivalent to some £700,000 today). Mr Alexander, the general manager at the bank, did not seem that concerned; presumably he had a good idea of the collateral. John and Michael's approach, like many other landowners then and now, was to offset Estate and farm losses against their investment income. We don't know if they were troubled by the accumulating overdrafts and the accruing interest. In the years between 1960 and 1965 the Estate had had one year with a loss of £8,000 and one with a profit of £10,000 (that was 1964, the year of the first home sheep sale at Clachan). Of the remaining years, two made small losses and two a small profit.

Whether or not John and Michael were unnerved by the scale of the overdrafts, if they had cast their minds back to what they had thought and written in the 1944 booklet they would surely have been discomfited:

It is within your knowledge that the income of the estate has fallen far short of the outgoings. [People on the Estate did not know this, either then, or ever.] We have had to draw on income from 'other capital' . . .

159

At the time, in the *Ardkinglas and the Future* booklet, they had explained that in the past the Estate had had to be dependent on the proprietors' external finances and they had gone on to say that this had two important disadvantages. The first was that if the Government increased personal taxation it would cause a reduction in the income which would be available for the Estate. It was not spelled out, but this is what had happened during the 1930s. And the second drawback, fundamental to their vision of 'Ardkinglas and the Future', was that dependence on 'outside capital, other income' was a bad idea because it indicated that 'the estate has too little vigour of its own, always being in need of outside support to keep it going. This will lead to decay – gradual or rapid.'

Their 1944 vision had been that an increase in production would close the gap between income and outgoings, reducing the dependence on outside capital. It was envisaged that this would happen through initiatives like market gardening, furniture-making, forestry, tweed-making, wool-dying, fishing and shooting.

> *Farming*. We must improve methods and try new things to become more stable and prosperous. Our stability should not depend on subsidies. We will make use of farm products rather than selling them in a raw state – i.e. introduce spinning and weaving, making cheese and gloves.

None of this had happened. So, though by the early 1960s the Estate and farms were certainly more productive than they had been in the 1930s, they were still heavily dependent on 'outside income' to finance debt, and on direct subsidies.

> *Garden produce*. Increased produce was to be sold locally and the surplus taken to the towns. Shrubs and flowers would be grown for sale.

By the 1960s the years of the early morning drives to the Glasgow flower market with dozens of daffodils were well over. The commercial enterprise of the market garden was represented by a small, muddy notebook kept in the potting shed. There, honouring the original concept, Elizabeth valiantly weighed out spinach and scarlet runners for the Ardkinglas and the Strone order, and scribbled down the date and the weight. Total sales for year in 1968 were £50.10s.2d.

*Forestry and timber*. Planting for commercial timber in the long term. In the short term more use was to be made of existing timber to employ people to produce simple furniture; it might turn into fine furniture production.

There was no furniture production. However timber was a success – it was lucrative; by the early 1960s there were some 340 acres of 'dedicated' woodland (i.e. registered by the Forestry Commission); some 70 acres of native oak and about 2,000 acres regarded as 'plantable' for commercial forestry. This was valued by the Scottish Woodlands Owners Association at about £50,000 (£650,000 today).

The plan had also been:

*Sport*. There are increasing numbers of people holidaying, who will like to fish, daily or weekly. There is also income to made from the sale of fish and game.

This continued relatively successfully, though decreasingly, to be a major source of income.

*Tourism*. In the past tourists have been regarded as something of a nuisance. In the future we should attract them, make them want to come back.

Little thought or input had gone into this; there were no tourist initiatives. As before, Glen Fyne Lodge was let for fishing or stalking, but regarded as being more for friends and family than a major income stream, and Inverchorachan was the only holiday cottage.

So what had gone wrong? Was it that it was an unworkable vision? Or that John and Michael couldn't work it? I don't know the answer, and there may not be a simple answer. It's probable that as the years passed the youthful enthusiasm that had brought the brothers together on the venture began to wane, and as the years went by their characters and their priorities diverged.

I found a diary entry I had written about a January pay-day in 1961, which hints at disharmony between Estate and farm.

Vehicles were drawn up around the gravel in front of the house. The joiners' lorry, the shepherds' Land Rover, the foresters' old jeep (the young son waiting, was looking grumpy) while the gangly David Brown tractor-man's son, sitting on the side of the trailer, was making faces. For some reason the gamekeepers have no issued vehicles, only cycles. The men stood in an untidy queue round the porch. Dogs lay and scratched around grumpily.

It was the January pay-day, the first after Hogmanay. Hands should have been wrung and best wishes and hopes for the New Year exchanged. Inside in the porch-room my father settled on his three-cornered leather chair was handing out pay-day beige envelopes of cash and commenting on the weather, the next curling match etc. Hands were being wrung, tradition is strong, but the well-wishing was muted, the atmosphere strained. Wednesday had been the annual Christmas party for everyone in the Big House. As usual all children got their presents off the candlelit tree in the drawing room. All employees were presented with a beige envelope by Mrs John. And after that, or rather, *but* after that, the farm men got another beige envelope, handed out by 'The Calf', Michael – their bonuses. But not for the Estate workers: there was no bonus for 'Sweetie' hunched all year over his glass frames, nor for 'The Heron', after foxes high on Ben Ahurn (SP) in all weathers, nor for Tammy (breakfast for him from 9–10 every morning back at his house, while my father has gone home to have his). There were innuendos and comments about that second beige envelope, that they didn't get.

I have since learnt that the second brown envelope was a 'bonus' given to the shepherds who had got all their tups back in before New Year's Day – presumably, no one had explained this to the Estate employees who, like me, didn't know it at the time.

A vision unfulfilled may have applied more to John than to Michael. Despite his political role, Michael was genuinely interested in farming. When I was seven he gave me a much treasured, beautifully illustrated book called *Both Sides of the Road* with the inscription: 'I hope she will enjoy the country and good animals as much as I do'. Over the nearly seventy years since I have looked out of car, bus, and train windows at cattle and sheep and crops, appreciating what *Both Sides of the Road* began in me.

Alistair Bremner, who worked on Achadunan farm, recalled:

Making hay was Mr Michael's passion. He would be in the Parliament and he would come up by plane, get into his Bentley and be non-stop till he was in the fields seeing if the hay was ready for baling . . . Everyone had to be involved getting the hay in, when it had been baled, into the shed, it didn't matter if it was the worst rubbish hay ever as long as it was in a bale and in the shed.

Michael became president of the Blackface Breeders Society and of the Highland Cattle Society. Indeed his enthusiasm and interest in farming may have been part of the problem in the brothers' partnership. There is a story that John was not pleased when Michael spent 1,100 guineas (£1,155) on a Mingary Highland bull. Michael became friends, a colleague even, with Brian Cadzow, an experimental sheep farmer from West Lothian and Mull. In Tam Dalyell's obituary of Cadzow in the _Independent_ (12 July 1994) he mentioned that Cadzow's particular friend in government was fellow sheep-farmer, Michael Noble.

Part of Cadzow's astonishing success was that he had a great gift for contacting the real decision-makers. In Holland, he dealt with the bankers of Amsterdam . . . in Hungary, with Communist bureaucrats; and, in Iraq, in 1973-74, with a young strongman by the name of Saddam Hussein. Cadzow gave a graphic description of how his farmer and Ministry of Agriculture contacts told him that he had to get up at 4 am to go to Takrit. 'Who the hell is this bloke in Takrit that wants to see me?' he asked. 'My friends looked glum, and pleaded with me to go, saying that the entire project depended on my going to Takrit.' Petulantly and reluctantly Cadzow agreed . . . He and his Iraqi contacts were rigorously searched. 'My friends, whom I had seen in Europe as dignified, self-confident senior officials and specialists in farming, were simply shit-scared as we were ushered into Saddam Hussein's presence. They really were cringing with apprehension.'

However, Cadzow recorded that Saddam was at that time extremely well-briefed about the major sheep project under discussion, and asked searching and relevant questions. The result was the establishment of a successful and viable joint venture in the Mosul area.

The obituary explained that:

Cadzow's particular guru was Hugh Donald, later Professor at the Scottish College of Agriculture. With the expertise of such friends and his own practical know-how, Cadzow brought a number of breeds to mix with his Scottish Blackface: Finnish Landrace, for their numerous litters of lambs; Westphalian Milk Sheep, carrying large amounts of suckling milk; Ile de France, famous for lean meat; Dorset Horn, capable of breeding all the year round. Cadzow skilfully mixed them all, with an eye to particular markets, in Britain, the EEC, or the Middle East.

Some of these sheep would soon appear as the 'Improvers' on the Cairndow Farms, not very successfully.

It is quite possible that John and Michael had differences of opinion about the farms, about the expenditure, and perhaps about the appointment of factors. However, on the surface things went on as usual.

Ernie MacPherson, son of Donald, grandson of Dougie:

I left school in 1961. I got a start as trainee shepherd in Ardkinglas Estate. I left school on the Friday, got an interview on the Saturday by Mr John, who said he was glad to see young boys following in their fathers' footsteps. I asked him what the wage would be and he said it would be £3.9s.6d and I asked him if he would make it up to £3.10s and he said he would see how we went.

There were two of us who joined at the same time – Angie MacDiarmid and I. We left school the same day and we started work the same day. Angie was Roddy's younger brother. The factor drove us round to the interview and when we were finished we asked Mr John when we would start, and he said see the factor. We went back out, the factor, that was Ben Coutts, and he said we were going to gather Ben Ime at 4 o'clock on the Monday morning. So we were delighted to get started.

Well, we had to be at work before 4 that morning. I had one dog. We met at Clachan farm which was the main farm for folk, the centre of the Estate and we got transported by Land Rover up to Butterbridge to start the gathering.

Recently a friend gave me a letter I had written to him after Hogmanay 1963–64. It illustrates the relationship between the brothers' family households around then.

As we had just sat down in the dining room 'Strone' arrived, thinking we expected them to dinner. We hadn't. They screamed with laughter about it and we laid more places and eked out the roast venison. They had brought a private copy of the New Year's Honours list from which Anne read out loud with comments like – 'Is that really *our* Ronnie?' . . . 'Just think of Popsie as Lady Phillipots' etc etc. After dinner in the drawing room Daddy played a Peter Sellers record which included a Tory political speech, it did not raise much of a smile. I thought midnight would never come. At last it was 5 to 12 and we all went outside for 'the bells', and everyone kissed everyone a Happy New Year. Back round the drawing-room fire, Daddy toasted the Queen, then passing round the silver 'loving cup'. Michael toasted 'to Alec!' and then the next round of the double-handled silver cup 'to Harold!'

My letter goes on to give an idea of 'first footing' 50 years ago and (because the TV reception was still so bad) before the White Heather Club and the breathalyser took over Hogmanay.

Then Strone left and I escaped the Big House and went from house to house drinking whisky out of tumblers and thimble glasses. Accordions played and people sang and mumbled, and danced solo or with their sisters, and pee-ed in the road and piled into cars. Sometime later we drove right up the glen. There, at Mark Park we sat around and found sodden people in chairs and drank cups of sweet tea and more whisky, and danced some more. One of the things about New Year is that everybody thinks they are looking after each other, though in fact they are all in as bad a way as each other. I got to bed at 8.30 and was up for breakfast at 10.30. There was a dance in the Hall that night, and then another singing and dancing and drinking bout at the Beatons till 7.30 am, which was good fun. Both nights were wonderfully warm and moonlit so that when the room became too smelly and smoky and breath-filled you could take a quiet clear walk by the loch.

# The Split of the Estate

In July 1964 the brothers' joint estate, called 'Messrs J. and M. Noble' was advertising for a new farm factor at Ardkinglas. Captain Ben Coutts must have been leaving. (John was never an enthusiast for Ben; had that been a source of contention?) There were many letters of application, all handwritten, no 'CVs' in those days. Then just a month later there is evidence that the division of the Estate had begun.

Back in 1942 the brothers had been committed to running the place together. In the already quoted letter from John to Elizabeth, written by a sunny waterfall in May 1942, John had said:

> So far as I can see at the moment neither Mike nor I could financially carry on Ardkinglas alone on a basis which would be tolerable. Apart from finance altogether I would not like to do so. We went into it as a joint venture and can get much more happiness jointly if it is properly handled.

Before I began this book I knew no more about the division of the Estate between John and Michael than that it had happened. I didn't know when, nor what had led to it. I am still not clear what led to it, but in August 1964 – twenty years after setting out their joint vision – it was over. I knew that the two wives had never got on and that there was some Estate-farm rivalry. Was there a last straw? The amount spent on the Mingary bull, or had John obstinately refused to support the Cadzow experiments? It's probable that increasingly John and Michael had different ideas of what they wanted to do and how it might be done, and how paid for. Whatever the reason, and whether or not it had been boiling up for some time, when the moment came it was acrimonious. I came across a wodge of papers in the Ardkinglas archive, 'Division of the Estate'. I was shocked, and sad, to read of the animosity between the brothers.

Some communication and each of their outline proposals must have been exchanged before the handwritten letter I found from Michael to John, dated 24 August 1964. Michael wrote that, as promised, before their next discussion on Sunday, he was putting some points on paper so that John could address them. Michael's suggested plan was to divide the Estate along the Kinglas, leaving Ardno and Laglingarten with John. Though he (John) would have fewer sheep (which was what he said he wanted), he would have all the productive woodlands, which, on the rough estimate of Mr MacGregor of SWAC, as Scottish Woodlands used to be called, was valued at £35,000–£50,000. The letter goes on to address what must have been John's already aired objections to this plan.

> The objection you have made to this was that you would be 'cut off' from the Glen. As far as the fishing on the Fyne goes it could be split into upper and lower beats, roughly like the present system. I would guarantee some access to stalking. I cannot, therefore, understand the argument about being 'cut off' unless you mean that physically you wouldn't own it. Any division must mean some 'cut off' and would apply to me with your half.

The main advantages of his scheme, as Michael saw it, was that both estates would be self-contained, with adequate housing, buildings, steadings etc; so a minimum movement of people would be needed. Though John would have only a third of the farm, as he had said he wanted, it was certainly the best part and the most economic and easy to run. Michael himself would have practically no commercial timber, but there were areas of natural woodland along the other side of the loch that could be developed. His plan envisaged a simple *ad hoc* division of the fishing and the stalking. He went on:

> Your scheme produces some particularly difficult problems for me, apart from equally hopeless ones from your point of view. They are –
>
> a) the natural division of labour for the two estates inherent in my scheme is totally upset. At least 4 or 5 of the people who work on 'my half' live on yours.
>
> b) I would certainly be faced almost at once with a massive capital programme on farm buildings, cottages, and forestry to make my half a reasonable unit and would have no timber sales to cushion this. We have for years agreed that to spend much more capital on the estate in this way – except on forestry – is absurd. In addition, much of what we have spent on steadings, cottages etc. at Clachan would be wasted as they are far in excess of what you would need.
>
> There may be advantages in your scheme, but I really can't find one and you haven't yet given one. I think it would be bad for the estates now and in the future and I am certain that any impartial person would agree with me.

I'm really not trying to be either selfish or greedy but with the essential fact that you chose to – and insisted on – living in Ardkinglas, there is no other sensible division than mine . . .

If you have a few spare minutes could you put your reasons for your division on paper so that I can study them on Saturday evening before we meet on Sunday.

John's response, handwritten, has no date, is perhaps a draft, presumably written before the Sunday meeting. The correspondence has become even more acrimonious.

First a minor point but perhaps of personal importance all the same. You write of my 'choosing' and 'insisting' on living here [at Ardkinglas] which I read, perhaps wrongly, as meaning odd or unfair. It seems to me natural, normal and not to have done so would have been more unusual and odd. [Why this was natural and normal isn't clear: because he was the elder brother?]

It has entailed carrying the burden emotional, and to some extent financial, of Daisy and Tasia. It was by choice – I do not complain, merely state the fact.

[Daisy, originally Sir John's personal secretary, then part of the team of women who ran the place during the war, had remained living in Ardkinglas as family ever since. Similarly Tasia, their younger sister, continued to live in Ardkinglas House.]

John went on:

Over the wider field what I see is that the estate provides at present sources of income from farming, forestry and sport, mainly fishing but to a lesser extent stalking. I have less interest in farming and have, perhaps because of that, less confidence in its future. I think that for the future the division should have consideration for those different factors.

As John saw it, Michael would have the best farming area, reflecting the latter's greater interest is in farming.

An objection to my scheme is you would be left with very little timber, but there would be ample planting ground without interfering with farming and if it turned out that the valuation went against me there would be the extra cash to do the planting and provide a death duty wedge.

John mentions a potential problem raised by Alastair Blair, the solicitor: that if they gave up joint farming it might be considered cessation of business and they would have to pay £20,000 tax, in one year, on the revaluation of the Clachan stock. (Ardno stock's value was more up-to-date, as it had been valued in 1963 at the takeover from the Weirs.)

John concludes: 'I think that sets out briefly why my scheme is better balanced overall and would have equal appeal to your – "impartial person".' [!]

Sometime over the next year, after a great many meetings and lengthy correspondence with solicitors and accountants, they came to an outline agreement which more or less followed John's scheme. What led to his scheme being the one that was largely adopted I don't know; it's not obvious in the correspondence. With the benefit of hindsight it's possible that Michael's plan made more sense.

The argument over who was going to have which area of the land soon moved to issues of value: who was going to get what value, and what was the Inland Revenue going to demand?

The ownership of the buildings on each estate were to go with the land. The Village Hall was to be made over to the community; John and Michael were to be included as trustees 'as a safeguard against it decaying through neglect'.

During the discussions on the division there were points, unforeseen, that would have significance in terms of future development.

Fishing on the Fyne was to be held jointly. However the upper reaches of both rivers were to be divided – from the new pool above the falls on the Fyne was to go to John, while the Kinglas from above the new Bendarroch bridge was to go to Michael. Unforeseen at the time, this was to be important in terms of hydroelectricity development for the future owners.

Foreshore rights above the low water mark on the sides of the loch were owned by Ardkinglas Estate. Would the right be retained if both sides of the loch were not in the same ownership? (It turned out that, fortunately in terms of the oyster farming of the future, foreshore rights were retained.)

John was to take on the masons and joiners and foresters. Their wages plus materials and added costs were about £3,000 p.a. They would work on either estate, by contract.

For the moment Jack Taylor was to continue to keep the books for both estates, farms and sport. As he did more for John (including looking after the turbine house and those innumerable odd jobs), he was to be on John's payroll with a proportion of his time to be charged to Michael's Cairndow estate.

To settle the problem of the contents of Ardkinglas, John had an arithmetically complicated proposal to make to Michael:

> To take Daddy's probate valuation, deduct 1/3 to cover what you, Paddy and Darling [his widow] had had, multiply the balance by 3 (to take some account of increased value) then half it as your share of the settlement. This is less than current values but I have had the upkeep and repair for 20 years.

There is no record as to how this was received.

There is a final (draft) valuation by Knight, Frank and Rutley (30 November 1965), after a meeting with the solicitors and accountants in Edinburgh. The 'heritable properties' of the land area of 34,000 acres 'which were currently jointly owned, are to be divided. The property going to John is to be called Ardkinglas Estate, the property to Michael the Cairndow Estate.' (Though it was initially called the Strone Estate.)

Knight, Frank and Rutley's considered the Cairndow Estate both larger and also more profitable.

8 January 1966 was the date of transfer. A document produced by Knight, Frank and Rutley, *The Disposition of the Estate* is useful in terms of this book as it details the values at the time. According to it:

The Ardkinglas Estate was to be about 13,200 acres. It would include Ardkinglas House and policies, Glen Fyne Lodge and Cuil House. Eight of the cottages were let, providing a rent of £305.10s p.a. Seventeen were occupied by farm and Estate employees (probably as 'tied' houses); there were two unoccupied and unmodernised houses and Inverchorachan was let as a holiday cottage without electricity.

The Cairndow Estate was to be about 20,800 acres; it included Strone House and policies (including the Pinetum which contained rare rhododendrons and conifers, and added to the value of the house and its amenities). Achadunan and Ardno farmhouses were included, also the Post Office, Laglingarten Farm (currently let at £330 p.a.), as well as the Hotel, which was let at the time to the Foulgers for £300 p.a. There were twenty dwelling houses, which included Ardno and Achadunan (let to Mrs Lang at £65 p.a.). Seven of the cottages were let at a total rent of £323; twelve of the cottages were occupied by farm and Estate employees (again probably tied houses), all but one was modernised.

The sawmill and joiners/masons shop were at Ardkinglas and there was a timber-yard and creosote tank and a turbine-driven saw. Knight, Frank and Rutley's view was that the yard being used by the maintenance staff would be too big for Ardkinglas Estate alone, unless outside contract work was sought.

*Farms.* The combined estate had been the subject of improvement schemes under the Hill Farming Acts. Some work was still to be done on this and John and Michael agreed to complete it as per the original plan. The main farming enterprise was the production of lambs. A few of them were sold off fat from the ewe, but most were sold in the autumn as store lambs.

*Ardkinglas.* At Clachan, which had been the main centre of the combined farms, the courtyard had been roofed over and the byre had been converted to in-winter 320 sheep. There was a large sheep fank outside capable of handling 2,000 ewes and lambs. Inverchorachan fank had been roofed over and could in-winter 200 hoggs.

There were about 180 acres of arable land.

The final figures for Ardkinglas Estate listed a sheep flock of 2,960 ewes and 300 wedders valued at £16,652, or £5 per head. The beef cattle were valued at £1,950, or £78 per head.

*Cairndow.* At Achadunan the buildings had been improved and the former byre was now a covered yard for in-wintering some 500 sheep and some cattle. At Butterbridge the fank had been covered, and was capable of handling 1,000 ewes and lambs. At Ardno there were two Dutch barns and a range of former byres, but some form of covered accommodation was needed and had been planned for.

A breeding flock of about 5,500 blackface ewes and 50 wedders would be carried, valued at a total of £34,138, or £6 per head, and 50 beef cattle valued at £5,974, or £119.10s per head. It can be seen that both the cattle and the sheep stock were of higher value than Ardkinglas's – perhaps boosted by the good quality Ardno stock taken over from the Weirs, and also because the land was lower and more fertile?

Between Ardno and Achadunan there were about 230 acres of arable land, and at Achadunan it was high-quality – fertile, flat and well drained (perhaps because it had been well tended by the Langs until relatively recently?).

As early in the negotiations as the autumn of 1964, the lawyers' and accountants' view was it was likely that the division of the Estate would 'mean a cessation of business', and that tax would be calculated accordingly. This would cause a retrospective revaluation of the sheep stock. For many years the Clachan ewes had been put through the accounts at 50 shillings each, and the ewe hoggs at 40 shillings. However the recently (1963) taken over Ardno stock of ewes had been valued at £5.10s and hoggs at £5. So now, if £5.10s was to be taken as fair value at the time of the 'cessation of business', the difference would be £21,000 and John and Michael would each have to pay tax on this. Ultimately the Inland Revenue agreed that the sum didn't have to be paid in one go: the tax owed on the profit arising out of this revaluation could be spread forward over six years (from January 1966).

*Woodlands.* Ardkinglas was to have about 303 acres of 'dedicated scheme' (registered with the Forestry Commission) commercial timber on a rotation of 30 or 40 years, and an additional 70 acres not dedicated. It was pointed out that about 1,000 acres of ground on the Clachan side of the loch could be planted.

Cairndow was to have about 118 acres of dedicated scheme areas (including the Pinetum). There were an additional 1200 acres which it was suggested could be planted with commercial woods.

*Sport.* Over the last fifteen years the average number of stags shot per year on the proposed Ardkinglas land had been 10, and the average grouse shot had been 27½ brace, whereas stags killed on Cairndow land had averaged only 7 per year over the same period, and grouse 22 brace per year. Oddly there is no mention of the salmon fishing.

On the date of transfer, 8 Jan 1966, according to the terms of the *Disposition*, the value of what had been the Ardkinglas Estate is based on Dr Bogie, the accountant's, calculation in regard to Capital Gains Tax (CGT). He stated that, as in 1938 the Ardkinglas Estate was 'acquired' (as per Sir John's probate) for £26,000 and that now, i.e. in January 1966, the Ardkinglas and Strone Estates together were valued at £375,000, there was an appreciation of £349,000 over twenty-nine years, which raised significant CGT issues.

At this time the District Valuer valued the new Ardkinglas Estate at £130,000, heritable – not including stock or timber.

During the period of discussion on the division, the Finance Act of April 1965 had brought in CGT, and what was or was not going to have to be paid now was much discussed. Moreover the CGT position established now was going to be important in the future, at John and Michael's deaths.

Michael was creating a 'Resettlement Trust', John wasn't. He died in 1972 within less than the seven years required to lessen inheritance tax.

As already mentioned, the joint Ardkinglas, both farm and Estate, had been running at a considerable loss and benefitting from John and Michael's tax offsets on their personal wealth. By the tax year 1966-67 the overdrafts on the joint farm and Estate accounts totalled about £54,000. John's share of this was £16,000 (he paid off £10,000 in March 1966); for Michael it stood at £27,800.

## After the Split: the Old and the New

From now on in this book Ardkinglas Estate (including Clachan Farm) will be the smaller area, divided out from what had been the old Ardkinglas, and now about 13,000 acres. (While the Cairndow Estate will be the other 21,000 acres.) Some parts of Sir Andrew's original 45,000 acres – Dunderave Castle and policies and some sections of hillside for commercial forestry – had already been sold.

From now on my focus will be on the Ardkinglas Estate as I have little detailed information on the Cairndow Estate. Michael died in 1984 and subsequently Strone House, and much of Glen Kinglas, was sold. The remaining land and buildings, including Ardno and Achadunan Farms, was divided between Michael's four daughters.

So while negotiations had been going on, what did employees think or know about the situation? Roddy MacDiarmid remembers how they were told about the division. Roddy and his brother Angus, Alastair MacCallum and his brother Colin, were asked to come over to Ardkinglas. Sitting in the billiard-room, John explained that the estates and farms were being split and that they were to be on his side, the Clachan side, and that Alastair MacCallum was to be head shepherd. They were told that the reason for the division was something to do with death duties. There was no discussion, no one was asked for their opinion about anything nor told of any future plans. Perhaps between employer and employees on a Highland estate in 1966 that is not so surprising. However, these were the lairds who in 1944 had stated:

> We want to arrange things so that we can more often and more regularly discuss matters of common interest. In this way you may have a larger share in directing your lives than you have had up to now, while we will have the benefit of your advice.

Had they forgotten what they thought then, and what they had written?

According to Roddy: 'We all thought nothing would ever happen, it would all always be there; it didn't work out that way . . .'

I asked him if they were sorry about the split, about being separated from their colleagues with whom they had been working so closely, and for many of them, like Donald MacPherson, for so many years. Roddy paused for a moment or two and said, 'Yes, but I think we thought it a bit of a challenge. We were young.'

So there were four shepherds, with Alastair as the 'manager', on the Clachan Farm and seven or eight on the Cairndow side, including Donald and Ernie MacPherson, Malcolm and Malkie MacDonald, Ian Bell, Jimmy Waddell, and Alastair Bremner.

I asked if anyone – my father, or Bob Hay (who was to become the visiting factor) – ever encouraged their work, said 'Well done'? Roddy smiled: 'No, people didn't tell lies in those days!'

# The 1960s

The 1960s were the Swinging Sixties in some places and for some people. In Cairndow the old and the newer co-existed.

John MacDonald was born in 1950. The following year at the May term, his father Callum had been offered a job on the Clachan hirsel on the old Ardkinglas Estate. They lived in the North Flat at Clachan farmhouse. When John started school in 1955, it was the year that Miss Munro retired after 50 years teaching and having taught several generations of Cairndow children, so it was the end of an era for the school. However, according to John, Cairndow was fortunate with the next teacher.

> For me Cairndow School was a wonderful seven years of primary school. We had the privilege of having Miss Muirhead as teacher. She taught seven classes and about twenty-five children. She sent them off to junior secondary school, probably at a higher academic level than children who came from other schools where they had different teachers for different classes. She used to read us a couple of chapters out of Enid Blyton books; it was directly after lunch and it was a bit like a soap opera. We used to sit and encourage her to read yet another chapter; we were all engrossed in it, it was one of the highlights of the day. She was a lovely person and a wonderful teacher.

*Kilmorich School in 1959. John MacDonald is third from the right in the right-hand block of desks.*

I asked if he had been a teacher's pet?

Probably! I stayed friends with her forever, even in my working life, when she had moved to Inveraray.

After that, when I went on to Inveraray Junior school, I probably didn't make as much of my abilities as I should have done. When you came to 16, if you wanted to go to work you weren't held back to do any extra education, you were let go. I was ready for out and to earn my living.

I left school in 1966 and came to work with the Ardkinglas Estate masons. I spoke to Mr John and asked if there was a position. And he said, yes, I could start with the masons. 'I think we have a position for you with Bolek.' Bolek was head mason at the time.

Bolek Kobiela had joined the Estate in 1946. As a young man he had been in the Polish cavalry. Poles who had been conscripted into the German army became prisoners of war; some were detained at Inveraray, at a camp above the Castle. After the war Bolek couldn't, or didn't want, to go back to Poland. He had met Mamie Cameron, daughter of old Bob, the game-keeper, while she was working at the George Hotel in Inveraray. He was a tall and handsome man, and she a pretty woman. They were to have three boys: George, Leon, Derek and a daughter Violet, named after her Grannie, Bob's wife. Initially Bolek worked with Jimmy Stewart, then when Nigel and Hamish Speirs came as apprentice joiners, Mr John suggested Bolek should become apprentice mason to old Archie MacVicar. That was how he learnt his trade. Nigel Callander claimed that Bolek was never as good a stonema-son, not such a craftsman as old Archie. 'He couldn't quite turn the chisel in the way Archie approved,' but Archie was a hard taskmaster.

The family lived for many years at Mid Lodge, at the front, where the Stewarts had been. He was good with his hands; everybody sent their boots and shoes to Bolek, who was a good cobbler as well as a mason, and in his spare time he made beautiful little leather boxes.

When John MacDonald joined the masons, Bolek was head mason and old Archie MacVicar was now semi-retired, working two or three days a week. Mr John suggested that John worked alongside Archie. So young John worked with old Archie who had worked with his father on the building of Ardkinglas: that represented sixty years of continuity for Ardkinglas masons. John recalled:

> By then Archie was doing little jobs like maintenance to the fountain and garden walls. It was only for a short period when I had started that I was sent along with him. It was quite an experience. We would do our bit and then he would say 'Let's have a smoke, John', but he didn't smoke, never had, neither did I! What he meant by that was, we'd sit down and have a break.
>
> He was an interesting old chap. He had old-fashioned waxed moustaches. He was an elder of the church and a Master Mason at the Inveraray Lodge. But he could call a spade a spade, as you might say. People said that if Archie was asked what he was doing, he would reply 'Making a cock for a wooden doll', meaning – mind your own business!

Archie's note in his time-book on 24 May 1967, his final day working on the Estate after 60 or more years, was 'jobbing and working on the pot holes on the front drive'.

# Ardkinglas Estate from 1966

In the first three years after the split, from 1966 to 1968, Clachan Farm made consistent losses: -£2,300, -£7,400, and -£3,200. The farm expenditure from the pre-divided days was obviously well down, but so was the income; wool prices were beginning to fall.

The Cairndow Estate farms also suffered losses over the same period: –£2,000, –£7,000 and –£10,000. The real problem was, as always, that there was insufficient income.

In 1967 John must have considered Clachan Farm's diminished sheep ground would be offset by the investment and/or grant and tax break (as suggested in the valuation by Knight, Frank and Rutley); the hillside between Clachan and Dunderave was planted with a large block of commercial, 'dedicated' forestry.

As Jack Taylor sat in his swivel chair at his commodious slant-top desk in the porch room, as he had, apart from the war years, for five decades, what did he think as he totalled income and expenditure columns and watched the deficit grow? He certainly wouldn't have talked about it to anyone. But was he concerned? Or were they just neat numbers in columns? By 1966-67 the overdraft for John was in the region of £15,846, and by the time he died it would be £41,000. But nobody on the Estate, except Jack, would have known.

∽

The Estate workers hadn't been split between the Estates: they were left with Ardkinglas. Work done by the masons, joiners and foresters for the Cairndow Estate or farms was done as contract work and paid for as such. Who paid who probably made little difference as far as the Ardkinglas Estate employees were concerned.

When John MacDonald began as an apprentice mason in July 1966 the split had already been formalised and his father Callum, a shepherd working for Michael, was shifted from the North Flat at Clachan over to Ardno.

By the time I started work, we had moved over from Clachan to live at Ardno farm. So I cycled the two miles along the shore road to the Square every morning. I remember leaving myself a bit short most mornings, you had to make it at 8 o'clock and stand there till Mr John cycled over from the Big House. He wouldn't get off his bike, he just came towards us, then stopped and put his foot down, still on the saddle, and said 'Morning' and everybody would say 'Good morning'. I was never consulted because I wasn't head of department, but he would ask 'What is it for you today, Willie?' Willie MacPherson and Nigel were the joiners. Willie would say 'I am going here or there' or 'We'll be jobbing at the shop'. It was just a routine, because people knew roughly what they were doing.

John commented:

So I was sixteen and I was serving an apprenticeship as a mason, but I only lasted about the first year, then Mr Kobiela and I had a difference of opinion. It was at the gable-end at Glen Fyne Lodge. We were roughcasting and hacking off the old render, some tools got misplaced, lost. So there was a bit of a thing about me being more careful with the tools. I was a young chap, I was a bit restless: I said 'Stuff this. I'm out of here'. So I went down and said to Mr John, I couldn't get on with Mr Kobiela, and he said more or less, 'well, alright, if you can't, you can't.' So I went off to work for W.H. Rankins, the civil engineers who were building the new road from Arrochar.

When I had started with Ardkinglas I got £5 a week, for 45 hours (we worked Saturday mornings in those days). With W.H. Rankin they did a bit more hours and I managed to get my wage packet doubled, so it was £10 (and I would have been 17 by now).

This was 1967 and there was an opportunity on the doorstep for a 17-year-old to double his wage packet compared with what he earned on the Estate. However it did have its risks.

The job with Rankins was petering out, and it was the last on, the first off. However, next there was an opportunity to go over to Finnart at Garelochhead, building the big oil terminals there. They wanted concrete workers, so I went with an Inveraray squad. I managed to get a lift with them, picked up at 6 in the morning at the Dunoon road junction. We were doing 12-hours shifts, we wouldn't get back home till 8 o'clock maybe. Monday, Tuesday, Wednesday and Thursday, maybe 4 o'clock on a Friday, Saturday was off and then Sunday we would be on till 4 o'clock again.

At Finnart John's wage packet went up to £19. So he had got himself from £5 a week as a sixteen-year-old to £19 a week at eighteen or nineteen. (Of course the disparity wasn't just between Estate pay and contractor's pay – it was statutory that eighteen-year-olds were paid more than sixteen-year-olds.)

As will be gathered from John's description of his working life, he is an energetic and organised worker, who takes a pride in doing his job well. He tackles a problem with nous acquired from experience. After Johnny's death he and I found a large stone in the bed of the Kinglas River as a gravestone (similar gravestones had been used for both my parents). In order to extricate it from far below in the river-bed, he created a remarkable system of pulleys around two trees, and slowly and surely manoeuvred it up onto the drive. He was a keen and agile sportsman, over many years of shinty, football, curling and golf.

> Wherever I was working I always managed to fit in my shinty. The shinty was fantastic, lots of friends from there that I still have. At Tighnabruaich, thanks to a Captain Duncan MacCrae, you went to the Royal Hotel. There would be a full table set for high tea, a bottle of whisky between four, and a packet of Senior Service cigarettes laid out for everybody. Captain MacCrae just loved the shinty aftermath. We would all be singing by the end and then we used to go via Drum Farm on the way home, for more entertainment and refreshments. I was quite young in the shinty team and I had to learn fast.

Shinty was the most popular sport, but young men played football too. Cairndow was always a predominantly Protestant locality, therefore, in the renowned tradition of Celtic (Catholic) and Rangers (Protestant) rivalry, Cairndow was largely Rangers-supporting. The late sixties was the era of the 'Lisbon Lions', as the Celtic team became known, when they beat Inter Milan in Lisbon to win the European Cup. It would be a while before Rangers could be so hailed – though there were celebrations in the pub when they beat Celtic in an Old Firm derby to win the League Cup final in 1970. Being a Protestant locality, Masons were strongly represented here, with the Lodge at Inveraray. John said he was never a Mason: 'it didn't appeal'.

John didn't stay that long at Finnart either. He had 'had enough of working on those huge jobs; with many "mental" men, it wasn't a nice environment'.

By then, 1969, Bolek had left direct employment from the Estate and started with his own business. I asked whether this was because there had been a difference of opinion.

No, I don't think there was any problem between Mr John and Bolek, I don't know why it had happened. Bolek asked me if I would like to come back. So I thought, well, it gets me back home, and so I came back. It was while I was working with Bolek that I got married, January 1970, I was 19. For that reason it was better to get back onto home territory. It was a reduction in wages, but it saved me all the long shifts and early mornings. I can remember getting 6s.8d per hour from Bolek, which was £14 or £15 pounds a week.

When I got married I went to see Mr John about accommodation. Sawmill Cottage [where the Beatons had been] was available, and because I wasn't working for the Estate I paid rent for it.

At the time Bolek had his sons George and Leon working with him, and also young Walter Beattie. After a couple of years Bolek and I fell out again. He and I were working three storeys up, at the very top, doing the apex party walls. We were working with a special plaster mix, and I was mixing all this at the bottom and then carrying it up three flights, to supply it to Bolek, and expected to do the coating as well. I knew that Walter and George were away somewhere else on a relatively easy job, and here's me working like a donkey. So I took so much, then said, 'Hey, I am not taking any more of this, this is ridiculous.' Bolek was quite a fiery chap, and I am known for being a bit quick myself. So again, one more time, I was told – 'you like it or you lump it'.

So I moved over to Douglas Campbell at Lochgoilhead. I was there for quite a period of time, maybe two or three years until 1974.

John explained that he never completed his apprenticeship, never 'done his time' in the traditional way as a mason. Over the years he learnt different types of building work, which stood him in good stead when he was to set himself up as a builder in the years to come. While he was working at Lochgoilhead he spent weekends working for a friend re-doing his house.

My friend was a self-employed joiner. I worked at the weekends for extra cash and he paid as much as he could afford. And that helped as far as gaining my confidence for building work. I had more responsibility and did things myself.

The Ardkinglas six-a-side shinty tournament had begun in 1961. It was held in the field at Clachan. It was a big annual event for twenty years or so; perhaps *the* big annual event. The tournament was in the summer, while the official shinty season was in the winter. John emphasised how important it was to him and to many others in Cairndow.

> I played shinty all my married life. I really enjoyed it, and all the banter and the social aspect of it. The kids and the wife would get into the car and off to the shinty – they still talk about it. When everybody went for a pint after the game, the kids were left in the car outside with crisps and coke, with the Ernie and Irene MacPherson kids. We would stop for fish and chips and they would have to listen to the Scottish dance music – they remember that too.

So as the 1960s ended, for some it was a time of independence and opportunity. Perhaps for others it marked the end of an old, safer order. Roddy MacDiarmid remembers his mother coming back from a WRI evening and telling her husband the news that Betty Manson and Mrs Taylor had been in the pub before the meeting. What – women in the pub? Unheard of until about then.

Roddy still lives in Cairndow, and, though now 72, is still not an entirely retired shepherd, and also a not-retired sheepdog trialist. He thinks the old days were treasured times, when:

> . . . people were happier in their lot, they weren't envious of someone else being better off than them. Both Mr Michael and your father were good at trying to find a wee house for someone to give them a start and that helped to make the community such a tight-knit place.

John Noble wasn't an obviously sociable person; he was, or perhaps became, relatively remote. He was respected; people say of him, 'He was a man of his word . . . He was always fair.' Janet Callander said, 'Mr John was a good boss. He was an honest gentleman, a right laird.' And her husband Nigel remembers him with affection.

181

*John Noble and Daisy Powell-Jones in the wall garden, 1970.*

Your father loved his cars, he loved them shining, and he used to praise me for looking after them. So I did that till he died . . . He wanted me to drive him to the hospital but the doctor said he was too ill, he needed an ambulance.

He died after a short illness in February 1972. The day after, Nigel drove us silently back from the Glasgow hospital. Coming down towards the bottom of Glen Kinglas in John's relatively new, mallard-green Triumph, my mother's surge of misery was palpable.

Was he disheartened by what hadn't happened on the Estate? Or were his other interests his priority? I can only speculate. Estate and farm matters were never discussed around the dining table. I am not sure why not. I don't think this was because it wasn't of interest. It may have been to do with Daisy and Tasia's presence; John wanted to preserve privacy in front of them. So what I gleaned about the goings-on was from my friends outside the Big House. It wasn't until Johnny took up the challenge that I shared the ins and outs, the ups and downs from the proprietor's viewpoint.

# The Entrepreneur: 1972 to 2002

## Johnny's Early Days

In February 1972, when John died aged sixty-two, Johnny was thirty-five. He had been at Eton and then served his two-year National Service in what he used to refer to as 'The Argyll and Suffering Highlanders'. His regiment was sent to Egypt in the Suez campaign of 1956. In 1957 he went, briefly, to Oxford University; when he flunked the French exam he had to leave after a year. From there he went to the university in Aix – where less time was spent at the Université and more in the cafés and working as an extra (sitting in a café) in a Jean Paul Belmondo film. This lifestyle must have led to a plea to his parents for funds. In response his father wrote (23 February 1959):

> Martins Bank has written to extend the Bank of England's permit to remit money [in 1959 there were still restrictions on the amount of pounds sterling you could take out of the country]. Martins say that your account is about £200 overdrawn . . . It seemed to me unwise of you to buy a share in a scooter when you had not the money. Please do not fall into the habit of thinking financial problems solve themselves. They don't . . . Not many of us have not overspent at some moment. The important point is to realise what you are doing. As you told me you were doing alright it seems that you may not realise it. [At that point in the late 1950s the Ardkinglas and farm overdraft was running at £50,000, around a million pounds today.]

And then 7 March brought a letter from his mother enclosing a bill.

> I sent you this account ages ago and I see you *still* haven't paid it. It really is so silly of you not to pay your bills. I thought of paying it myself and deducting it from what I owe you, and then thought that is treating you as if you were a child. But DO PAY IT NOW. Janet [Callander] had a son on Friday night, all well after a bad labour. He is exactly like Nigel and is called Colin.

Despite the parental outrage (to a twenty-one-year-old son), the letters didn't change his habits. Complaints about unpaid bills continue over the years. In August 1984 New and Lingwood, the Jermyn Street shirt-makers, complain about an accumulating bill standing at £1,065: 'You will appreciate that in the present economic climate we are not able to permit extended credit.' And in 1985 from Sullivan and Wooley, Tailors, Saville Row: 'I must point out that at the present reduction of £10 per month it will take a further 4½ years to clear your outstanding balance. You will appreciate I am sure that this is unsatisfactory as it is not our practice to charge interest.'

Johnny sends a cheque for £569 and barks back, 'could you let me know if you have ready for fitting a suit I ordered some time ago of grey flannel?'

As to overdrafts, in 1977, five years after Johnny inherited the Estate, the manager of the Royal Bank of Scotland, Inveraray, wrote that he had passed on to Head Office information which would reduce the net borrowing on the Estate accounts to within a figure of £70,000. But this overdraft was not all (or even mostly) of Johnny's doing. Massive loans from RBS had been inherited from his father, who had so admonished him over his Aix extravagancies and had written at that time, 'One cannot get away with things for too long. In the end they land back on one and are often doubled in the process.'

Johnnie's next step, in 1960, after the' terraces' of Aix, was to the desks of S.G. Warburg's investment bank offices in King William Street, London. It was a step he didn't relish. At his father's instigation, and as a nephew of the co-founder, Johnny was taken on as a trainee by Siegmund Warburg. Many years later, asked by someone who had worked at Warburg's at the same time, which department he had worked in, Johnny replied, 'Frankly I moved from department to department with ever-increasing bewilderment.'

Johnny's next employment was with a Yugoslavian wine-importing business owned by an elderly Dr Teltscher and his son Willy, situated in a less prestigious area of London, Kingsland Road. This was much more his cup of tea. By the mid 1960s he had bought a fifth of the shares of the company.

For a young man with the CV described above – running up overdrafts, bills unpaid, sent down from Oxford University after a year, not often seen at the Université at Aix, not a success at Warburg's Merchant Bank, with experience of the Yugoslav wine trade and a recently set up London wine business of his own, Johnny wouldn't be an obvious candidate to make a success of Ardkinglas Estate. As John Keay put it in the obituary in the *Glasgow Herald*:

184

In 1972 his father died leaving Johnny heir to a large, loss-making and heavily indebted estate plus the magnificent Ardkinglas House, a Robert Lorimer creation incorporating the entire catalogue of Scottish vernacular features, superbly sited, and designed with a fine Edwardian disregard for maintenance and manning costs. Seventy per cent death duties and responsibility for a loyal but financially crippling ensemble of shepherds, stonemasons, joiners and gardeners added to the burden.

When John died he was only sixty-two. In the previous year, 1971, Johnny, a mere thirty-four, had set up his own wine importers business, called 'French and Foreign Wine', based in central London. A knowledgeable friend said, 'It progressed extremely well due to Johnny's discerning palate and complete indifference to fads and fancy names per se.' It must have been tough to have to divert his attention from his fledgling new business to his grieving mother and the challenge that Ardkinglas presented.

For fifteen years Johnny had a more or less regular weekly commute between London and Ardkinglas – weekends and Mondays at Ardkinglas and the week at his office in London, and enjoying the company of his friends. An exchange of views and the fun of friendship was always important to him. I remember him saying then that without time in London he would have found it all too difficult.

# The Daunting Task

Though John and Johnny might have discussed the latter's succession to Ardkinglas Estate in principle, with John dying at sixty-two after an illness of only a few weeks, it is improbable that they had practical discussions about the Estate as Johnny was to find it.

In an 'Information and Discussion' paper of 1999, Johnny looked back on these earlier times: 'The Estate had been run along traditional lines with masons, joiners, shepherds, garden and sporting. None of these could be disbanded overnight because many long term old employees were involved.'

Nigel Callander remembered:

Johnny tried to do it like his father. He came over a couple of times to the garage arch in the mornings, but he couldn't do it.

He was funny, after your father died he came up to see me in the joiners' shop and he asked me, 'Could I borrow my father's car to go to Edinburgh?' I said, its nothing to do with me, it's not mine, it's yours, you should take it. It was the Triumph, quite new at the time.

It was hard for him at first. Such a young fellow. He didn't know the ropes, he hadn't been about the place. He was down in London, he wasn't here.

I'm sure that in Johnny's mind at the time there was no question but that he would take on the challenge: Elizabeth, Ardkinglas house, the Estate, Clachan Farm all required someone at the helm, but he can hardly have relished the prospect. Ardkinglas had always been home to him, but he had been away at school, and most of the subsequent years, as with previous generations of proprietors, had been spent elsewhere; though with regular holidays at home with his family and fishing and stalking. He didn't have a wife to share the responsibility. His mother was at Ardkinglas, but her great grief and anxiety only added to his burden. And there were others to think about. What must poor Jack Taylor have felt? After over forty years of loyal and deferential service, he might well have been thinking of retiring. He couldn't have anticipated that his employer, eight years his junior, would die first. There he was in his orange-leather swivel chair, surrounded by those old portraits of 30-pound salmon and antlers and our gumboots. He must have been shocked and wondering what was to happen.

*Jack and Mrs Taylor in 1971.*

Johnny may have thought that he could handle the 'ropes' that Nigel referred to, but the state of the Estate finances, or the lack of them, when they began to unravel, were a real challenge.

Elizabeth and Sir Alastair Blair, the family solicitor, and Johnny were the executors of John's estate. A cousin, Robin Jessel, a lawyer and an ex-Warburg's employee (as well as a close friend to both Johnny and Elizabeth), luckily was able to step in to advise and to help in those crucial early years.

In March 1972 the 'confirmation' of John's will, signed by the Sheriff Clerk, lists values as follows:

| | |
|---|---|
| *Heritable Estate* in Scotland the Estate of Ardkinglas | £150,000 |
| | |
| *Moveable Estate* in Scotland (i.e. non-heritable) | |
| Farm stock, crops, and implements | £18,000 |
| Household furniture &effects | £10,000 |
| Silver, silver plate & jewellery | £25,000 |
| | £55,300 |
| | |
| *Moveable Estate* in England | £221,559 |

[including 79,466 Mercury Securities (i.e. Warburg's) shares @180p – £143,038 –almost the same value as the entire Ardkinglas Estate, including the house]

In addition to the above there were some assets/liabilities left over from previous generations – Sir Andrew's share in foreign companies and also Sir John's Revisionary Trust.

In July a letter from Robin Jessel suggested that Elizabeth should sell 15,000 shares of her own holding in Mercury Securities (Warburg's). This would realise £36,000 to be put towards:

The Royal Bank of Scotland farm and estate overdrafts totalling £41,000,
The first instalment of the anticipated estate duty,
The anticipated estate duty on the revisionary interest on Sir John's Trust,
The anticipated capital gains tax.

It was agreed there wasn't a need to discuss this with Elizabeth at the moment. (She would have gladly used her money, but would have been anxious about the predicament of the Estate and the worry for Johnny.) In the same letter Robin says: 'We agreed that Elizabeth should eventually be asked to meet the balance of the Estate Duty on the Ardkinglas Estate . . . but we agreed to leave a decision until the tax position is agreed.'

At this stage, i.e. July, the money owed was roughly estimated by Robin as follows:

Estate Duty on the Ardkinglas Estate, say 63% on £150,000 =

|  |  |
| --- | --- |
|  | £104,500 |
| Less Agricultural relief of 45%, £47,025 | £57,475 |
| Overdrafts at RBS Inveraray: |  |
| Estate | £33,500 |
| Farm | £8,022 |
|  | £41,500 |
| Estate duty on Revisionary Interest in Sir John's Trust | £23,000 |
| Cost of admin, valuations etc for first year of Trust | £10,000 |
| Estimate to be paid | £132,000 |

[The above didn't include capital gains tax liability on estate or personal income.]

In November there was relatively good news from the District Valuer regarding the heritable property. He suggested the following to be adopted for estate duty:

| Principal value | Agricultural value |
| --- | --- |
| Mansion House and Policies £25,000 | £25,000 |
| Farm £50,000 | £50,000 |
| Solum of woodlands £6,000 | £6,000 |
| Cottages £24,000 | £65,000 |
| Fishing and shooting £15,000 | £15,000 |
| £161,000 | £120,000 |

[Not included in his figures above was timber of the value of £22,500.]

So the calculation of the Ardkinglas Estate overall value had gone up from the estimated £150,000 to £161,000. This increase meant the rate of estate duty went up to 70%, amounting to £112,700. However, as fortunately the District Valuer had decided that £120,000 of the total qualified for agricultural relief (at 45%), it brought the total owed down to £57,000. To this would have to be added the duty on moveable personal property, plus the duty on the interest on Sir John's Revisionary Trust, plus the £41,500 overdrafts at RBS Inveraray and plus capital gains tax.

I have included the above detail making as much sense of it as I can because, as the family solicitor explained to me in 2016, 'the fear of death duties (or estate duties) has hung over decades of landowners like a sword of Damocles.'

(I knew that Elizabeth Noble's money had been needed for the Estate – at this time and later too. Until I began this book I didn't know to what extent. It was money left to her by her brother Harry and it was used as she would have wanted at the time. But thinking about it with hindsight, I might have thought my sister and I should have had a say in our inheritance?)

# The Burden of Ownership

In the early 1970s Johnny may have felt like the laird described in Roderick Grant's *Strathalder* who had inherited the estate when he was thirty-one, his father having died young, with heavy estate duties to be paid. Grant explained that this laird had substantial businesses outside the estate and could exist perfectly well financially without it, but just as the tradition of working on an estate had been bred into many of the men he employed, so he felt the need to fulfil an obligation that came his way as a result of his ancestry. And 'If I go under financially it won't only be me and my family; if I have to sell, all those who work on the estate will suffer. Their lives, as their fathers', are bound up with this place, to them it's their home. I try hard to remember they have just as much a right to it as I do.'

For Johnny, as for many others who inherited estates, there was an onus of responsibility for long-term employees and also to the extended family who considered the house and estate an ancestral home. There is a letter to Johnny from Lady Gainford, a fond and sympathetic cousin, who had been at Ardkinglas when her grandfather, Sir Andrew, processed to his new house in 1907, and regularly since then.

I do enjoy so very much the sense of continuity at Ardkinglas – changes come, as they should do, with each generation, each adding something of interest and something good, never cutting the thread that runs through the years of which I have seen so many and have such happy memories. Grandpapa and Lorimer did a good job when they made Ardkinglas, long may you and it flourish!

The letter may have, as she certainly intended, encouraged Johnny. But when times were hard he felt alone amidst everyone's expectations.

## So What Was the Estate that He Inherited?

Though, as Johnny commented, the Estate had been run along traditional lines with a way of life much as it had been for the previous generation, there were changes. Some of the old had gone: 1974 had seen the last coal boat and the last Christmas Tree Party.

Angus MacGillivray had retired, so he and May – the laundry maid for so many decades – left the laundry; and Alice Beattie (née Sinclair) and Walter and their six children moved in. Tina MacCallum, after so long in Glen Fyne, moved down to the North Flat at Clachan Farm, below her son Alastair and his wife Christine. Bolek and family had left Mid Lodge and gone to Callander; John and Sandra MacDonald had moved in there, back to back with Janet and Nigel Callander. Jack Taylor took semi-retirement; he continued to live at Dacia Cottage at the Square until he died in 1980. Now, a few months after John's death, in July 1972 Bill Smellie was appointed; not exactly in Jack's place, Bill had a more managerial role. The dairy cows were moved out of the byre (where Tasia and I used to eat grapefruit segments straight from the tin on hot summers' evenings) up to the Top Byre. And the byre was converted into the Ardkinglas Estate Office, where Bill and his assistants worked.

Bill had a very different style from Jack: it was a different era. He was a self-deprecating, portly man, with watering eyes, and suffered in the heat (we were amazed when he emigrated to hot Perth in Australia). He came from Lanarkshire, from a farming background, but had been living and working in Glasgow with a firm of transport contractors, doing their book-keeping and general office administration. Johnny and Bill became fond of each other: they shared jokes and anxieties. Bill would go to Glasgow airport on a Friday evening to collect Johnny, and driving round Loch Lomond would bend his ear with the latest Estate ups and, more often, downs; Johnny would dread Bill's latest bad news.

The Estate was short of builders as Bolek Kobiela had left to run a boarding house in Callander. In 1974 John MacDonald was asked to come and fill the void. John and Johnny had always got on well, and Bill Smellie had come to trust John, to confide in him, perhaps. According to John, people were aware that:

> Johnny had come back to take over the reins and things were not going very well for the Estate at that time. We tried to make ends meet. The Estate started what was known as the Works Department, we were contracted out to go and do work for clients. Bill got sort of landed with that, and we all had to try and make it work.

For the next nine years he and Nigel's team worked as Ardkinglas Estate employees. Nigel and Janet's son Colin worked with them and there were others who came and went. There was no lack of work. John looked back from 2014:

> In 1974 I started back on the Estate. At that time there was quite a bit happening because they were building a new hatchery for Golden Sea, [the salmon smolt business] on Rhumore, and also a house there. The hatchery was a big job. And there was also an extension to the back shed at Clachan Farm, that was for beef cattle, and a sileage pit.

Nigel Callander:

> Johnny was trying to keep the Estate going because he had a lot of problems. He had nothing that they have nowadays, there was no income in the Estate in these days, not a thing. Contracting out, we were the Ardkinglas Works Department, but it wasn't too successful I don't think, there was too much competition in these times. We built the hatchery for Golden Sea. John did the block work, he was working for the Estate, and I was working for the Estate, and Roddy [MacCallum, joiner, Janet's brother] he came back, he was working for the Estate too. He gave us a hand, that was quite a contract in these days building that big place.

The Works Department operated in the same way as the Estate joiners and masons had after the division of the Estates: tendering for work on the Estate and elsewhere. At the time there was a Mr Bernard Preston, an architect/surveyor who worked with the Estate teams. By 1974 there was a lot happening. After Tina moved down to Clachan, there were alterations to be done to Glen Fyne Cottage. There were additions and alterations to No 2 the Square; Tasia was moving out from the Big House into it. There was the replacement of the fank at Clachan as well as a stock shed and sileage pit. There was a new sawmill to be built beyond the head of the loch. Then there was Johnny's sister, Sarah, and Peter Sumsion's new house to be built at Bachie Bhan. John remembers:

> Bernard Preston was around then doing the shed at Clachan and the hatchery house, and then Sarah's house. Bernie used to come through once a week and go around the jobs, and he and Bill would go for lunch and they used to have a few drinks, gin and tonics. Bernie was quite seasoned to that way of life, but Bill wasn't; he would come back a bit bleary-eyed.
>
> That reminds me – Bill had a bit of a problem with his eyes, they would water a lot. Johnny knew that of course and I remember him teasing Bill one day when there was a bit of a problem over something: 'It's alright, boy, it's not that bad, don't cry about it!'
>
> Bill tried his best, he was a bit out of his world when it came to the construction side. We all had to muck in. Bill was good at jokes, but less good when it came to estimates, not that I was that experienced myself, but at least I knew how long a job should take.

Bill had many attributes, but construction estimating and strong management may not have been among them. This might have been part of the reason the Ardkinglas Estate Works Department was not a success. When, later on, Johnny appointed a Mr Ronald Baird as a part-time Factor, Johnny wrote:

> I am sorry to say that at the moment I am rather as sea as to what our real outgoings are . . . On the whole, I think we have quite a good team but they certainly need motivating under tighter management. This is the moment to make it clear that the old days of private subsidy are finished. The losses, the cost of investments of buildings, saw-

mills, sheds, cattle, machinery etc., have put us seriously into debit. We cannot continue merely to sell assets to keep a large loss-making affair going.

The management side is not without its problems. Bill has the quality of honesty, he has a lot of practical sense and is well informed on the local setup. Perhaps he is more inclined to join the men rather than playing the firm manager . . . I think you will find it important to pin him down fairly carefully to the programmes as they emerge.

I asked John MacDonald whether he thought the Estate workers' inherent frame of mind might also have contributed to the lack of success of the Works Department.

Well, that might have been part of the problem, when you had worked for the Estate it hadn't really mattered, the time you took . . . While for instance working for Douglas Campbell in Lochgoilhead you had to produce what he expected you to produce.

So Mr Campbell oversaw what was happening better than Johnny or Bill?

Well, with Douglas Campbell you had somebody in charge of the job. He was a great man for saying it would be so much an hour – you'll get £500 for doing that: a price for doing it and get on with it. While on the Estate we were left to your own ends a lot; it wasn't that we skived but it was just the time we would take, for instance we went home for our dinner every day.

Along with the initiatives by Nigel and John described above, some things changed at the domestic level. After John died a flat had been created downstairs at the Big House, in what had been the servants' bedrooms, next to the wine cellar, so that there would be company for Elizabeth. Bill Smellie and his wife Anne lived there for the first few years; then, when they moved to Pier Cottage, the Knights moved in.

Elizabeth and Johnny were fortunate to find George and Kathy Knight. George's role was to look after the dairy cattle and the milking, the pigs, and the kitchen garden (this had been moved up from the wall garden to a fenced-off section of Dallegate, in front of the Big House), and also to look after the house itself. It turned out he did all that and much more. He was a miller's son, proud to be from the north east, born into a horse-powered world. He was a large handsome man, and a beautiful old-style dancer; at his funeral his niece said when you'd danced with George you knew you had been danced. He and Kathy were a mainstay to Elizabeth in her frailer old age and George became loyal to Johnny to the 'nth degree; indeed he was the embodiment of loyalty. George called him 'SJ'. He would settle into a chair up in the dining room and suggest ideas – for the boilers to heat the house or a new variety of potato. As John Keay put it: 'George could turn his hand to almost any task . . . The ability to solve problems without recourse to the retail trade was perhaps typical of his generation, but George elevated it to an art.'

He sourced the free-range Christmas turkey and cured the hams of the pigs he had fed. As the house, increasingly, became used as a movie and TV set, he guarded every item meticulously; and often featured in the resulting films himself.

*Elizabeth Noble by Pier Cottage, going brambling.*

*Elizabeth Noble making bread at Ardkinglas, 1970.*

Elizabeth cooked in the kitchen, which hadn't been changed since Lorimer envisaged it: she was adamant it was not to change. Early in the morning George would bring over clanking milk cans from the top byre at the Square. Wide pans of milk stood in the milk dairy, the rich yellow Jersey cream to be skimmed morning and evening. Elizabeth would churn the butter: the familiar thump, thump of the churn as reassuring to me as it must have been to others during the war years. Alice Beattie (née Sinclair), Janet Callander (née MacCallum) and Sandra MacDonald (John's wife), came in to help and to clean. And at the 10 o'clock teatime there would be gossip and teasing over the girdle scones.

*Teatime in Ardkinglas kitchen – Janet Callander, Kathy Knight and Sandra MacDonald in 1980.*

Soon after John died, perhaps thinking about the Glaswegian evacuees and feeling the house big and maybe empty, Elizabeth invited the children of the Maguire family from Springburn, Glasgow, for holidays. Various of the eight siblings visited, but Lizzie was a constant. She was nine when she first came. Recently she wrote about it. She was met by Elizabeth:

> On first meeting her I was struck how small she was and what huge hands she had. I was quite scared, and given the big house as well, on my first night I wondered if I would even survive till the next day. I soon found Elizabeth had a giant heart of gold, which manifested itself in never-ending kindness and generosity.

Elizabeth showed her the wall garden, pointing out what grew where. As Lizzie had never seen fruit and vegetables actually growing she couldn't immediately follow what she was being told. A day or two later she was asked to go and fetch a cabbage, which grew 'past the carrots'. Lizzie remembers this as a daunting challenge, 'as you can't see carrots when they are in the ground'. She continued her early memories:

Janet, Alice and Kathy helped in the house and you would see them cleaning, polishing and dusting in the mornings and stopping for tea and scones and a chat. Alice's daughter Dot was my age, and Janet had daughters just a bit older. I would often visit their homes to play – and in Janet's case get a bit of her delicious shortbread.

She remembers that Ardkinglas offered many experiences; many in contrast to life in Springburn. She saw the Estate as structured but also a relaxed place:

People went home for their lunch and then at half past five would be home in time for their tea which would be on the table as soon as they walked through the door – it all seemed to work like clockwork . . . I will always be grateful to Elizabeth Noble who gave me an opportunity to be at Ardkinglas and to the Noble family who enriched and continue to enrich my life.

As already mentioned, after John's death Tasia moved out of the Big House to No 2, the Square. Not enough has been told about her in the post-war years. She never married; she was an unusual woman, undaunted by any situation. She continued, until her death, to be a bastion of community functions – WRI, all the dances in the Hall (she taught me to dance the 'La Va', which I can remember but no longer get an opportunity to show it off), all the whist drives, every wedding; and she always had the time to talk to everyone. Soon after the war, first land girls and then cowmen were employed to look after the dairy cows, so her role on the farm declined. She was dedicated to her increasing numbers of prize-winning Scottish deerhounds – she bred 125 litters, travelled the country to shows and coursing events, exported dogs to Australia and America and travelled there as an esteemed judge – but she also bred hens, ducks, geese and hackney horses. She liked breeding animals and was knowledgeable of their care. For me and others she will be remembered fondly for the way she never treated you like a child: she almost never praised you, she gave you responsibility, you learned how to do things properly from her, you became part of her world.

Alice Beattie's daughter Dot, like me, but twenty-five years later, spent many childhood years with Tasia and gave us a lively picture of her childhood at Ardkinglas and of Tasia. She called her Miss Anastasia.

*Tasia and her deerhounds, getting off MacBraynes' bus at Ardkinglas Gates during the 1950s.*

The bones for the dogs were sheep and beef bones and came from the butcher in Inveraray or Lochgilphead. They were delivered to the Big Gates at the entrance to the Estate, and eventually someone from the farm would bring them down to the Square. It was okay if they brought them down when they had just been delivered, but if they had been left for a day or two in the summer, they were absolutely stinking with maggots crawling all over them! The boiler used for boiling the bones was in the stable. The smell was terrible, the (soup?) from the bones was used to soak the dried dog biscuits. If you got the soup on your clothes or hands they really stank and it was near impossible to get the smell away. When the bones were boiling you could smell them all around the Square, it was BAD! As they boiled there would be a layer of maggots floating on top!

When the pigs got killed, someone came to do it, sometimes it was Archie MacCallum or sometimes Jake Speirs. The pig was shot in the head and then its throat was slit to let the blood out. The trough at the end of the Stable was filled up with boiling water and the pig was submerged in it, this was to remove all the hair from the pig; then it was wheeled in the barrow to the larder which was just outside our window at Laundry Cottage. There Miss Anastasia and either Old Willie or Peter Manson would remove the guts and hang the carcase until it was butchered. As children we would watch all this and didn't think a lot about it, it was just what was done. But my big brother John never watched it; he couldn't stand what they were doing to the pigs.

Tasia and I would take the dogs for a walk up by the wee dam above Mid Lodge, or away along to the Crofters Cottage above Bachie Bhan; Miss Anastasia would show me where the badgers' sett was, or the foxes' den, she would continuously talk to me telling me all about the surrounding areas in the Estate. In the winter nights when it was frosty and we were out a walk she would tell me all the names of the clusters of stars.

She let us wash the hens and take them to the Pet Show at Inveraray during Inveraray Week; we took the hens on the bus and we won a prize!

*Tasia, Nigel Callander, Willie MacPherson and John Martin, the plumber.*

Often Miss Anastasia would go away to dog shows and Mum and I would be left in charge of the dogs. She would leave a tiny note on the small table in the feed room; sometimes she didn't tell us she going away or when she was coming back! The small note would have instructions on every spare space in every direction and it was hard to decipher it, plus her writing was so bad.

During the winter I would go into Miss Anastasia's house and we would play cards or board games, I would be there for hours; she taught me how to play backgammon, mah-jong, and lots of different patience card games.

I don't know what I would have done during all my childhood years at the Square if Miss Anastasia had not been there, every day was taken up by helping with the dogs and animals even after school. She taught me lots, and probably put up with me lots. When I think about it now, I wish my kids had been able to have the carefree childhood that I had. I think my daughter would have loved it, I'm not so sure about her being permanently stinking though!

# Scraping the Barrel

He was scraping the barrel, but for Johnny life was hardly ever all gloom and doom. He was good at finding or creating fun in any situation. French and Foreign Wines were going through hard times. Johnny's response was to take the 1932 Rolls Royce Phantom 1, inherited from his father, out of the museum to drive it to Burgundy, then to race back with the Beaujolais 'nouveau', and to be the first to deliver the 1977 vintage to London's West End. Admitting his bad driving he hired a specialist driver of old Rolls. At three in the morning on the Autoroute suddenly smoke and flames started coming through the floorboards. With himself, three of his weighty customers and the heavy cases of wine in the car, the wooden undercarriage of the Phantom had pressed down on the exhaust pipe. Johnny ejected his passengers and was driven on and delivered the Beaujolais to the Stafford Hotel, St James's, in time for dinner that evening.

But at Ardkinglas the repercussions of those estate duties and overdrafts continued and for Johnny the barrel was just about empty. He sold some objects at Christies, the London art auctioneers, to raise cash. Some Japanese objects were sold, presents to Sir Andrew from Admiral Togo – in the far-off days when Armstrongs was an important world business; the profit from this had to be shared with Michael as a part of Sir Andrew's Residuary Trust. Johnny encouraged silver experts to value items from John Noble's collection as being of 'museum importance', and thus would escape death duties if sold. Two dark and dull old Italian still-lifes of grapes, that had always hung in the dining room, were sold for a 'useful bob or two'.

His scraping of the barrel sunk even as far as garden gnomes. Early in the 1980s he let a bit of the old Clachan steading to a concrete block and garden gnomes company. The rent soon dried up as the gnome company, not a successful business, didn't last long (but the concrete blocks were useful later in the construction of my extension at Policy Gate).

He was searching for sources of income. Johnny had set up a mini seatrout farm by the old bathing hut beyond the pier. First a wild autumn storm crushed the cages, and then a fierce frost shattered the wooden platforms. That was the beginning and the end of his own fish-farm ventures.

The Golden Sea salmon hatchery has already been mentioned. Johnny had brought in Gilkes, the hydroelectric specialists, with the idea of refurbishing and recommissioning the original, Lorimer-day, hydroelectric scheme on the Kinglas. However Golden Sea then required more water for their hatchery, and at the time it looked to be more remunerative to sell the water to them than to reinstate the hydro. The late 1970s and early 1980s were a time when several West Coast estates made essential income from letting fish-farm facilities; increasingly the successful salmon farmers were Scandinavian enterprises.

Andy Lane, a young recently qualified marine biologist, had come to work with Golden Sea at the hatchery. He and Johnny met for a pint in the pub; he described to Andy how there used to be oysters in the loch, and how as a boy during wartime his daily task was to grind up oyster shells for the hens. As explained in *The Story of Loch Fyne Oysters* (Christina Noble, 1993):

> Noble was anxious about the rising cost of hay and cake for his cattle. So when Andrew Lane suggested the idea of growing oysters, Noble said 'Great idea!' Oysters, unlike cattle, were self-reliant little creatures. They quietly pumped water through themselves, sieving out the nutrients.

And that was how LFO began, registered as a company by Johnny and Andy in 1978.

Many years later, after Bill Smellie had left Ardkinglas in 1985 and emigrated to Australia, he and Johnny continued to correspond and Bill thanked for Johnny for a recent letter: 'You would be hard put to realise what a letter of this nature means to both of us here with a genuine interest in the well-being of Ardkinglas and all those connected with it.' Johnny must have mentioned LFO's progress, as Bill continued: 'As you so often remarked when discussing the plans for the LFO enterprise, it represented the optimum use of the available *natural resources* of the Estate.'

# Estate Plans

In 1979 Johnny took on a part-time factor, Ronald Baird, probably because Ardkinglas Estate's finances hadn't improved or because by now he had taken stock of the situation. Johnny wrote Ronald a detailed letter which explained how he viewed it. This letter is useful in terms of the story of Ardkinglas Estate, as it highlights the key issues at the time.

> A priority is to get the sawmill on a viable footing [this was a recent venture, not at the old mill at Bachie Bhan, but up beyond the head of the loch]. The farm will take longer to improve, better use of our low ground could save a lot of money in winter keep, apart from the labour cost a major problem is our low lambing percentage [this was to be a constant problem]. The sport could break even. The Works Department has the objective of breaking even by taking on a greater number of outside contracts.

The purpose of the letter was to set out the management structure. At a monthly meeting, overall performance would be discussed and Ronald and Bill would report to it. David MacIntyre would attend the meetings (David was recently appointed as accountant and was to become close to Johnny and a source of strength and advice). Johnny explained that he would be at home on Mondays but Ronald should feel free to discuss anything with him at any time, even if he was in London. (At this time he still had a fairly regular Friday–Monday commute to Glasgow via British Midland.)

Perhaps the letter was to be circulated to each head of department. It begins 'Dear . . .' and continues:

> All the activities and departments of the Ardkinglas Estate are very vulnerable in these acutely difficult economic times. This cannot continue. Indeed every department must pay its way or be disbanded . . .

The intention of this letter is to clarify the areas of responsibilities. An enormous united effort is required by all and I hope this will avoid further redundancies and provide stability of employment. Wages and conditions now compare very favourably with those elsewhere and performance must also compare with those outside levels.

*Factor: Ronald Baird* is responsible to the trustees [Johnny, Elizabeth and Sir Alastair Blair, solicitor].

*Manager: Bill Smellie* will report to Ronald Baird. He is responsible for the everyday running of the Estate and those working on it. Except Clachan farm where Alastair MacCallum is responsible. Bill will liaise between Clachan farm and the Ardkinglas low ground. He will be responsible for this low ground and the garden.

*Farm Manager: Alastair MacCallum* is responsible directly to Ronald Baird for the performance of Clachan and the hill sheep and the supervision of farm workers, with the help of Bill Smellie for the paperwork.

*George Knight* [with his wife Kathy living in the flat at Ardkinglas since 1977] will be responsible for the preparation of the low ground fields and the stock while at Ardkinglas. Also the garden and certain mansion house duties. Notably furnace fuelling for the central heating.

*The Works Department.*

*Nigel Callander* will be responsible with the active assistance of John MacDonald.

*Sawmill: Stuart Keith* will be responsible for sawmilling production, completing orders, and all sawmill sales.

*Woodlands: Willie Manson* will carry out a programme in the woodlands including the provision of firewood, the improvement of the sporting amenity and the day to day work as Forester.

*Sport: Peter Mason* will be responsible for functioning of all sporting activities including the sale of game, with the assistance of Bill Smelllie.

*Garage: Lachie Beattie* will act as Estate mechanic and will be responsible for all Estate machinery.

Then the concluding item is:

Loch Fyne Oysters

This is an entirely separate activity to the Estate and is under the management of Andy Lane. *However its success is an integral part of the future prosperity of the Estate* [my italics] and close co-operation is looked for.

# Loch Fyne Oysters – A Castle in the Air?

Envisaged as 'integral to the prosperity of the Estate', Loch Fyne Oysters soon became Johnny's driving force. In 1979, only a year after it was set up, despite early setbacks, Johnny was already convinced, or determined, that it would be a success. Andy Lane described those early days in his piece in the *S. J. Noble Scrapbook* (privately published as a memorial after his death).

In 1978 LFO was capitalised at £100 with assets comprising one wooden pleasure boat (great for mackerel fishing but of no practical use to an oyster farm) one plastic dinghy (minus seats and with a large hole stuffed with a sack at waterline) and one wet suit riddled with punctures.

Johnny invited our Inveraray bank manager to view our facilities and discuss an overdraft facility. Our bank manager was a man of cautious habit. We stood on the shore on a blustery autumn day. It was raining and the manager had not brought his mac.

I think it was Johnny's idea to get him round when the tide was in; because the oyster enterprise of our imagination was likely to impress more than its meagre reality.

Johnny was at his most expansive and lyrical. Attention was drawn to the huge potential of the loch, the vast numbers of oysters consumed annually in France and historically in the UK, the eighteenth century, when at oyster howffs in Edinburgh Dukes and artisans had caroused with comely lasses, and now we would resurrect this tradition on Loch Fyneside and throughout the world.

Afterwards Johnny likened it to playing to the Glasgow Empire on a wet Monday.

The Bank Manager was of a sceptical character. Once Johnny's magical oration was over I remember a chilly pause and then 'Thank you Mr Noble. That was most interesting'.

In the event Johnny's bravura performance played off. We were granted a small facility secured against the company's assets and backed up by a personal guarantee from Johnny. Bearing in mind that Johnny was already carrying 70% death duties this was an onerous and risky step. It was typical of the man that he bore this with the stout conviction that LFO would eventually prevail.

In 1980 Johnny was writing many 'out of the blue' letters. He would say 'It's always worth the cost of a postage stamp'. A Mr Hales, M.D. of Hales Snails Ltd, must have responded to one: he was treated to lunch in St James's with wine and oysters. However his 'thankyou' letter indicated a cautious view of the LFO project: 'I certainly feel that you have a very good project with the oysters and we could market them . . . But I think a great deal of promotion and advertising will have to be done to educate the public to eat oysters throughout the year.'

This Johnny was doing with zest.

*Oyster Farmer* was now Johnny's profession as written in his passport. In May he wrote 'out of the blue' to Sir David Orr, M.D. of Unilever. There are two scraps of paper pinned to the copy of the letter. The first is a small cutting from the London *Evening Standard* of 1 May. It reports that Unilever are abandoning their efforts to keep on the remaining MacFisheries retail shops but will be investing in their wholesale business. The second scrap pinned to the letter is the back of an envelope – literally (the envelope, empty, had come from an importer of lobsters, oysters and prawns in Brussels). The back flap of this re-used envelope has calculations in Johnny's handwriting – projections for oyster production, for both gigas and edulis oysters, from September 1980, through September 1981 and on to September 1982, increasing from 20,000 to 50,000 and 50,000 to 200,000 respectively. He had wasted no time; his letter to Sir David is dated 2 May, the day after the *Evening Standard* article. He says to Sir David that he very much apologises for writing somewhat out of the blue, but that he has seen the *Evening Standard* article, and though Loch Fyne Oysters have nothing to market just at the moment, they anticipate having very substantial quantities of oysters in the not too distant future. And the projected quantities (as per the back of the envelope) are listed. No reply from Sir David is attached to the correspondence. This was Johnny the inveterate marketer.

Were Johnny and Andy's oyster ideas castles in the air? Was Johnny clutching at straws? The cautious view held by the RBS manager and Mr Hales of Hales Snails was probably shared by many. Indeed there were to be troubled years before the hoped-for prosperity had any impact.

Required for his membership at Lloyds underwriters was a 'certificate of means'. To prove his means Johnny commissioned a valuation of his revisionary interest in John Noble's Trust – which he managed to have calculated to be £400,000.

At the same time, October 1980, in order to back up his guarantees and loans to the bank, he commissioned Ronald Baird (chartered surveyor as well as factor) to value the estate. Ronald's estimated total was £1,202,100. This hardly seems in line with the valuation at the time of John Noble's death a mere eight years previously. However that was for probate, and for the bank Ronald may have been encouraged to look favourably on the assets. And moreover in some areas of the Estate there had already been considerable additions – various land rents, including Golden Sea's hatchery and their house, and more recently the old sawmill leased to Loch Fyne Oysters Ltd. And there were optimistic predictions for the future – the 'potential' revenue from Bonar's about-to-be-excavated gravel quarry, the new sawmill, and newly planted commercial woodland. All of this within eight years of taking over the Estate.

If Ronald was generous in his estimates, it produced the hoped-for result. There is a letter from Mr Smith, RBS Inveraray, of January 1981, saying that in order to enable the payments of the outstanding capital gains tax of £17,000 plus £22,500 he is pleased to advise that head office has agreed to increase the overdraft facilities up to £300,000 until April/May, when he understands that £20,000 'should become available from the expected sale of items of silver'. He adds that he hopes that the sale of the enlarged Drishaig block (for forestry) will be concluded soon to reduce the borrowing.

And he goes on to say:

> We have been asked to send to head office a 'negative pledge' letter undertaking that so long as you or the firms in which you are a partner are indebted or committed to the bank you would not divest yourself of your rights to the estate. You will recall that this was discussed when you and Mr David MacIntyre met our Mr Buchan at head office in September last year and we will be pleased if you will send us a letter couched in the above terms as soon as convenient.

At Ardkinglas Johnny was treading on eggshells; and for his wine business it was worse. These were turbulent times nationally; the stock market collapse of the mid-1970s and the financial downturn of the early 1980s had contributed to French and Foreign Wine's instability. It is also probable that

Johnny's need to focus on Ardkinglas had diverted his attention from the direction of his wine business. It was a bad time for him, and I can remember his breaking down in tears in a London taxi. In the summer of 1981, French and Foreign Wine went into liquidation. One of Johnny's obituaries recalled: 'Rallying some of his many friends they placed his stock [of wine] amongst themselves and a number of City institutions within the day, thanks to Noble's reputation.' A friend, James Joll, explained this to me:

> Johnny had given a personal guarantee to the bank. Thus the liquidators of the company would have been content to sell the stock off cheap, knowing that any shortfall against the bank overdraft would have had to be paid by Johnny personally. We wanted to avoid this. What we did was circulate the stock list at either the original prices or some slight discount. I was delighted and rather surprised quite how quickly his many friends snapped up the wines on offer.

The financial damage may not have been too bad but Johnny suffered: he felt he had failed and that he had let people down.

Over the years he didn't exactly recover but he weathered it. He would say in the face of difficulties – his and others – that they were character-building. His outside business interests carried on. He continued to be involved in the wine trade with what became a very successful company called Wine Importers Edinburgh. He was a non-executive director of Noble and Co., an investment bank in Edinburgh. For many years he kept a London toehold with a flat in St James's; however increasingly his home was Ardkinglas, Cairndow, and his driving focus was Loch Fyne Oysters.

## On the Estate and the Farm, What Was Happening?

John Macdonald described what happened next on the Estate:

> Well, we had worked away with the Ardkinglas Works Department, and then in 1983 Johnny must have sat down and thought, 'This is not the way to go on.' I don't know how much influence Bill had on it. He came to me and said 'What do you think about going self-employed?' And I said I would bite his arm off for it. I think it may have been Bill who had dreamt up the idea to make us all redundant and then offering us the opportunity to go self-employed. Or it might

have been David MacIntyre, Johnny's accountant. I said I had been thinking about an opportunity for my own business, but I was in a tied house, I had got a young family, and there was nothing wrong with my way of life. Ardkinglas Estate was a fantastic place to bring up young children, you were home every day, no pressure, good quality life, even if you weren't making a fortune. So I hadn't made the move to set up my own business.

I was 33. They put a proposal – would I accept nine years' redundancy, which was to be cash in your hand. We were offered to take over our department, which in my case was with all the tools, equipment, scaffolds, cement-mixers and the van. They valued it, put a price on it all and Johnny said OK, you can pay me back over 30 months at no interest. Which was fantastic; this added offer added to the nine years' redundancy.

And about the house, the offer was that the first year we would pay 25% of the rentable value of the house and the second year we would pay 50% and the third we would pay 75% and then we would pay full rent.

These were very generous terms and illustrated the sense of responsibility Johnny felt for the wellbeing of people of the community.

It was also offered to Stuart Keith and Willie Mather at the new sawmill. Stuart said no. And he went to work for the Hydro Board. A Bill Warnock had come to make garden furniture and gates and stuff at the new sawmill. But he was really a shop joiner, he hadn't done of that kind of work and it didn't really work out.

Nigel got the same opportunity to set up his own joinery business. Lachie Beattie the mechanic, Alice's son, set up his workshop at the garage in the Square.

I asked John if he knew what influenced those who did or didn't take up the offer?

Both Nigel and Lachie had a good go at the new idea. For me, and Nigel, there was already work on the book, work in hand, for instance the proposed work at Dr Lachlan's at Hirsel Cottage; it passed on to us, straight away.

The sawmill seemed a bit daunting for Stuart, I don't know, it was complicated. Maybe the fact that they had to generate a market. Anyway self-employment didn't suit everyone.

I asked, 'Was it different for you working for yourself, for Cairndow Builders, with all the responsibility?'

No, I didn't find the transition too difficult because actually for the Works Department I had been involved in pricing work and estimating the time of the job, and getting the materials ordered. So it was doing the same thing for myself . . .

Colin Callander, Nigel's son, had been working with me, but when we went self-employed I decided I had to go carefully for a start, so Colin so went on the dole for a time. Six months later there was an opportunity from the government, if someone had been on the dole for at least 6 months you could apply to have half their wages paid as an assistant. So I took Colin back on with me. And he stayed with me for eight or nine years. Nigel never had anyone working with him, he always just worked on himself.

For me it was an opportunity that came, it was like a gift from heaven, I had always wanted the chance.

# 1983 on the Estate

In 1983 there was George Knight at Ardkinglas House and garden and Penny White and Angie MacDonald, John's daughter, in the Estate office. And there were the long-term employees like Peter and Willie Manson. Their father Willie, a cousin of the MacCallums who had been brought up in the Glen, had been a keeper here from when he left school until he retired. Unlike the Mac-Callums, who were Tories, he was a staunch Labour supporter, as was Betty his wife, from Dundee. When, soon after the war, Bob Cameron had moved up to No 3 at the Square, the Mansons had moved into Lorimer Cottage. Betty was sociable and 'a character'. She was a good friend to all the children who called in at her house for a 'jelly piece' or sweeties on their way back from school. Old Willie, always with a pipe, wore voluminous tweed plus-fours; he kept a ferret and yapping little terriers. He nailed the skulls of foxes he had shot to the trunk of the big silver fir, on the far side of the Stable Field (where Tasia's dogs were taken to be shot, when they were too old or too ill). He retired in 1978.

The sons, Peter and Willie, were both clever at school. Peter went into the Argyll and Sutherland Highlanders for his National Service (along with Johnny). After that he was in the Police and then a warden in young persons' remand homes. In 1978 he had come back and took over his father's job as a keeper. Young Willie also went into the Argylls, but as a regular, missing National Service. After a year or so he bought himself out and went to Australia, where he joined the Australian army and went to Vietnam. He got wounded there and was invalided out. He too was in the prison service for a while. Back at Ardkinglas with his parents, he worked for years alone in the woods; brashing the lower branches from the growing trees and keeping the place tidy, clearing fallen trees – making big bonfires – and crashing about with machinery and chainsaws. He was not an enthusiast for training courses nor for health and safety.

After Willie died in the 1980s, the two unmarried boys continued to live with their old, increasingly deaf mother in Lorimer Cottage with its Triplex stove. There was no indoor toilet, they didn't see the need.

# On the Farm

On the Farm there were four shepherds/farmworkers. They were Alastair MacCallum, his brother Colin, Roddy MacDiarmid and his brother Angus. At the time many estates were selling off land for commercial forestry. High-income-tax-bracket investors could write off the costs of planting against their taxable income and so justify the high purchase prices for new planting land – famously Terry Wogan among others. Johnny, constantly looking for income, took advantage of this market, cashing in his hillside assets, clearing sheep and selling for forestry. (By now the issue was less deer versus sheep, more commercial forestry versus sheep.)

To an extent the same thing happened on Cairndow Estate. Ernie MacPherson, son of Donald, was shepherd at Ardno for Cairndow Estate: 'The sheep went off Ardno in 1978 because the hill ground was sold to forestry. But there was one hirsel kept on, so I still had a shepherd's job from 1978 until I left in '84, I was on my own at Ardno, plus helping out on Cairndow/Achadunan or Ardkinglas as well.'

However, unlike John, Michael had always had a real interest in cattle and sheep, and therefore was more involved with his farm employees than John had been. Alistair Bremner, shepherd, remembered: 'I suppose Michael was wanting to make the best of what was there. Oh aye, he was quite innovative.'

Dot, who was recording him, asked if Michael was approachable.

Oh yes, he was approachable. Even then when he was so old, he was interested, still had an enthusiasm for the land and for sheep. Lots of times, you would be summoned to the kitchen at Strone, he was a heavy smoker and he smoked, I don't know what they were but they were in a tin and I mean he shouldn't have smoked, because, Christ, he would go into a fit of coughing and you didn't know what to do, whether he would come out the other end or not! And then he would tell – he would tell you any changes that were going to happen.

He was always there and involved, and that was the difference when he died, there was nobody and he had been the figurehead, and if he said yes, it was yes, and if he said no, it was no.

Ernie agreed, Michael was always interested in the land and the stock.

At that time we did quite a lot of improvement to the fields at Laglingarten. We re-seeded them and managed to get the lamb crop up from about 80% to over 100%. The ewes, if they were just on the hill, you were lucky if you got average of 80% lambing, but by improving the ground in-bye, we re-seeded some of the hill parks, so we were able to bring the ewes in in October. It was what we call 'flushing' them, putting them on to better ground, in these parks they got into better condition, so when they went to the tup they were producing more eggs and were producing twins and suchlike. After that they were put back onto the hill. Then in the spring we looked after them better. Because we didn't have so many we would feed them better and put blocks out for them so that was a help to them for the lamb crop. We managed to get the lamb crop up to just over 100%.

On the Clachan side (the Ardkinglas farm) Alastair was in charge. The '80s and '90s may not have been great times for commercial cattle and black-face sheep. Like his father Johnny lacked interest in animals or agriculture, which may have had an impact on Alastair and his colleagues. It was not the farm that was the focus of Johnny's drive. A factor from a neighbouring farm commented recently:

You have to have an interest, though it helps to have an outside taxable income. Well-run hill farms have supported sustainable employment from the 1970s right through to the present day and they continue to do so. The European and the Common Agricultural Policy has played a major role supporting hill farming right through the period from the 1970s . We have to wonder what would have happened to farm support without the EU and what will happen now when power is returned to Westminster or Edinburgh?

Roddy MacDiarmid, recorded in June 2016, recalled:

Colin was on Ceanngarbh hirsel, Angie on Clachan, Ally [Alastair MacCallum] was on Newton and Beinn Chorranach, I was on Cuil. Cuil was the first to be sold by Johnny for the forestry. Yes, I did mind, it was a great hirsel . . .

No, it wasn't in the slightest bit of an encouragement, I was very, very disappointed to say the least when part of Cuil was sold off and then the whole lot. I was disappointed. I don't actually know why it was sold, I really don't, there was probably a good reason but I'd like to know why.

I suggested to Roddy that people assumed there was lots of money and that jobs were going to go on forever, but there was financial difficulty. All these estates had depended on outside money.

I think that would be right . . . We did hear at the time that that was the case. Johnny never explained one word, whether he did to anyone else I don't know, but not to Angie or me, but we had heard that he was financially insecure and that it was through necessity that he sold the land. Cuil and some of Clachan was sold, and some of Trosgiche. That was not such a good hirsel, it was very, very unhealthy, a cobalt deficiency, the sheep would be wasted – skin and bone. Then we learnt to dose with a cobalt bullet as hoggs.

Later Roddy left Ardkinglas and went and worked for two or three years as a shepherd on Cairndow Estate and briefly at Luss on Loch Lomond. Then in 1974 he became self-employed, working as a shepherd all over Britain, and travelled internationally to sheepdog trials. He says:

212

*Roddy MacDiarmid and sheepdog trial cups in 1980.*

Yes, I was pleased to have made the decision. You've got to travel to see how the other half lives in the world, and it's the same with shepherding, I have seen how other people do things, you can pick out the best of it. The dog-trialling took me: I went to a lot of interesting places, met an awful lot of nice people. England, Ireland, Wales, Canada and America.

I asked if he ever thought of a farm of his own. 'Yes, but the opportunity never arose of setting up on my own. The opportunity doesn't arise for most people. Occasionally it does, but not often. I would have liked to have had a go.'

## Diversification: the Mid-1980s

Elizabeth Noble died at the end of 1983. Johnny and his mother were close, in many ways alike in character, and, since John's death, Johnny had been his mother's strong shoulder. Grieving as he was for her and for the loss of continuity that her death meant, in a way it was a relief. He could take the ups and down on his own head without the anxiety of how it might affect her.

Mrs Thatcher and her Tory government had been elected in 1979, and individualism and materialism became a way of thinking, perhaps even in Cairndow. People began to go abroad for holidays; few of the previous generation in Cairndow had gone on any holiday more than a visit to relations.

Some of what was happening on Ardkinglas Estate was simply to do with changing times, and some of it was to do with direct interventions, largely by Johnny. An incident of around 1986 illustrates this.

As already mentioned, Golden Sea Produce salmon hatchery had been set up at the mouth of the Kinglas River in 1974. In the early 1980s a Norwegian called Finn Rostaad arrived and took it over. Many local people worked there – Archie and Dot Beattie, Alastair Bremner and also Ernie MacPherson (Donald MacPherson's son).

Ernie (recorded by Dot) looked back from 2014 to the role of Finn and the impact of diversification.

I had been in Ardno for 11 years when Michael Noble died, it was 1984, I was made redundant. The day after I was made redundant I got a letter from the family, telling me I had ten days to vacate the house and sell my cattle, which was a bit of a shock after 24 and a half years with the Noble family. But we had nowhere to go so we just stayed put till we found somewhere to go. We actually got a chance to buy a house off Johnny Noble, on the Ardkinglas Estate, which was Clachan Beag, and I moved to there. That was the end of the farming career for me.

When I moved from Ardno for six months I didn't have a job, I just helped out with farmers, and planted trees and suchlike. Then I got word that the local fish farm was looking for a handyman, so I went down there and applied for the job. And I got it.

That was working for a man called Finn Rostaad. And he had the hatchery there, so I got the job as the handyman. And then one day he sacked his manager and the next day he called me into his office and said he wanted me to be the manager for his hatchery. I said well, I didn't know anything about fish and didn't want the job. He said, yes, you'll take the job and I'll get someone who knows something about fish to help you. That's what happened and we got this good chap who helped me, a chap called Ian Gillies.

It produced smolts for the salmon trade. We would buy in eggs and we would have to hatch them out and take them from eggs to fry. And then breed them right up till they were smolts at about six months old. Then we had to acclimatise them to the salt water, which was quite a tricky job to do, and then they were sold on or put into our own sea sites.

It was at this point that Finn was building what we were told was a feed shed further over on Rhumore, and I was put in charge of that along with his M.D. at that time, Ian Booker, and we built it.

Ernie refers to the building, which was to became a bellwether of the times, as 'what we were told was a feed shed'.

John Macdonald described what happened.

Finn . . . was an independent type of person. Yes, the shed on Rhumore was meant to be going to be a feed shed, I remember there was quite a bit of a to-do from some people about the construction of the Rostaad salmon place because of the visual impact from the village, there was some whingeing about that. Johnny didn't realise what level Finn was heading for. Johnny came back from London to find a large full-framed fish shed being put up and he was gobsmacked, he had thought it was going to be the size of a garage or something. He obviously said – hang on, what's going on?

But some people were thinking it was a chance to get good employment. Finn was pushing ahead and promising people big things. Johnny was annoyed at the wool having been pulled over his eyes. To come home to find out this had happened. There was a big meeting in the pub.

I remember him setting off to the meeting, he was anxious, nervous. John continued:

So some people were saying it spoiled their view, from the village. More people were saying they wanted the good jobs. And Johnny didn't want to be seen blocking that. At the end of the day, and when he thought about it a bit, probably he thought: it's got to happen.

So the 'little feed shed' became Finn's large salmon-processing plant.

He became a notorious character. He surreptitiously brought in salmon eggs, hidden in an old plane, which he then buried in the pond in front of Garden Cottage. Entertained to dinner by Johnny at Ardkinglas, he tore up pound notes and tossed them into the drawing-room fireplace bellowing, 'I don't care anything about money', as the flames took the notes up the chimney, 'it means nothing to me.' On another occasion Johnny had entertained Finn and his Norwegian bankers. Next morning Johnny found the bankers still in the drawing room, stretched out asleep behind the sofas. Finn's seaplane regularly flew in bringing jerry cans full of vodka. His midsummer barbecue parties were long and lavish. This all was a new style for Ardkinglas Estate.

But soon those recumbent bankers began to wake up and take over. Ernie continued:

After three years Mr Rostaad went bust for a total of three million pounds and another company took the place over, called Volvo. Next step was they upgraded the processing, they had all women working. Then again it changed hands and it was upgraded a bit more. I think it was a company called Concordia and then it changed hands later on again to Pan Fish. They spent a lot of money in the processing area and made it bigger still with machinery to gut fish.

So I was in charge of the processing and latterly there I had sixty of staff. We were producing about sixty to seventy ton of fish a day, it was quite a bit of handling.

Pan Fish bought other sites on Loch Fyne, more and more sites, so they owned their own salmon which came from these farmed sites into the factory. And just before I left, another company, Lighthouse of Scotland, took it all over. Then it was sold again to the company that has it today – the Scottish Salmon Company.

The fish was mostly going abroad, to France, some to Britain, but not a great deal, mostly went abroad and latterly into China and suchlike places. It was transported by refrigerated lorry from Cairndow to Bellshill, Glasgow, by the Inverdell Company, a local man from Strachur. He had the business of taking it from Cairndow to Glasgow.

I retired after 26 years, between the hatchery and the processing plant. I enjoyed the farm more than the fish farm, working on the land, the hills, just because it was in my blood I think.

It can be gathered that, as described by Ernie, the diversification, initially just a lease from Ardkinglas Estate for a hatchery and a manager's house, soon spread out into a large industry, Scandinavian-owned, with a beneficial impact on a variety of local jobs and initiatives.

Johnny was still searching for cash injections; still suffering from the estate duties and the borrowings he inherited, and also increasingly needing cash for his new ventures. He saw Clachan Farm as something of a financial drain; in particular because of the rising cost of feed for stock, the low lambing percentages and falling prices, and anyway he wasn't really interested in farming.

In 1983 Danny Bonar took on a lease from Johnny for a gravel quarry beyond the Clachan Power Station, beyond the old Clachan fanks above the Whirlpool (where the exhausted haymakers had bathed on their way up the Glen on 21 August 1939). The quarry brought the estate 50 pence royalty per ton at that time, and turned out to be a very useful income-stream for the estate.

Johnny read about the potential of windfarms in the *Scottish Farmer*. He was a voracious reader of books on a wide variety of subjects and also newspapers and periodicals – the *Financial Times* every day, the *Herald*, the *Oban Times*. In partnership with Border Winds, he tried to further the development of a windfarm on Clachan Flats. At that time Scottish Natural Heritage scotched the idea, they considered it would spoil the view for hill walkers on Beinn an Lochan. Had it gone through then, the agreed percentage of turnover would have come to Ardkinglas Estate and the Cairndow community. However by the time it did go through, there was a new landowner on the Clachan side of the hill who forbade access. Access had to come from the Inveraray side, so Cairndow community and Ardkinglas Estate have had to share the benefit with Inveraray and the Duke of Argyll's estate. The Clachan Flats Wind Farm is owned by Oberdrola Renovables, an international company with bases in 23 countries: all this grew from Johnny spotting a small column in the *Scottish Farmer* in the 1980s.

As already mentioned Michael Noble, by then Lord Glenkinglas, died in 1984. After his death both Achadunan and Ardno Farms were let, for 10 years, to the Findlay family. Several years passed while his daughters carved out an amicable division of land and property. Ultimately Cairndow Estate was divided into five parts. A large part, including Glen Kinglas and Strone House itself, was sold to Johnny Turnbull in 1993. The remaining land and buildings, not already sold to forestry companies, were then divided between Michael's four daughters. Catherine How had Ardno Farm and Anastasia Delap

*The Tree Shop as it was in 1990.*

had Achadunan Farm. (The Findlays' tenancy of these ended about this time.) The other two daughters had property but little land.

This meant that by the 1990s Ardkinglas Estate was the largest land entity at Cairndow, some 13,000 acres, and it, combined with Loch Fyne Oysters (which was more than 50% owned by Johnny), constituted the largest employer in the community.

On Ardkinglas, as already mentioned, significant areas of land had been already been sold for commercial forestry, then Loch Fyne Oysters bought some of the land at Clachan and some of the foreshore on the Ardkinglas side of the loch. Around this time John MacDonald was able to buy a plot to build a house for himself. 'I got the offer of a piece of land, the Estate had a pre-emption right over it if I ever sold. They had had planning permission on it, to build a house for an oyster farm manager, but at the time they decided against it, they didn't have the funds maybe. So that was where I built my house, Arleigh.'

In addition to Loch Fyne Oysters Johnny had set up another Estate-owned enterprise at Clachan, the Tree Shop, combining a shop selling wooden goods and a garden centre.

Probably the most significant change to the locality was to house owner-ship. There were now fifty-two privately owned houses, including the Hotel and the Post Office. There was Kilmorich, a new development of fourteen houses built by Fyne Homes Housing Association, some of which were or became privately owned. Ardno Estate owned three houses, Achadunan six, Strone five. Ardkinglas Estate still owned twenty houses, of which about 50% were leased.

## Loch Fyne Oysters: A Cottage Industry

During the 1980s, tentatively at first, Loch Fyne Oysters began to play the promised 'integral role'.

As indicated by Andy Lane in his account of the RBS Manager's visit to the oyster beds, it wasn't all plain sailing. Like the sea trout farm before it, the oysters suffered from local weather: the waves rolled them into heaps and they didn't grow; they were too far up the shore and got frosted; they got killed by an anti-foulant used on boats. The 'back of the envelope figures' were not as quickly achieved as Johnny had envisaged.

Andy and Johnny were not deterred, and in the meantime set about cre-ating some alternative products in the old joiners' shop (which had been the Old House of Sir Andrew's day). Christine MacCallum, Alastair's wife, remembers that in 1984 and 1985 trout and salmon were smoked on the upper floor by David Graham, better known as Heedie, who had fish-smok-ing experience. The herring-pickling 'section' was on the floor below. Chris-tine membered:

> The herrings arrived salted, they had to be put into big troughs and then you hosed off the salt and put them into the marinade. Andy had the recipe of how it had to be done. Sandra MacDonald [John's wife] and I were doing the herring.
>
> Oh, there was lots that went on there! One time there was no sherry for the herring marinade because someone had drunk it all.

The next year Greta Cameron, niece of Donald and Willie MacPherson, joined the herring team. She had been employed for half a day's work, to do the purchase ledger, in the 'office', in the byre at the Square (she had done bookkeeping before). Half of what had been the byre was the Ardkinglas Estate office and the other half was the oyster/herring/smokery office. Greta was looking for more work, so she took on the scrubbing out of the herring barrels. She did the barrels in the mornings and then changed her clothes and her shoes and went up to do the ledger in the office in the afternoons. Mary Munro kept the sales ledger, but she too worked at the herrings. David Weir, who had joined as a sixteen-year-old fish-farming student, was the salesman, but like everyone else he did a bit of everything as needed – accounts, smoking and filleting. Andy did everything too. There were four in the office. Johnny was the marketer, when he was at home he would be there every morning. He had to sit in the Estate Office as there was no room for him in the fish half. He would study the accounts and the sales ledgers and talk about the marketing.

In *Local Heroes, The Story of Loch Fyne Oysters*, David Erdal acclaims Johnny's bravery and his marketing flair. This was true, but his reading of Johnny as a shy misfit was never true. Greta:

> It was cheery, it was funny, there was excitement and fun. The joiners' shop had no planning permission or anything like that. When visitors were expected, Johnny would say, 'Don't let them see here. Take them straight into Ardkinglas House.'
>
> When an order came in at the office you would rush down to the old joiners' shop in the woods with the fax or whatever it was. There was always something happening and humour. Andy, David Weir or Heedie would go off to Tayinloan, Tayvallich and Crinan and places to pick up the prawns, you could never be sure when they would be back. And the prawns had to be cooked and rushed off to catch the London sleeper train at Arrochar.

In 1986 they opened a stall by the old bridge at the head of the loch. At first it was a table made of fish-boxes, under an umbrella, then it became a small shed with a hatch. There were two shifts – 10 am to 2 pm, and 2 pm to 6 pm. Mary Munro, and also her daughter, worked there, as well as Sandra MacDonald, Irene (Ernie MacPherson's wife), Amelia Mirrlees (wife of John), and many children, including Daniel Sumsion (Johnny's nephew) and Colin, Christine's son. Christine kept the rota. They sliced salmon and opened oysters on the spot.

Ideas for development moved on at speed. At Clachan, they took over some of the old farm buildings and began to renovate them for a smokehouse. The architect was Archie Proven. He had bought a building plot from the

*The Loch Fyne Oysters shed at the head of the Loch, with American
tourists in 1986.*

Estate, up by the bothy in Glen Fyne. Johnny was in a hurry to get the smokehouse up and running, but Archie was busy building a house for himself. John
MacDonald remembers:

> I got involved in the situation. Archie was doing the drawings for
> the new smokehouse. But he was too busy getting his own house
> built and not pushing on with LFO. Johnny was not at all happy
> about Archie dragging his feet and that I was tied up working with
> his housebuilding rather than getting on with the LFO job. Looking
> back on it I think Archie did an extensive thing, ahead of what LFO
> were anticipating, they wanted a basic smokehouse but he went ahead
> and designed something more. If you could see into the future he was
> right. But at the time they lacked funds to go to that level . . .
>
> Yes, a lot of development was happening as compared to ever
> before. This was diversification. People were happy to go along with
> it. I don't remember people being critical of any of it. The things that
> were happening were creating employment. There was no opposition,
> no, because people could see the estate had been going nowhere fast.

Until now no proprietor of Ardkinglas Estate had used estate assets to fund a commercial enterprise. Land was sold to raise cash. As already described, the resulting income was used towards settling capital gains tax bills and reducing bank overdrafts in order to free funds to develop Loch Fyne Oysters. Parts of Drishaig and Cuil hills had already been sold; then in the mid-1980s lower Cuil, higher Clachan, Larige and Newton were all sold.

Because of the continuing developments, Johnny was not out of the woods; not for a while, if ever. The major business bank accounts were moved from RBS at Inveraray to Adam Bank, Edinburgh (founded in 1983 by Johnny's cousin Iain Noble and others). There is a letter of 1986 from Sandy Dudgeon, Manager at Adam Bank: Sandy very politely explained that he had written to land agents for valuations of the Ardkinglas Estate for inheritance tax purposes and also for bank lending purposes. 'In the meantime you suggested that you would consider further the practicality of realising further cash from some of the existing assets of the Estate, including forestry. You also confirmed that you and Andrew Lane would be considering the development of the Loch Fyne Oyster company in the next five years.'

In due course the renovations at Clachan were ready; or rather, that is not exactly true, because development there moved at such a pace that expansion demanded new construction almost yearly. But the smokehouse was moved from the old joiners' shop over to Clachan.

Now the office too moved to Clachan. Loch Fyne Oysters was hardly an industrial showcase, it was still more of a cottage industry; the office was like a box with a window that looked out into the yard, at the time still a sheep yard. Greta, Mary Munro, David Weir and Andy were based in it. Johnny drove backwards and forwards to the Estate office to send or pick up faxes (Clachan must have lacked a fax line). One afternoon Angie MacDonald saw him dash off with his pigskin briefcase left on the roof of his Subaru. As he rounded the head of the loch, speeding on his way with a fax to Hong Kong, it slid off. The driver behind noticed, picked it up and kindly followed him down through the village and into the Estate all the way to the office.

Clachan was in a fortuitous position on a straight section of the A83; motorists could see it from a distance and turn off without too much danger. The 'shop' moved there from the head of the loch, though it was still not much more than a stall. There was a small signboard out in the road and people in the know would be queuing before it opened. Christine worked there from its beginning, with Jenny Speirs (daughter-in-law of Jake). There were oysters, and smoked salmon and prawns, and if you wanted to eat on the spot, there was bread and paper plates. There was no tea or coffee, just beer and wine; though there was no drinks licence 'we just did it'. The customers had to stand outside, which wasn't great on a wet day, so it was decided to build a picnic area. Johnny said to Greta 'would you like to run a picnic area?' The picnic area never happened; instead it fast became the Oyster Bar.

Morag Keith, wife of Stewart:

The first hot food we ever did was for some people camped nearby. They wanted hot food. But how would we do it we hadn't got a cooker? I said to Andy, 'what about a challenge?' Alastair MacCallum dug out an ancient gas cooker from an old shed somewhere in the steading. Mary Munro and Greta and I cut up an old blue carpet to cover over the muck in the yard. And we boiled up a salmon and some potatoes.

The Oyster Bar took over what had been the byre, where the cattle had chewed their expensive feed. Nigel Callander built 'booths'; the idea was that they were reminiscent of the old cattle stalls, they were cosy and provided privacy to the diners. The Oyster Bar opened in April 1988. It was a great event, and top-class food writers were flown up from London. The concept was explained to them: 'It was to be a simply furnished bar where at any time of day or evening passers-by could drop in for a Guinness and half a dozen oysters, or settle to a three-course dinner, washed down with fine wines.'

In 1988 this concept was unusual, unheard of even.

Loch Fyne Oysters began to offer employment opportunities that local people, particularly women, had never had before. There were no professionals, no consultants. I don't think that was exactly a conscious decision, more a matter that at that time Johnny and Andy couldn't afford outside assistance and also didn't see a need for it. Greta was the manageress. Morag was the cook; she had been a hotel manageress before she was married, but not a cook. 'Most of what I knew I learnt in my mother's kitchen.'

Greta explained how everything just grew out of demand. They advertised for staff.

It grew and grew. It was a big opportunity for local people, opportunity for women and young people. I would say three-quarters of local people worked with LFO. In the shop, office, restaurant, slicing room, packaging, and on the shore with the oysters of course. For

223

instance, Jackie from Strachur, she had never even been to Inveraray, never come up the loch this length before!

It got so busy. We kept going and kept the ideas going. It grew from absolutely nothing. I went to Johnny and Andy and said we needed more space. Then a proper kitchen was built the other side of the hatch. We didn't do all that much planning, we just responded to demand. If we wanted to do anything we had to make the money to do any improvement.

Johnny and Andy always listened to ideas. The Oyster Bar was a brilliant idea, seafood fresh and simple. I would say it was one of the first restaurants in the whole of Scotland which did the fresh and simple. Initially it was thought to be a joke to have an Oyster Bar at the head of Loch Fyne. There were a lot of things said at the beginning. Local people didn't come to eat much, it was a different style that they weren't accustomed to. In those days they weren't seafood enthusiasts.

The list is long of those who worked there at one time or another and gained experience of various sectors of Loch Fyne Oysters. Boys and young

*Greta Cameron and Johnny at the opening of the Oyster Bar in 1988.*

men started off on the shore with Dom Adams grading oysters, moving those ready to sell higher up the shore so that they learn to 'harden' or practise clamming shut, before their long journey to Hong Kong or Singapore. Dom claimed that oyster farmers knew their water like a sheep farmer knows his hill. 'You should see the loch on an evening in late spring or early summer. The surface of the water is crisp and luminous with phosphorescence: that's when the plankton is blooming.' (Oysters absorb plankton as they pump water in and out of themselves.)

Dom, waxing lyrical, continued the comparison with hill farmers: 'We live according to the tides like a farmer does the seasons. We have to plan our work according to them – a fortnight in advance. Whenever I come out of the pub, even if its pitch dark, I can tell the state of the tide by the smell.'

## Loch Fyne Oysters, the International Company, Puts Cairndow on the Map

1990 saw the opening of the first Oyster Bar outside Cairndow, in Notting-ham. Greta and her team went down to open it. It was soon followed by one in an old dairy outside Peterborough. Again the home team went down to train staff, and I was given a lavish lunch party for my 50th birthday.

Loch Fyne Oysters had gone from nothing to a business with a £3-mil-lion turnover in twelve years. The Clachan Oyster Bar was serving 100,000 oysters a year; you could buy one for 35p or a dozen for £3.50. They were producing a million oysters a year, nearly half for export; every Friday a consignment went off to the Hilton in Hong Kong. These figures well out-did Johnny's 'the back of the envelope' estimates of the early 1980s. Loch Fyne Oysters now employed sixty people; though Andy was quoted as saying 'It's important to retain a family atmosphere, which is why our expansion is controlled.'

1990 saw the first Seafood Fair. Johnny had been to a mushroom fair in Northern Italy and thought a seafood fair in May on the field at Clachan would be a good idea. It was. The sheep and lambs were moved off the field, marquees were put up, the sun shone, local pipers, jazz musicians and ceilidh bands played, Johnny and Andy opened hundreds of oysters, there were tubs of langoustine and of mussels, there was a champagne and wine bar, and everyone lay around on the grass among the daisies and thanked the Lord. And in the evening we all made merry dancing at a ceilidh in a tent.

Loch Fyne Oysters put Cairndow on the national, even international map. The Big House played its part. Useful income came from hiring it out for feature films, TV ads and fashion shoots. And it was a useful icon for the Loch Fyne Oysters 'brand'. The high heid-yins of the restaurateurs and food writers stayed here; Johnny would choose which of them would most appreciate the Lily Room, or the four-poster in the Veronica Room (where Lady Noble's Oban Ball guests had once nestled). As Greta said, Johnny liked entertaining, he liked a houseful, especially of young people; and everyone went over to the Big House to help with the catering.

*Off to open the Oyster Bar in Nottingham, 1990: Morag Crawford, Greta Cameron, Lorna MacGillivray, Arlene MacDonald, Johnny and Andy Lane.*

The dining-room table with its backdrop view of Loch Fyne was used for photoshoots. The food gurus of the time – Keith Floyd, Jennifer Paterson of the Two Fat Ladies, Rick Stein and Christopher Sykes, writer and photographer, all made TV programmes here. I don't know if there was a payment of cash from Loch Fyne Oysters to the Ardkinglas House coffers, but it meant that as well as continuing to be a well-used family home, the House played a significant role in the Loch Fyne Oysters business. As with most estates, the mansion house was a financial drain due to the cost of repairs, in the absence of an estate squad of joiners and masons. In the pre-war days slates had been sorted and the gutters and rhones cleared every year.

John MacDonald:

Johnny tried his best for the house. He had a fund for it, I had an allocation of money from the fund every year, for materials and work on the house. I can't remember how much the fund was, maybe it was £25,000. For three or four years I was employed every summer, to replace any broken slates, clean down all the roofs, clean all the moss off the roofs, put copper in below the slates – trying to stop the moss and the algae growing on the roof.

To catch up or keep up with the maintenance, it's a very big milestone for anybody. It's not just the roof, at Ardkinglas, it's also the stone, the dressed stone, and the ingress of water in the gables that face into the prevailing wind and take a battering from the Southwest.

(The dressed stone is the sandstone from Dulitter quarry near Cumbernauld that Lorimer, mistakenly, decided to use. It may have been alright on the drier east coast, but in Argyll it's been an endlessly expensive problem.)

Being so much on the map meant that those who worked at Loch Fyne Oysters met a wide variety of people. Robbie Coltrane got stuck in a booth; they had to remove the table to get him out. Leslie Grantham who played 'Dirty Den' Watts in EastEnders, was surprised to be turned away; however famous he was, there was no table available. Famous food journalists like Jane Grigson and Derek Cooper were kept up to date with the latest news from Loch Fyne Oysters and there was regular contact with the *maitre d'* from the Ritz and Stafford Hotels in London.

Exports grew, of 'Bradan Rost' – hot smoked salmon, invented accidentally by Loch Fyne Oysters – and also of traditional smoked salmon, particularly the 'Kinglas Fillet', to Europe, Hong Kong and Singapore. Simon

Briggs, who became sales manager for Loch Fyne Oysters, described an incident in Hong Kong. 'Johnny and I were at a promotional lunch in the Hyatt Hotel when the General Manager was introduced to Johnny as "Sir Johnny Noble". I was about to put him right, when Johnny pulled me aside and told me that no harm would be done if he was known to be Sir Johnny Noble when in Hong Kong!'

(Wearing a kilt or passing himself off with a knighthood would make Johnny cringe at home, but for the benefit of Loch Fyne Oysters it wasn't a problem.)

When they didn't win the Queen's Award for Export, Johnny wrote to find out why; a year or two later they won. There was particular pride and excitement when Loch Fyne Oysters began to export oysters to France, the home of twentieth-century oyster cultivation and eating.

For some years Johnny had been nurturing the idea of launching a Loch Fyne Restaurant company, separate from Loch Fyne Oysters, but of course using its products, widening its market. In 1998 Johnny was preoccupied by this. He had broken his arm with a fall on the curling rink and was in pain. He sat in the dining room night after night, drinking too much, thinking and worrying about how they were going to raise £3.5 million (about £5.5 million today) needed to launch it.

Bob Craig, Chairman of Loch Fyne Oysters, remembered that Johnny's original idea was to find a venture capital company to fund Loch Fyne Restaurants, but at a meeting in the drawing room of Ardkinglas, the advice was the venture capitalists would charge too much; it would be better if the promoters could raise the initial capital themselves.

Mark Derry and Ian Glyn, with experience in the restaurant trade, had come into the venture. They said they could find £1 million if Johnny could do the same. Johnny did some furious mental arithmetic and obviously decided that if he stretched a few friendships, he might be able to match that. However in the end Johnny was required to find a further additional amount. He succeeded, due to some input from family, trusted friends and city contacts.

The expansion of the business had an impact on wide sections of the community: electricians, plumbers, transporters, builders, all benefited. It wasn't only that there was work available; Loch Fyne Oysters had an impact on raising confidence and aspiration locally, particularly for women. The Estate had never been able to offer anything like this. Many who worked at Loch Fyne Oysters had left school at sixteen. Looking back, all of them mentioned

*Johnny in the dining room at Ardkinglas, 1994.*

the excitement, the passion, being proud of what happened. Morag said it gave a lot of people the best experience of their lives. Greta recalled that it opened up the whole of Cairndow. And Christine said, 'I looked forward to every day of my work, there was a good spirit, cheery times that reflected to the customers. It was quite an achievement when you think of the humble beginnings to get to the standard it did. It was exciting. There was a lot of devilment and fun, but we were all keen to achieve.'

At the end of our conversation about it she said, 'I think I had an exciting job. Doing appraisals and being in charge of staff. I would never have imagined that I could have been doing that.'

Greta summed it up: 'It grew, it never stood still, it was a challenge. To prove it, to make it work: that was the challenge, for Johnny and for Andy.'

I think she is right. Johnny used to say to people that the point of Loch Fyne Oysters was to underwrite the continuity of the Estate and to 'keep slates on the roof' at Ardkinglas. Initially that was the aim for his initiative, as stated in that 1979 document – 'its success would be an integral part of the future prosperity of the Estate.' However as Loch Fyne Oysters grew, his driving force became to make it work; not exactly for the money, though the money was a measure of it, but the challenge of making it work, proving it. That was his goal. Alan Cameron, translator for Johnny on a visit to an Italian winegrower, noticed that. He commented, 'Johnny appeared more interested in the business of business than in business as profit, or business as power.' And Ian Jack wrote in his obituary, 'His work came to mean everything to him.' The staff were crucial to this. Christine described how he would come in every day: '"How's things Christine? How's it been?" He loved to hear, he was always quizzing me – "How's it been today?"'

## By 2000, What Was Ardkinglas Estate?

At this stage of the book, increasingly I refer to 'Cairndow' rather than Ardkinglas Estate because, increasingly, it isn't possible to disentangle Ardkinglas Estate – the place and its community – from other entities at Cairndow, particularly Loch Fyne Oysters.

In the 1944 booklet *Ardkinglas and the Future*, John and Michael stated 'we need to increase the feeling of community to give it a more definite purpose'. Among the surprising aspirations aired in that booklet, this is one of the most surprising. The recognition of the role of a community wasn't usual then: indeed it was not until decades later. These days it is much discussed. The term 'community' assumes people who are in the same boat, but the boat can vary: it might be a geographical area or people who have a shared way of life or a shared interest.

Even Alice – highly intelligent as she is – found it difficult to reflect on the concept of the role of the community in the Estate in the past; or of equality or inequality. Things just were as they were:

> We were more together then: it was how things were then. More people all together. Women were at home, they didn't go out to work. They would chap on each other's doors and chat. Now no one will do anything anymore; in those days there was the WRI, and whists and dances and bowls. Then the telly came along.
>
> Equality . . . ? I don't know, people didn't talk about it. We had come out from being poor, and then we got an electric cooker and kettles and things. I got my first carpet when I went to Cuil, Mrs Lang gave it to me. I didn't think about things like that, the Brodies and the Mirrlees probably had more, but they were just doing a different job, and were away a lot. We didn't talk about what others had.

*Cairndow village from Clachan.*

Work and your house might cause a worry. You just shut your mouth and didn't rock the boat . . . In some way you were looked after – a bit like a family – that was probably due to your mother. Other wives of proprietors mightn't have been so concerned. Most of them weren't there all the time like your mother and father were.

Whether or not Elizabeth had a view on the role of community as we refer to it today, she certainly understood and valued it. As Alice suggested, she was the one who fostered it. She masterminded the WRI; she was always involved with the school; there were the Christmas parties; jumble sales; fancy-dress parties; her presents of venison – cut and chosen as suitable for each household – and her warm concern for people. All this contributed to the sense of wellbeing, of being looked after, on the Estate.

The endlessly imaginative nicknames, and long, long-running jokes depended on community cohesion and shared context, everyone knowing each other and meeting each other at work and socially: a daily feed of very local news. Ernie Macpherson:

> The vans carried the news around the village, and the gossip and the jokes – that's how nicknames spread too. In those days there were travelling vans which came round the doors and you got your groceries off these vans. Grocers, and the butcher and the fish man. Campbells from Inveraray [grocer] would come, Archie MacNair from Strachur; Ronnie MacLeod from Lochgoilhead had a grocer's van too, the butcher was from Arrochar, and the fishmonger combined with shoe shop was Johnny Dewar from Inveraray.

Roddy 'Birdy' MacDiarmid explained his nickname: 'A tree had blown down at the back of the school. Miss Munro hid some money in it. Our PE exercise that day was to search for it. Miss Munro said, "Oh Roddy, you're going through that tree just like a little bird." So that's how I got my name.'

Birdy's glasses may or may not be rose-tinted, but looking back fifty years, this is how he sees it: 'People, I am firmly convinced of this, people were happier in their lot, they weren't envious of someone else being better off than them. There wasn't the opportunity. Everybody in the village of Cairndow, and I'm sure it was the same all over, everybody helped everybody. Village life was a happy life.'

During the war and into the 1950s and 1960s the Estate was the community, the community was the Estate. This probably lasted even after the division of the estates, into the late 1960s or early '70s. With a great reduction in sheep and cattle numbers, houses for so many employees weren't needed; though the new initiatives like fish and oyster farms needed accommodation for workers. New people began to come in. Also the estates began to sell off houses, which were bought as holiday houses, weekend houses, or for retired people from elsewhere. These changes meant that the Estate and the community became more mixed, socially and economically.

In March 1999, Jean Maskell, the recently appointed Estate Manager, myself and others proposed a meeting between Johnny and the heads of the various different departments on the Estate. At the time Johnny was so absorbed by setting up Loch Fyne Restaurants that other departments and enterprises were feeling left out. We asked for information on what was happening on the Estate and what the plans might be. (I was back living at Cairndow and had just set up Here We Are, a community organisation, with a £1 lease p.a. from the Estate, to build a centre at Clachan.) Johnny circulated an Information and Discussion paper for the meeting. He thought it would be useful to set out 'the background covering the salient points of current ownership, structure, tax implications, approximate financial picture and present management framework.'

For this book it is one of the all too rare documents which give an overall snapshot of the context of the time. Johnny outlined the current 'convoluted ownership, created because of tax considerations; capital gains and inheritance tax in particular. In an ideal world such a format would not be chosen, however from the tax angle it is very far from being an ideal world.' He explained that if he died after five years the inheritance tax which would be due on Ardkinglas Estate would have tapered down to zero. (He died within three years of this meeting.) He wrote that the current grants schemes on farm and forestry provided a reasonably encouraging cashflow for the immediate future. However his father's death duties and debts still had an impact on the Estate. Some £500,000 of bank loans still existed, though they were more or less contained with the assistance of funds derived from outside the Estate. The hope was that the outside funds would pay off any residual inheritance tax, and also pay off any existing loans; and provide a 'financial cushion, historically essential to subsidise a Highland estate and mansion house.'

Johnny concluded: 'In the early years mere survival, at times by no means certain, was the preoccupation. Now there is a more optimistic financial scene . . . though complete financial security is not yet in place.'

He said that in the twenty-seven years since he took on the Estate he had seen:

> . . . almost all the received opinions on farming and forestry – economics and practice – turned upside down. I approach most new fashionable nostrums with great interest but a degree of scepticism and patience.
>
> Once a more solid platform of financial stability is gained I would aim to withdraw from more 'hands on' management.

I don't think such an open meeting had ever happened before. But there is a certain air of reluctance on Johnny's part, a sense of being on the back foot. Johnny said that updated information and management accounts would be available for all to see in the Estate office, but I don't think they ever were. It was also suggested that meetings like this might happen every six months, but I'm not aware there was another. The tone of the document and of the meeting was a little wearied; he has had enough of Estate matters: it was burdensome.

In 'The Laird and the Community' (McKee, A., in Glass, J., Price, M.F., Warren, C. and Scott, A. (eds.), *Lairds, Land and Sustainability*, Edinburgh University Press, 2012), McKee asked what role the private landowner should play in sustaining a community. She asked who comprised the contemporary 'estate community'; and then defined it for the purpose of her study as:

. . . the landowning family or organisation, estate employees (direct and indirect) and estate tenants (residential, agricultural and commercial) . In some cases 'estate community' also included . . . owner-occupiers within estate boundaries, estate visitors and those with *a sense of belonging to the estate* [my italics].

Does a sense of belonging to a place bind someone to a community? In June 2016 I asked Roddy MacDiarmid if, when he was working elsewhere, he had missed the terrain, the place itself.

Yes, I was born in Glen Fyne, worked here when I left school in 1959 and worked right on here. I knew every hill like the back of my hand,
    You can ask Ally [Alastair MacCallum], he will say the exact same thing as I am going to say. We belong here. Supposing I had settled away down in England, I would still say I belonged to Cairndow.
    I know Ally never left Cairndow, I could never imagine him leaving Cairndow, he wasn't interested in going anywhere else.
    Though I have worked all over, home was always Cairndow. I don't know if I could have settled anywhere else . . . it's such a nice area and I know everyone, and I knew all the hills here.

McKee suggests that some people in estate communities consider the low wages and lack of opportunities a disadvantage, though they appreciate the benefits of estate work, its low cost housing and the rural lifestyle. But she saw that a dependency on estate employment can perpetuate low confidence and aspiration.

Ardkinglas was one of the six Highland estates McKee's study was based on. Reading between the lines, though no names are mentioned, John Macdonald may be her example of an estate offering someone a new opportunity. She quotes the, unnamed, person saying that the chance to become self-employed turned out to be a great opportunity – 'you got complete independence. It's been hard work but it's paid dividends'.

McKee suggests that now there is some breaking down of traditional hierarchies.

Landowners and community members both believe that modernisation includes, crucially, a change in the social distance between landowner and community. For example, one community member

*Alastair MacCallum and Christina high on Newton in 2001.*

describes the change since her childhood: 'then you were never to enter the front door of the landowner's home'; today she is happy to go in and shout for him/her.

However McKee goes on to say that her research demonstrated that the key constraints to partnerships between the landowner and his estate, and the community, relate to inequalities in power relations:

> Community members highlight the social differences between the land-owner and the wider community . . . as an indicator of persistent historical roles. This social difference is not explicit but may be considered an intrinsic element of long-established estate-community interactions.

McKee quotes a member of an estate employee family.

> There is a certain residual kind of loyalty to the Laird idea . . . It's partly to do with work . . . and it's partly deference . . . it's not exactly

'tugging the cap' deference but . . . to disagree is not something you don't do.

Towards the end of the chapter McKee states:

Crucially, despite the many examples of positive engagement and the potential for partnership approaches, a fundamental weakness of private landowners is that partnership approaches between an estate and the local community maybe be unavoidably unequal owing to the greater economic power of one party.

Still, today, for people in Cairndow there is an accepted recognition of the disparity between the proprietors' assets and theirs. Day to day this doesn't cause discomfort, but it does have an impact on the relationship of many of those in the community to the Estate owners. On the one hand, for some, there is the inherited deference, and for many the reality that to an extent work and rent still depend on the proprietor's goodwill; it's unwise to rock the boat.

The economic power imbalance could be similar in a commercial business – the owner(s) and managerial levels' wealth in comparison to the shop-floor staff. So, in a business is the employer-employee relationship different to that on an estate? And if so, why? I think it's an interesting question. For Ardkinglas Estate and Loch Fyne Oysters I think it was different. Johnny and Andy and all the staff involved from the earliest days worked together, shoulder to shoulder, with shared enthusiasm. Listening to the stories about Loch Fyne Oysters, the relationship between employer and employee does seem different to what it ever was on the Estate. That might be because it was the beginning of something exciting and new. It might be because of the individuals involved. In later years, as Loch Fyne Oysters grew, this could have changed. But McKee well describes the continuing undercurrents on an estate and the lack of open communication. A landowner is so often haunted by death duties and a martyr to inherited responsibility; while those living on an estate, even today and even if not direct employees, have the uncertainty of work and rent; are aware of the contrast of visible assets; and have the feeling of having no say in and no knowledge about what happens.

Writing about Johnny as an estate owner and Johnny as a businessman has brought this into focus for me. And it highlights the question that lurks throughout this book: an estate, what's the point? For whom? There were times when the responsibility got him down – I remember him with a characteristic emotional exhalation of breath, sighing, 'I'm not a fucking charity!'

So for Johnny, at the end of the twentieth century, the fourth generation laird of Ardkinglas Estate, what was the point? Sadly I missed the opportunity to have that conversation with him; I can only speculate.

Several of a landowner's conventional attractions were not the point for him:

Status, 'This is all mine!'? – No.

Farmer? – No, he wasn't interested in animal breeding, nor the state of the fields.

Amenities? – No, as time passed he became less interested in the shooting and fishing.

Garden? – He occasionally walked round the garden; he didn't know much about plants or botany, but he was interested in what grew to be eaten.

Forestry and the Woodland Garden? – Yes he was interested in trees, both ornamental and commercial.

The inherited responsibility? – Yes, for the wellbeing of the place and people.

The mansion house? – Yes, he loved his home, whether on his own or enjoying the company of friends young and old, businessmen, and always his family. His warmth and empathy meant people quickly felt at ease with him. He greatly appreciated Lorimer's esteemed craftsmanship of Ardkinglas, and respected Historic Scotland's five-star rating. But the maintenance of the heirloom was a burden.

A sense of belonging and of home? – People who lived here, their warmth to him and also their quirks were important to his idea of home, as were the policies, the hills, the glen, and of course the shore. He claimed that if he felt homesick and down at heart in Mayfair or Manhattan he would have a Loch Fyne oyster and the savour of the 'terroir' would make him feel at home, at ease!

# The End

At Christmastime 2001, Johnny was clearly not well. In January he was diagnosed with liver cancer; the doctors suggested there was no likely cure but also no imminent danger. On 9 February, 2002, he died.

Just a day or two before he died, there had been a meeting about the future of Loch Fyne Oysters in the dining room at Ardkinglas. After it he needed help to get back to his bedroom. I went for Old George, sixteen years his senior, still an upstanding big man, dignified and tender in the task as he helped Johnny along the corridor. By the following day Johnny had lost consciousness.

The funeral service was at Kilmorich Church. Eilidh, Angus Paterson's daughter, and Kate, Mary Speir's daughter, played the pipes. Stan Lupton from Lochgilphead was the undertaker and George, John, Nigel and Alastair carried Johnny's coffin into and out of the church. There were so many people and so many cars, the road round the head of the loch was closed to other traffic. He was buried in the old graveyard above Loch Fyne Oysters. I continue to gather large, native oyster shells from the bay along the shore from Policy Gate, to place at the foot of his gravestone.

All local papers carried an obituary and all the national papers too. From the *Oban Times*:

> While savaging Highland pretension, he championed Highland tradi-
> tions, crafts and pastimes, delighted in the pipes, sang without inhibi-
> tion, and curled with gusto.

*Johnny Noble's funeral in the old graveyard, Clachan, 2002.*

238

*At Johnny's funeral: George Knight, Alastair MacCallum and
John MacDonald.*

A laird who lambasted status and ducked regard, Johnny cared
intensely for his community and served them handsomely.

From Ian Jack in the *Guardian*:

He was an oyster farmer, fish exporter, wine importer and restaura-
teur; and also a laird and owner of one of the finest and most welcoming country houses in Scotland. His largest achievement – a rare
enough one in the Highlands and Islands – was the prosperity and
optimism he brought to his own small community in Argyllshire . . .

In recent times, very few Scottish lairds can rest as content as he
should.

When Johnny died in 2002 there were about two hundred and fifty people
employed in Cairndow as a whole, fifty of them women, though the resident

population of Cairndow was a mere one hundred and eighty. People came in to work from a thirty mile and more radius – indicating plenty of jobs and a lack of housing.

The Sheriff's Office's confirmation of Johnny's heritable and moveable estate in Scotland was some £6,500,000, with another £300,000 in England. *Of course this didn't mention his liabilities!*

# Afterword

## July 2017

Our pub, the Stagecoach Inn at the heart of the village, has been owned by the Fraser family since 1966; it's now run by Dougie and Kathy and their family, the second and third generation. Keats visited (and taking a dip in the loch was bothered by 'gad' flies). Dorothy Wordsworth admired the trees in the policies and commented that Ardkinglas House looked deserted (it would have been the one in Dallegate field that predated the 'Old House' and which burnt down in 1830). The main road from Glasgow runs above and behind the pub, along the 'bypass' built in the 1930s, so it is on the quiet village road. On its loch side is the garden; my daughter had a wedding ceremony there before the dance in the extension, where the stables used to be.

These days at early evenings on Saturdays, it's become a habit that we (mostly older people) go for a drink (and a few more); we refer to it as 'The Club'. Jamie Fraser, or whoever is barman, stands in front of the traditional gantry and we sit or stand up at the bar or nestle round on the curved bench at the window, which looks out to the garden and the loch. Rum and Coke is popular and 'Vital Spark' and 'Highlander', brewed by Fyne Ales at Achadunan Farm. Many people who feature in this book are often here at The Club – Alastair and Christine MacCallum; Roddy MacDiarmid and May MacPherson; Alice's sons, Lachie and John Beattie; Stewart Keith, son of Sam the forester, and his wife Morag, Loch Fyne Oyster's cook for many years; John MacDonald; Elsie and Dom – who used to look after the Oysters and claimed he could smell the state of the tide when he came out of the pub; June and Brian Wilson, grandson of John Lang, the Ayrshire cattle farmer. And there are 'newcomers' who have been here a mere fifteen years, like Craig and Celine MacIntyre who bought Honey MacLachlan's croft across the loch; and Owen, who manages the Smolt Farm where Finn Rostaad began.

We buy rounds of drinks for those we happen to be sitting with. Alastair and Roddy are particular – Alastair's whisky has to be in a wineglass and Roddy's in a small tumbler. The Club is not at all exclusive, often weekend visitors find themselves amongst us and are welcomed into conversations about the afternoon's shinty score or the anti-landslide expenditure on the Rest and Be Thankful, or oft-repeated jokes referring to people by nicknames, the origins

*Bar at the Stagecoach Inn.*

long forgotten. Pete and Jeannie, a couple from South Dakota, called in just for a drink twenty years ago on their way to Iona. That evening they found everyone in the pub so friendly they stayed on for the weekend, and now come for months at a time to the house they bought in the village.

In 1910, probably every schoolchild would have known that Sir Andrew Noble owned everything as far as the eye to see. Today even those of the 5 o'clock Club have a problem naming exactly who owns what.

In the final section of the book I increasingly wrote about Cairndow rather than the Estate, because what was happening in Cairndow as a whole was more significant than what happened on Ardkinglas Estate; in the fifteen years since Johnny's untimely death the trend has continued.

John MacDonald says: 'Cairndow still has a strong community spirit because of a hard core of people. There are still a lot of people who have known each other for many years; many who are part of several generations of families. Though there are people who have bought houses who we never see.'

The proportion of second homes in Cairndow is now over thirty per cent, and increasing. When a house comes on the market it's at a price local people can't afford; a trend all too typical in rural areas. The most recent sale – a simple semi-detached house in the village – was for £225,000. Ardkinglas Estate currently has a 30 x 30 metre building plot on the market (with planning permission) for offers over £80,000; to build on this would mean an outlay of around £300,000. For a young couple on, say, a combined income of £35,000 (and Argyll's average wage is below the national average), this would be a challenging sum to find.

On Johnny's death, ownership of Ardkinglas House and the Estate passed to his nephew David Sumsion (my sister Sarah's eldest son). As well as looking after the Estate, he had been, and continues to be, a practising architect. Ardkinglas Estate remains the largest landowner in Cairndow, with some 12,000 acres and twenty dwelling houses; all are rented out, except for the Bothy up the glen, which is self-catering holiday accommodation. Since 2002 only five new houses have been built in Cairndow. David designed one of these, a semi-detached house at the top of the Pheasant Field. Neil Coburn, the Tree Shop manager, and family live in one side and in the other Scott Mirrlees (John Mirrlee's grandson) and family. All the farming – the fields and also the hillsides – are contracted out to the Jackson family of Pole Farm, near Lochgoilhead. These days Ardkinglas Estate has few direct employees. There is Jean Maskell, who is still Estate Manager, with two part-time assistants, and there is one other Estate employee, a forester/gardener who works principally in the Woodland Garden. Others, like a gamekeeper and a fencer, are employed as needed, as is John MacDonald. What has expanded since Johnny's day is the Tree Shop/Garden Centre/Café at Clachan, which is still owned by the Estate; there are at least four full-time staff and several part-time.

So today, in addition to subsidies and timber sales, as in Sir Andrew's day, the large proportion of Ardkinglas Estate's income is from rent. Scottish Power pays rent for the Estate's share of the land used for its wind turbines. Most of the land and shore used by Loch Fyne Oysters was sold by Johnny to Loch Fyne Oysters, but there is some on lease to them. The smolt hatchery pays rent, as do the salmon processing plant on Rhumore and also Bonnar Sand and Gravel Co. Ltd at the foot of Newton Hill, in Glen Fyne. The latter is still an independent, family-owned business. Danny Bonnar, the company founder, began his career shovelling sand by hand with a second-hand lorry.

He now employs twelve people and has a turnover of more than £1.5 million. The community organisation Here We Are's new renewable energy plants also pay rent to the Estate. Our power is a woodchipping plant with premises near Bonnar's weighbridge at the head of the loch. The Merk Hydro LLP is a hydroelectric scheme on Newton Hill owned by Here We Are and three other partners.

David and his wife Angela and their two daughters live in Ardkinglas House. The flat there, where George and Kathy used to live, is now a holiday let; the drawing room and the grounds, with a marquee, can be hired as a wedding venue and David and his wife host chamber music concerts in the house. When I asked David what he thought about a Highland estate today, he wrote that 'the underlying criteria' of the surroundings had not altered much, the change had been the transition from a typical nineteenth-century model where the estates survived only because of their recreational value to their wealthy owners, to an estate being more of a commercial business. As he sees it:

> Despite this new business-like approach, many (not all, of course) estates benefit from longstanding relationships between many of the people involved, resulting in a degree of cooperation, exchange of ideas and mutual support that would be very rare in urban businesses or in other more intensively farmed rural areas.

After Michael Noble's death, his daughters divided the Cairndow Estate. Strone House and 7,500 acres were sold to the Turnbull family. Jonny Turnbull was an early example of a Highland estate owner seeing the income benefit of hydroelectricity. He installed a 'run of river' scheme on the Kinglas, commissioned in 2004. The estate advertises itself as 'an outdoor pursuits organiser' and offers stalking for one or two rifles for 'the fit and agile' at £450 a stag.

Ardno is owned by Michael Noble's eldest daughter Kate, who has made a magnificent garden there. The fields and the hillsides here, those not covered by commercial woods, are farmed by the Jackson family from Pole Farm. Ardno's comparatively fertile fields are home to their high-class blackface tup lambs; the hardworking Jackson family also farm Highland cattle and commercial sheep.

In the twenty-first century it is Achadunan Estate which has been the most entrepreneurial. Tuggy Delap, Michael Noble's third daughter, and her husband Johnny, began a brewery there in 2001, in the old byres where once lines of Ayrshires stood to be milked. Sadly, Johnny died in 2010, but Tuggy and her son Jamie have continued to expand the Estate's activities. From four Highland cattle at the beginning, they now have a fold of over seventy. Meantime the brewery has flourished: it had a £2 million expansion in 2014 and it now rivals Loch Fyne Oysters and the salmon-processing plant in the numbers of staff it employs. It has a congenial bar where you can enjoy a Highland beef pie and a pint of Fyne Ale on tap.

Here We Are is a community-owned organisation; it is a charity run by a community committee, its office and exhibition centre (architected by David Sumsion) is at Clachan between the Oyster Bar and the Tree Shop. At the Ardkinglas Estate management meeting in 1999, Johnny said that the embryonic Here We Are was to be 'most actively encouraged, with the closest possible liaison in the future'.

Here We Are explains what a Highland parish is really like – our past, our present and our future. It combines local history with community development; as the reader will have gathered, that is where my interest lies. The idea is that, becoming aware of the changes as they happen, we will have a clearer understanding of what underlies the changes and be better able to make decisions for our future.

As part of this we held an exhibition about weddings in Cairndow. We showed old studio portraits like Archie and May MacVicars' of 1912 (they would have had to go to Glasgow for it). Interestingly, the first groom to wear a kilt was Dougie Fraser in the early 1980s; before then grooms wore suits, and ever since then everyone sports a kilt and a fancy jacket. We showed wedding dresses (Isobel Brodie's, still in its 1938 Co-op box), 'favours' and telegrams – 'When at night you seek repose, keep your nightie round your toes' – and we had a dance in the Hall; Janet and Nigel waltzed under the photograph of them at their own wedding in 1956. Here We Are's archive of memories, anecdotes and photographs have been invaluable to this book, as well as to Here We Are's prestigious exhibitions. 'Our Houses, Their Stories' was an exhibition (and now a website) showing every house in Cairndow and who has lived in them; it has been exhibited at our centre, in the Village Hall, in Inverness and even in the Kelvingrove

Museum. The initial work was instigated by Alice Beattie and continued by her daughter Dot.

With the help of European funds we made a film, 'To See Yourself as Others See You', comparing life in an Irish village with Cairndow. And the Scottish Government has supported and encouraged us (particularly our renewable energy initiatives). John MacDonald is the Chair. Dot Chalmers, Alice's daughter, works with us, also Lorna Watt, Archie MacCallum's great-granddaughter, and Greta Cameron (née MacPherson). Alastair Mac-Callum is a founder director, as is Alice Beattie herself. And Roddy MacDiarmid has been essential to our current study, masterminded by Dot, about a hundred years of shepherding.

We were the instigators of a 'high head' megawatt hydroelectric scheme on Newton Hill, and own a 25% share in it - the Merk Hydro LLP. We own Our Power, a biomass plant which sells wood chips to heat water for the smolt hatchery, a halibut farm and housing associations. Now we are beginning to be able to progress economic and social development; we have a Post Office at Here We Are, we have produced walking maps for the area,

*Alice Beattie.*

*Nigel Callander, Dot Chalmers and John MacDonald recording at
Here We Are.*

are creating a path round the head of the loch to avoid the busy trunk road, and are exploring the idea of a pontoon. 'Recent' members of the community have joined our committee; Celine MacIntyre has been a driving force for the projected path, and Alexander Miles, with his wife Ketki, are regulars at The Club. I asked Alexander what it was like, living here. Alexander wrote:

> We bought a house on Ardkinglas Estate in 2003. We kept it as a holiday house for a couple of years before moving up permanently in 2005. Cairndow has been an unusually friendly and welcoming place, with no sense of the social divisions which I have experienced elsewhere. The Estate is a significant but easily unnoticed part of life in the village. It provides a sort of glue to the experience of living in Cairndow – the source of countless stories, ranging from the eccentricities of the previous laird, Johnny Noble, to tales of salmon poaching on the Fyne and Kinglas rivers.

❧

On a recent Saturday evening, as I cycled home from the pub I thought about ownership. Not many people in Cairndow would know that the salmon hatchery, across the river from the pub, is now owned by Cooke Aquaculture, an American/Canadian-based company which is a 'leader in the global seafood industry' with branches in Argentina, Uruguay, Chile and South Africa.

The prototype is widespread. Many years ago there was a hullabaloo about Finn Rostaad's 'feed shed' for fear it would be an eyesore when seen from the village. Now the increasing numbers of huge sheds for salmon processing and packaging which are fully visible, belong to the Scottish Salmon Company, as does Loch Fyne Oysters itself.

The year after Johnny died, Loch Fyne Oysters became a company owned by its employees, with a set up similar to John Lewis's 'partnership' structure, a development encouraged by David Erdal, who had assisted in the introduction of employee ownership to the family papermaking firm Tullis Russell of Fife. The Royal Bank of Scotland agreed a large loan while Andy Lane was still at the helm; there was a Waitrose partner on the board, and the various departments of Loch Fyne Oysters elected members to it. When Greta and Morag and others retired, they benefited from their shareholdings. Andy Lane soon moved on, and some of those that came in were less committed to the vision. The recession of 2008 hit them hard – too hard – they struggled, and in 2012 Loch Fyne Oysters was bought by the Scottish Salmon Company. It now owns it all – the foreshore and the oysters, the grading shed along the loch from Ardkinglas, the salmon smokery, the Oyster Bar and Restaurant and the shop at Clachan. Few in Cairndow are aware that the Scottish Salmon Company is now a part of Scottish Seafood Investment, whose major shareholder is Northlink, a private equity firm backed by Yuri Lopatinsky, a Ukrainian banker.

Loch Fyne Restaurants Ltd, registered in 1998, was always a separate company from Loch Fyne Oysters. Its launch had caused Johnny a lot of anxiety and the intake of a lot of whisky in front of the fire at Ardkinglas; many of his friends and family had invested in it; Johnny and Andy were large shareholders. Two years after Johnny's death there was a buy-out for around £30 million supported by a private equity firm. In retrospect it seems a pity that Loch Fyne Restaurants wasn't kept in the control of its existing shareholders. Those who had been Enterprise Investment Scheme investors, including Ardkinglas Estate, and also some of Johnny's friends, wanted to realise their tax-free gains at the end of the qualifying five-year period, in 2004. My son Rahul and I wanted to stay in, but were discouraged by the directors. The continuing directors – Mark Derry and Ian Glyn – further developed the Company, opening new oyster bars. Then, within three years, Greene King, the pub-owners and brewers, bought the company for about £70 million. There are now thirty-seven Loch Fyne Restaurants, which buy smoked salmon and seafood from Loch Fyne Oysters. It is a public company with recent profits of £184.9 million. On the front page of its website is a photograph of Ardkinglas standing above the loch with the caption 'We work hard to stay true to our roots'. However, its business expansion has been criticised in some quarters for its over-active acquisition policy, and it is sometimes known as 'Greedy King'.

These global companies' remote owners will continue to buy and to sell. As I cycled on down the shore road, I wondered how much difference this makes to us and to what happens here and to the employees? Does it matter?

The light began to dim. I love it when it's like that, when the familiar line of the hills is a silhouette, the landscape becomes one-dimensional and you can imagine it as if unchanged for centuries.

The windfarm up on Clachan Flats, the blade-tips just visible on the horizon, is owned by Scottish Power; it in turn is owned by Iberdrola, a Spanish multinational utility company.

The dark blanket of spruce trees across the loch, the hirsel where Roddy MacDiarmid was shepherd until the late 1970s, is an asset in someone's investment portfolio (as are swathes of the hillsides in Glen Kinglas and on the Ardno Hills). These benefit from certain tax advantages for commercial woodlands. The benefits include tax-free income from sales of timber; if it's commercial woodland it will be free of inheritance tax; Capital Gains Tax is only due when a commercial woodland is sold on the solum (land) gain and not on the increase in timber value; and any Capital Gains Tax can be 'rolled over' if the proceeds from the sale are used to buy other woodland.

As I neared home, the rising moon's light on the water meant I could just make out the reflection of Dundarave Castle across the loch, where Sir Andrew's widow lived until she was a hundred. I thought about the generations who have cycled along the shore road. And I thought about the days when my great-grandfather bought it; it is unlikely that many people on the Estate then would have known that the purchase was largely financed from armaments sold to the Japanese. But everyone would have known his name, they would have recognised him, seen him at church. I doubted if any of the shareholders in Cooke Aquaculture have ever been here.

By then I had wobbled home and was soon snuggled into the box bed; as would Maggie or Julie Luke have been a hundred years ago. And I thought, who owns what does matter.

# Books Consulted

Blythe, Ronald, *Akenfield*, 1969 (Penguin edition, 1999)

Bryden, John and Houston, George, *Agrarian Change in the Scottish Highlands*, Glasgow Social and Economic Research Studies 4, 1976 (Martin Robertson)

Campbell, Marion, *Argyll – The Enduring Heartland*, 2001 (House of Lochar)

Darling, F. Fraser, *West Highland Survey, An Essay in Human Ecology*, 1955 (Oxford University Press)

Darling, F. Fraser and Boyd, J. Morton, *The Highlands and Islands*, 1964 (Fontana)

Devine, T. M., *The Scottish Nation, a Modern History*, 2012 (Penguin)

Erdal, David, *Local Heroes*, 2008 (Viking)

Forrester, Chloe, *Ardkinglas and the Historical Connection*, 1992 (University of St Andrews, Department of Art History, Senior Honours Dissertation)

Fearnley-Whittingstall, Jane, *The Ministry of Food*, 2010 (Hodder and Stoughton)

Garfield, Simon, *Our Hidden Lives*, 2005 (Ebury Press)

Gainford, Veronica, *Looking Back*, 1991

Gaskell, Philip, *Morven Transformed*, 1996

Glass, Jayne, Prince, Martin F., Warren, Charles and Scott, Alister (Editors), *Lairds, Land and Sustainability*, 2013 (Edinburgh University Press)

Graham, Angus, *Skipness, Memories of a Highland Estate*, 1993 (Birlinn)

Grant, Roderick, *Strathalder, A Highland Estate*, 1978 (Gordon and Cremones)

Hunter, James, *Last of the Free, A History of the Highlands and Islands of Scotland*, 1999 (Mainstream Publishing Company)

Johnston, Tom, *Our Noble Families*, 1909 (Argyll Publishing edition, 2001)

MacKenzie, Osgood Hanbury, *A Hundred Years in the Highlands*, 1921 (Birlinn edition, 2007)

Noble, Timothy, *Noble Blood, A History of Noble of Ferme, Ardardan, Ardmore and Ardkinglas*, 2007

Noble, M. D., *A Long Life*, 1925

Orr, Willie, *Deer Forests, Landlords and Crofters*, 2003 (John Donald)

Raven, Hugh, *Ardtornish*

Smout, T. C., *Scottish Woodland History*, 1997 (Scottish Cultural Press)

Smout, T. C., *A Century of the Scottish People 1830–1950*, 1986 (William Collins)

Taylor, Craig, *Return to Akenfield, Portrait of an English Village in the 21st Century*, 2006 (Granta Books)

Thorpe, Adam, *Ulverton*, 1992 (Minerva)

# Unpublished Sources

The Ardkinglas Household Diary of 1947, kept by Daisy Powell-Jones, Elizabeth and Tasia Noble

John Noble's Estate Journal, November 1949–December 1950

Alice Beattie, recorded in 2012

Patsy MacPherson, recorded in 2012

Ian Stewart, recorded in 2008

Roddy MacDiarmid, recorded in 2016

Peter Beaton, recorded in 2016